Transformers and Philosophy

Popular Culture and Philosophy® Series Editor: George A. Reisch

Volume 1 *Seinfeld and Philosophy: A Book about Everything and Nothing* (2000)

Volume 2 *The Simpsons and Philosophy: The D'oh! of Homer* (2001)

Volume 3 *The Matrix and Philosophy: Welcome to the Desert of the Real* (2002)

Volume 4 *Buffy the Vampire Slayer and Philosophy: Fear and Trembling in Sunnydale* (2003)

Volume 5 *The Lord of the Rings and Philosophy: One Book to Rule Them All* (2003)

Volume 9 *Harry Potter and Philosophy: If Aristotle Ran Hogwarts* (2004)

Volume 12 *Star Wars and Philosophy: More Powerful than You Can Possibly Imagine* (2005)

Volume 13 *Superheroes and Philosophy: Truth, Justice, and the Socratic Way* (2005)

Volume 17 *Bob Dylan and Philosophy: It's Alright Ma (I'm Only Thinking)* (2006)

Volume 19 *Monty Python and Philosophy: Nudge Nudge, Think Think!* (2006)

Volume 24 *Bullshit and Philosophy: Guaranteed to Get Perfect Results Every Time* (2006)

Volume 25 *The Beatles and Philosophy: Nothing You Can Think that Can't Be Thunk* (2006)

Volume 26 *South Park and Philosophy: Bigger, Longer, and More Penetrating* (2007)

Volume 28 *The Grateful Dead and Philosophy: Getting High Minded about Love and Haight* (2007)

Volume 29 *Quentin Tarantino and Philosophy: How to Philosophize with a Pair of Pliers and a Blowtorch* (2007)

Volume 30 *Pink Floyd and Philosophy: Careful with that Axiom, Eugene!* (2007)

Volume 31 *Johnny Cash and Philosophy: The Burning Ring of Truth* (2008)

Volume 32 *Bruce Springsteen and Philosophy: Darkness on the Edge of Truth* (2008)

Volume 33 *Battlestar Galactica and Philosophy: Mission Accomplished or Mission Frakked Up?* (2008)

Volume 34 *iPod and Philosophy: iCon of an ePoch* (2008)

Volume 35 *Star Trek and Philosophy: The Wrath of Kant* (2008)

Volume 36 *The Legend of Zelda and Philosophy: I Link Therefore I Am* (2008)

Volume 37 *The Wizard of Oz and Philosophy: Wicked Wisdom of the West* (2008)

Volume 38 *Radiohead and Philosophy: Fitter Happier More Deductive* (2009)

Volume 39 *Jimmy Buffett and Philosophy: The Porpoise Driven Life* (2009) Edited by Erin McKenna and Scott L. Pratt

Volume 40 *Transformers and Philosophy: More than Meets the Mind* (2009) Edited by John R. Shook and Liz Stillwaggon Swan

Volume 41 *Stephen Colbert and Philosophy: I Am Philosophy (And So Can You!)* (2009) Edited by Aaron Allen Schiller

Volume 42 *Supervillains and Philosophy: Sometimes, Evil Is Its Own Reward* (2009) Edited by Ben Dyer

Volume 43 *The Golden Compass and Philosophy: God Bites the Dust* (2009) Edited by Richard Greene and Rachel Robison

Volume 44 *Led Zeppelin and Philosophy: All Will Be Revealed* (2009) Edited by Scott Calef

Volume 45 *World of Warcraft and Philosophy: Wrath of the Philosopher King* (2009) Edited by Luke Cuddy and John Nordlinger

Volume 46 *Mr. Monk and Philosophy: The Curious Case of the Defective Detective* (2010) Edited by D.E. Wittkower

Volume 47 *Anime and Philosophy: Wide Eyed Wonder* (2010) Edited by Josef Steiff and Tristan D. Tamplin

Volume 48 *The Red Sox and Philosophy: Green Monster Meditations* (2010) Edited by Michael Macomber

Volume 49 *Zombies, Vampires, and Philosophy: New Life for the Undead* (2010) Edited by Richard Greene and K. Silem Mohammad

Volume 50 *Facebook and Philosophy: What's on Your Mind?* (2010) Edited by D.E. Wittkower

Volume 51 *Soccer and Philosophy: Beautiful Thoughts on the Beautiful Game* (2010) Edited by Ted Richards

Volume 52 *Manga and Philosophy: Fullmetal Metaphysician* (2010) Edited by Josef Steiff and Adam Barkman

Volume 53 *Martial Arts and Philosophy: Beating and Nothingness* (2010) Edited by Graham Priest and Damon Young

Volume 54 *The Onion and Philosophy: Fake News Story True, Alleges Indignant Area Professor* (2010) Edited by Sharon M. Kaye

Volume 55 *Doctor Who and Philosophy: Bigger on the Inside* (2010) Edited by Courtland Lewis and Paula Smithka

Volume 56 *Dune and Philosophy: Weirding Way of the Mentat* (2011) Edited by Jeffery Nicholas

Volume 57 *Rush and Philosophy: Heart and Mind United* (2011) Edited by Jim Berti and Durrell Bowman

Volume 58 *Dexter and Philosophy: Mind over Spatter* (2011) Edited by Richard Greene, George A. Reisch, and Rachel Robison-Greene

Volume 59 *Halo and Philosophy: Intellect Evolved* (2011) Edited by Luke Cuddy

Volume 60 *SpongeBob SquarePants and Philosophy: Soaking Up Secrets Under the Sea!* (2011) Edited by Joseph J. Foy

Volume 61 *Sherlock Holmes and Philosophy: The Footprints of a Gigantic Mind* (2011) Edited by Josef Steiff

Volume 62 *Inception and Philosophy: Ideas to Die For* (2011) Edited by Thorsten Botz-Bornstein

Volume 63 *Philip K. Dick and Philosophy: Do Androids Have Kindred Spirits?* (2011) Edited by D.E. Wittkower

Volume 64 *The Rolling Stones and Philosophy: It's Just a Thought Away* (2012) Edited by Luke Dick and George A. Reisch

Volume 65 *Chuck Klosterman and Philosophy* (2012) Edited by Seth Vannatta

In Preparation:

Neil Gaiman and Philosophy (2012) Edited by Tracy L. Bealer, Rachel Luria, and Wayne Yuen

Breaking Bad and Philosophy (2012) Edited by David R. Koepsell and Robert Arp

The Walking Dead and Philosophy (2012) Edited by Wayne Yuen

Curb Your Enthusiasm and Philosophy (2012) Edited by Mark Ralkowski

Dungeons and Dragons and Philosophy (2012) Edited by Jon Cogburn and Mark Silcox

The Catcher in the Rye and Philosophy (2012) Edited by Keith Dromm and Heather Salter

Jeopardy! and Philosophy (2012) Edited by Shaun P. Young

Planet of the Apes and Philosophy (2013) Edited by John Huss

Boardwalk Empire and Philosophy (2013) Edited by Richard Greene and Rachel Robison-Greene

The Wire and Philosophy (2013) Edited by Joanna Crosby, Seth Vannatta, and David Bzdack

For full details of all Popular Culture and Philosophy® books, visit www.opencourtbooks.com.

Popular Culture and Philosophy®

Transformers and Philosophy

More than Meets the Mind

Edited by

JOHN R. SHOOK

and

LIZ STILLWAGGON SWAN

OPEN COURT

Chicago and La Salle, Illinois

Volume 40 in the series, Popular Culture and Philosophy®, edited by George A. Reisch

To order books from Open Court, call toll-free 1-800-815-2280, or visit our website at www.opencourtbooks.com.

Open Court Publishing Company is a division of Carus Publishing Company.

First printing 2009

Printed and bound in the United States of America.

Library of Congress Cataloging-in-Publication Data

Transformers and philosophy / edited by John R. Shook and Liz Stillwaggon Swan
p. cm.—(Popular culture and philosophy ; v. 40)
Includes bibliographical references and index.
ISBN 978-0-8126-9667-7 (trade paper : alk. paper)
1. Transformers (Fictitious characters)—Miscellanea. 2. Comic books, strips, etc.—Moral and ethical aspects. I. Shook, John R. II. Swan, Liz Stillwaggon, 1973-
PN6728.T67T73 2009
741.5'973—dc22

2009009549

Contents

Making Proper Introductions

JOHN R. SHOOK and LIZ STILLWAGGON SWAN

> I am alpha and omega, the beginning and the end. I am that which is, which was, and is yet to come . . . and you will know my name is Megatron when I lay my vengeance upon you!
>
> —Beast Wars, "Nemesis Part 2" (1999)

The search for extraterrestrial life is over. Aliens have been discovered in great numbers and great variety. They exist, at the very least, in the human imagination. Their stories are told in novels, short stories, movies, comic strips, cartoons, and folklore. In science-fiction stories, aliens are often depicted as horrible little creatures who visit Earth to wreak havoc on its inhabitants. And a common theme of alien abduction stories is the horrific nature of the invasive experiments to which abductees are subjected at the hands of their alien captors. But the pervasiveness of all kinds of alien stories that exist in our culture today suggests that humans find these frightening stories far more compelling and spell-binding than the alternative—that there are no aliens at all and we are alone in the universe.

Transformers comprise a unique example of possible alien life for several reasons. First, they are robotic in nature and thus very different from the "little green men" cliché of mid-twentieth-century science fiction. Seth Shostak, Senior Astronomer at the SETI Institute, thinks that First Contact will be with a civilization of artificially intelligent robots. It's quite likely that if an alien civilization has existed long enough to develop the technology for space travel, they will also have figured out how to build intelligent machines that are not subject to the limitations of biological life and are designed to endure the rigors of space travel. Second, while many traditional alien stories involve the good humans versus evil aliens dichotomy, Transformers are unique in having their own dichotomy to deal with—evil Decepticons and good Autobots. Humans immediately get caught in between, on a moral plane as well as a physical plane.

The fact that the Autobots remain on the Earth to protect the planet and its people from the evil Decepticons makes them immediately endearing to us. They had an independent reason for coming to Earth, namely to recover the All Spark and restore peace on their own home planet of Cybertron. Yet they are now determined to protect the human inhabitants of the planet throughout their mission on Earth. In the 2007 movie we see the Autobots develop deep and moving relationships with a few humans and begin to witness in them a new kind of transformation: from mere machines or robots to more thoughtful, compassionate, *humanlike* subjects. Transformers bear little resemblance to the little green men of the horror-scifi genre that wanted to harvest the human race for food or make us their slaves; they are instead an admirable race of beings in their own right, with their own history and future, concerns and motives, one of which includes the protection of the young and weak human race from the tyranny of the evil Decepticons.

This book presents a collective inquiry into the nature of this alien, robotic civilization that so many have grown to admire and love. Its chapters take a close look at Transformers on a deeper, more philosophical level. They ask and answer many questions about their fundamental nature, such as: Do Transformers have moral status? Are they morally accountable for their actions? As smart robots, they can pass the Turing Test with flying colors, but do they have *minds?* How about souls? Are they heaven-bound? Are they capable of love, and if so, which kind of love: Platonic? Erotic? And what makes Optimus Prime always Optimus Prime, whether robot or vehicle? What makes him the same being despite his changing form? Some chapters adopt a particular philosophical stance from which to analyze Transformer nature, such as phenomenological or Aristotelian. And others choose to focus on a particular Transformer character: John Shook's chapter postulates that Megatron is best understood as a fascist, while Swan and Stillwaggon Swan's essay portrays a broken down Optimus Prime seeking guidance through psychological counseling.

In our imaginations, Transformers are so *real,* so *humanlike.* But what does that really mean? One of the most significant features of Artificial Intelligence is that it objectifies what before was only subjective. AI creations such as robots provide a kind of mirror for us to see features of ourselves from a new perspective. It's impossible to look into someone's mind (which, you'll note, is not exactly the same as looking into someone's brain, which we can do!). Yet it is possible, and also fun and interesting, to watch robots do things that require what we think is going on in the human mind when humans do those things. And Transformers are certainly no exception. By probing more deeply into the cognitive, moral, and metaphysical features of Transformers, we're really probing more deeply into human nature, since Transformers are our creations after all!

And what a stunningly successful creation Transformers has been. From its humble beginnings as a marketing tool to sell some Japanese-made toys, the Transformers have used every modern media to expand into the planet's collective consciousness. The recent Transformers blockbuster movie was a huge success in 2007, but many people still easily recall the original cartoon TV series (1984–1987) and also the comic books, which continue to be published around the world. Over fifty different series of Transformers toys and matching storylines have been released to date (see http://tfwiki.net/), and there are no signs of slowing down. Needless to say, Transformers now has an immense web existence as well, propelled by an amazing amount of fan energy.

Transformers turned out to be far more than a marketing ploy to sell children's toys. Excepting only the *Star Wars* saga, no science-fiction story has reached as many people around the world. While countless science-fiction writers have explored future scenarios of humans encountering and dealing with robots, Transformers has been the single greatest entertainment vehicle to explore the potential scenario of humans confronting an alien robotic civilization in our own time. Their influence on the way that the world thinks about First Contact is undeniable. Furthermore, if Seth Shostak's prognostications have any validity, Transformers may be prophetic as well. Our first communication and contact with an alien civilization may be with AI life forms. Are we ready?

There may be Megatrons out there . . . but hopefully there will be Optimus Primes, too. First impressions really will matter. Can we make proper introductions?

EPISODE ONE

We Have Company

1
The Changing Shape of Things to Come

J. STORRS HALL

Suppose we, the people of Earth, were to be visited by robots from another star. What could we say about them in advance? Perhaps surprisingly, we can say quite a lot.

First of all, we shouldn't be surprised that our visitors are indeed robots. Emmisaries from Earth have visited the other planets in our own solar system in the past few decades, and all of them have been robots. Humans have stepped only (and briefly) on our own moon. Any civilization sending explorers to the stars is almost certain to send robots first.

We ourselves can't send anything to the stars (except TV commercials). A civilization capable of doing so would have to be more advanced than ours. How much more?

Stages of Civilization

Futurists sometimes use the Kardashev scale to put the different stages of civilization in perspective. On the Kardashev scale, a civilization that uses all the energy available on one planet is called Type 1, and one that uses all the energy from a star is called Type 2. It's a logarithmic scale: each type uses a billion times more power than the previous one. Type 0 works out to be a village of stone-age humans. Human civilization on Earth today is about Type 0.7, which means we still have a factor of a thousand or so to go just to Type 1.

Several remarkable developments are expected in our own technology within the coming century. The ones most important to the subject at hand will be artificial intelligence and nanotechnology. By "nanotechnology'" I mean the ability to build machines with atomically-precise, molecular-sized parts. By the end of the century (and most likely, by the end of the 2020s), we'll have robots who can talk and think like people. Not quite as soon, but still comfortably in the century, we'll get to a level of nanotechnology that will give us broadly general control over the structure of matter at the atomic level. And in roughly the same timeframe, we'll become a Kardashev Type 1 civilization.

Here's a simple way to be a Type 1 civilization, if you have nanotechnology: put a layer of tiny balloons in the high stratosphere, covering the entire Earth. Each one contains a wisp of aerogel that consists of switchable molecular-scale antenna elements. Taken together, they form an optical phased-array with an eight thousand mile aperture. You have a planet-sized solar power plant, which is incidentally a planet-sized telescope and laser as well.

Alternatively, you could launch ten million square-kilometer-sized solar satellites, something that nanotechnology also puts within the range of economic feasibility.

Sending a spaceship to another star, which would involve accelerating it to some decent fraction of lightspeed, would use more energy than our current civilization can produce in a year. But it would be doable for a Type 1 civilization, if still a bit expensive.

So it's hard to avoid the conclusion that the civilization the visiting robots come from is at least Type 1. Having reasonable predictions that our own civilization will reach Type 1 sometime in the coming century, including fairly detailed technical roadmaps of how we can do it, allows us to make a good estimate of what the originating civilization would be like, at least as regards their technological capabilities. They'll have true artificial intelligence (unlike our current planetary explorer robots, which are not too smart), and nanotechnology.

Physical Bodies

Probably the most compelling feature of the Transformers of fiction is their shape-changing bodies. The bodies combine two different essences that are powerful and, more importantly for the movies, eye-catching. They depict complicated mechanisms with many, many moving parts, and they alter radically in overall form. This makes them seem like living machines.

We're used to seeing machines with lots of moving parts, and we know how fast and capable they can be. Watch a printing press sometime: a decent-sized one can produce several books or newspapers per second. Imagine how long it would take you to write out several books by hand. To anyone with a gut-level understanding of technology, a machine with thousands of smoothly interacting moving parts conveys the impression of an almost limitless capacity to do something.

Our machines, however, don't change their overall shape much. The most that real cars do is to open and shut their doors, with a very few which can raise and lower roofs. We humans and indeed most animals, on the other hand, can't even move without changing shape. We change shape to walk, sit, pick up things, climb trees, and so forth. Watch a bear change from a big furry cushion, curled up for sleep, into a powerful hunting machine. Watch a moth change from an almost invisible lump amidst the tree bark to a multi-winged flying marvel.

Put these two notions together and you get the sense of something transcendant, with both the power of the machine and the ineffable spark of the living creature. This is in fact what we can expect of the bodies of our visitors. There's only one minor caveat.

For visual appeal, the Transformers are shown as being made of parts of about the size and moving at about the speeds of the parts of machines we're used to. But in reality, our most advanced machines already use parts that are too small for the naked eye to see and which operate at billions of cycles per second. Our own bodies have moving parts, the molecular machines inside the cells, that operate on that scale if not quite at that speed.

A robot built with nanotechnology would, to an outside view, be as seamless and fluid as a living creature. Internally, it would consist not of thousands, or even millions, of moving parts, but trillions, just as your own body does. But the parts would be thousands of times faster than your body's proteins, hundreds of times stronger, and capable of operating in a much wider range of temperatures, pressures, and atmospheric compositions (including none at all).

A human-sized robot, with human strength, built with nanotechnology, could be able to fold up into a package the size and weight of a ball-point pen. A human-sized nanotech robot with human weight could be stronger than a locomotive and fly faster than a speeding bullet.

Minds

Our most advanced machines today are our computers. I'm writing this essay using a computer that is frankly overkill for the task. If you took the technology of just a century ago, and tried to build a computer of equivalent processing power using electromechanical parts such as relays and gears, you'd need more than the budget of the entire United States (then), and the machine would fill a fair-sized city.

Our computers today are within hailing distance of the biological technology of our brains, in size and speed (they are nowhere near as efficient in power usage, yet). We can't build a computer with the processing power of the brain that's the same size as the brain today, but such a machine would fit in a bedroom. Given the historical trend of power-to-size of computers, known as Moore's Law, we should expect computers to match the brain's power within its size in about ten years.

Then add another century of development to that.

We can reasonably expect our human-sized, human-strength robots to have humanly-smart brains that fit into the ballpoint pen as well.

But of course, nobody's going to stop there. If a century of progress can put a city's worth of computing into a desktop box, a century from now we'll have a city's worth of human thinking in a desktop box. A "big brain" robot the size of, say, a tractor-trailer truck, could have a mind with the intellectual power of the entire current human race.

We can't come close to saying what the optimum configuration of these possible bodies and minds would be. The ten-ton supermind would use about as much material as a million ballpoint-pen (human size, human strength) robots. Obviously you'd want some balance between wise, insightful governance on the one hand, and distributed manipulating and sensing capability on the other. The human brain is about two percent of total body mass, but this is quite a bit higher than for most other animals. Let's suppose the evolutionary trend continues and the percentage of brain goes up in the interstellar robots. Then we could imagine a two-level society, consisting of physical robots that did things with matter and energy and who typically had roughly human intelligence (and a two-percent brain-to-body ratio), and "big brains" which were much less mobile but did the heavy intellectual lifting (taking up, say, another two percent of the overall mass of the robots, for a total of four percent). To some extent our society is already trending in this direction: the "brain" part consists of everybody who works in an office.

Society

To all appearances and best estimates, we will build such robots within this century. They will then proceed to build other robots themselves, and so forth, producing a society much more diverse than our current human-only one. There would be a wide range of different body types in the robots who did physical work. There would be insect-sized robots who kept the floor clean, and robots the size of cities who were interstellar spaceships—and everything in between. But will the robots' home civilization have any humans (or other biological forebears) at all?

There are at least two reasons to think probably not. First is that given the ability to build robot bodies and brains of the kind we've been talking about, the most adventurous and ambitious of people will be the ones to copy their minds over into electronic form—"uploading." This is particularly true of anyone who wants to go into space, but the prospect of having a bigger, faster brain will be a powerful draw for anyone. Although there will be plenty of people who want to remain in biological human form, they will become essentially the Amish of the civilization as the human uploads, pure AIs, and mixtures of the two continue to improve in productive and intellectual capacity. Nothing nefarious would necessarily happen to them—they would just become a steadily dwindling proportion of the total.

The second reason is simply that it's almost certain to be the robots, not biological humans, exploring and settling new worlds and star systems. Thus even if the original civilization retains many organic citizens, their colonies and colonies of colonies and so forth will probably be all-robot. These will be more numerous than the original worlds, and will form the outer and expanding parts of any civilization's sphere of influence - so they are where we expect our visitors to come from.

But why expand in the first place? Interstellar travel is expensive, so much so that our current civilization can't do it at all. Part of the answer is simply evolutionary: given a few civilizations, some with the itch to explore and colonize and others without, come back in a few centuries and the galaxy will be full of the explorer types and not the others. But even if you don't have that territorial urge, it might be a good idea to settle a buffer zone with gentle, peaceful cultures that are compatible with yours before the noisy, gung-ho types take them all.

Culture

It's tempting to say that a civilization that spent all its time fighting wars amongst itself wouldn't have the time or resources to waste on interstellar exploration, and so that if we get visitors from the stars, they'll be from a unified, peaceful culture. But unfortunately history says differently: the great age of exploration and colonization in the sixteenth and seventeenth centuries originated in Europe, where there were numerous countries often at war with each other, while China, though unified, peaceful, and technologically more advanced, sat in a self-imposed isolation.

So we should expect our visitors, if not necessarily out-and-out warlike, to be from a competitive culture. But what else can we say about such a culture? Will it be greatly different from a human one because it's composed of robots and not biological humans?

One obvious way robots might differ from humans is in their reproductive arrangements. For example, it might be much more efficient for robots to build factories, which then build robots, which build factories, and so on, than the human method. When species of biological life follow this pattern, it is called alternation of generations. One could think of ant colonies and bee hives as pursuing a similar strategy. The social insects exhibit an enormously higher group loyalty than humans, and also a fairly vicious inter-hive rivalry.

But there are also pressures that are likely to make the robots more like humans. The most important is that they will be intelligent. Consider the technological advantages the European explorers had over the native Americans in the Age of Exploration: perhaps more important than the guns, germs, and steel was the printing press. In European culture, knowledge propagated, was tested, and improved much faster. The Europeans were smarter, not because of anything about their physical brains but because those brains were populated by more advanced ideas. Ideas evolve in a way that is not necessarily linked to the physical substrate, and it is the evolution of ideas—memetics—that determines the ultimate shape of a culture.

The printing press was a quantum jump up in communication from manuscripts and word of mouth; the internet is a quantum jump up from the printing press. A robot culture would be connected by communications of such high bandwidth that the only thing we have to compare them with in our experience is the corpus callosum, the connection between the two hemispheres of your brain. (Its bandwidth is just about the same as a current-day high-speed Ethernet connection.) Imagine a society of geniuses who could co-operate as seamlessly as the two halves of your brain do. That's what a robot society would be like.

Technology

Why would a solar-system-wide civilization of robots—or, more precisely, some faction of such a civilization in competition with the others—send representatives to Earth? There might be many reasons, but given the dynamics of the evolution of interstellar cultures, there's a very high probability they would be prepared to take any opportunity to reproduce their civilization around the new sun. The galaxy is simply much more likely to be populated by cultures that do that, than by ones that don't.

Before proceeding, it's worth reiterating the difference in capability between our civilization and one which could send starships. It's difficult to convey the power, speed, and pure volume of effect a combination of artificial intelligence and nanotechnology would bring to bear. Imagine that Columbus had arrived in the West Indies, not with three wooden sailboats, but with a nuclear carrier task force—but one where the technology was aimed at exploration and development instead of fighting another navy. They'd have chainsaws instead of rifles, earth-movers instead of tanks, well-drilling equipment instead of artillery, and prefab factories that built more pre-fab factories. Now imagine that all of the islands were uninhabited, except that one of the smaller ones was home to a band of monkeys.

In other words, given the technological mismatch, we couldn't put up enough resistance for them to be able to "conquer" us in any meaningful sense. It would be more a question of whether the footnote beginning "Incidentally, the indigenous life forms of the third planet were . . ." ended with the word "displaced" or "preserved."

Ethics

Probably the best we could hope for would be that the small island Earth with us monkeys on it would be left alone as a nature preserve. Luckily for us, that turns out to be a fairly minor concession. Science-fiction writers have a propensity to imagine biological visitors who would find the surface of a life-bearing planet useful. But given that the visitors are robots with polymorphic bodies, they will need only matter and energy to rebuild their civilization and send their descendants on to other stars.

Most of the matter and energy in the solar system is not on Earth. Virtually all of the available energy comes from the Sun, and the Earth gets less than one part per billion of the Sun's output. Most of the matter (outside the Sun itself) is in the large outer planets, starting with Jupiter. But the low-hanging fruit, so to speak, is in the smaller planets, moons, and asteroids. Mercury is an obvious place to start, with relatively low gravity and close proximity to the Sun for power. Smaller but closer than Earth, it picks up about the same amount of solar power as does the Earth—the Kardashev Type 1 level. Or if you disassembled it and used the mass to build solar collectors in its current orbit, it would provide a hundred million times as much energy—well on the way to Type 2.

So for the robots to avoid wiping us out, they would only have to have a fairly minor moral concern for indigenous biological species. It's not as if we had anything they really needed.

Why might they have such moral concerns? It seems likely that they will have descended from biological creatures similar to ourselves—that's the only way we know that they might exist in the first place. Their ancestors are reasonably likely to have given them at least a human level of ethics—if for no other reason than that many of the robots will originally be uploads (and besides, as robot ethicist Ronald Arkin points out, it's a pretty low bar).

Let us think of an ethical scale for civilizations in the same spirit as the Kardashev scale. I'll modestly call it the Hall scale. The Hall scale rates a civilization's ethics in terms of how many individuals can co-operate productively without breaking out into physical warfare. For primitive human hunter-gatherers, who lived in tribes of about two or three hundred which were constantly at war with each other, we can say order of one hundred people. For current Western civilization, it's about a billion. We'll simply use the logarithm of the number of co-operating people (or robots!) as our scale, so the hunter-gatherers have Hall Level 2 ethics and our globalized economy has Level 9 (there are more than a billion people on Earth now but we don't all co-operate!).

A Kardashev Type 1 civilization probably needs Level 10 ethics—or more—to sustain the kind of co-operation necessary to launch interstellar probes. Over the past century, in moving from the colonial era to our present world (or at least Western) culture, we've moved up from about Level 8 to Level 9. In doing so our moral concern for things like indigenous peoples, species preservation, and the like has increased dramatically. It is at least not unreasonable to hope that a civilization with Level 10 ethics would be concerned enough about such things to make the minor accomodations necessary to let us survive.

I can already hear the outraged objections of any philosophers who may ultimately read this. There is a lot more to a system of ethics than the number of people who co-operate within it. Ethical development doesn't proceed in a straight line, such that by measuring one aspect (number of cooperators) you could say anything about some other one (concern for other lifeforms). Yes, indeed, the Hall Scale is a very crude way of measuring ethics.

Yet there are some strong overall correlations between number of co-operators and the other concerns we're worying about. In a hunter-gatherer society, there is a major distinction between a member of your own tribe (not to be killed) and someone from another (kill if you can get away with it). The higher on the scale the level of ethics, the more people have to be in the "own tribe" category - and concomitantly, the more kinds of people. People with different accents, who wear different clothes, and eat different kinds of food. People who speak different languages and worship different gods. Even people of different races and sexes fall under the expanding umbrella of inclusiveness.

But every expansion of inclusiveness contributes to a general background sense that increased inclusiveness is a major component of ethical betterment. Co-operation and tolerance go hand in hand. We can only expect this to become stronger in civilizations whose members vary as radically as we can expect AI nanotech robots to.

Level 10

Would the interstellar robots then bother to contact us at all? They might simply go about their own business, leaving us here to develop naturally. I like to think, however, that they might have some interest in us. We ourselves have a great interest in nature, studying creatures of all stripes. And again, it would be a minor investment for a Type 1 civilization to make to learn a lot about us. Just one "big brain" of the kind described earlier would be able to be personally acquainted with every single human and hold a separate conversation with each of us at the same time.

We Earthlings would soon enough be living in a Level 10 society. Perhaps we would see the robots, and decide we had to grow up quickly if we wanted to take part in the galactic civilization as a member instead of as a zoo. Perhaps the robots would see it as their moral duty to educate us. Or perhaps, even without the robots, the long, slow historical climb up the Hall scale will simply continue in the long run.

Big Brains, whether visitors from the stars or ones we build ourselves in the coming decades, will be a crucial part of the next moral development. The ability to know (and be known by) many more people than natural humans can, will be key to establishing wider networks of trust and co-operation. Deeper understanding of everything from economics to cognition will allow smarter systems of interaction to be designed.

To close on the same note that I opened with: We can say a lot about what interstellar robots would be like because we are tantalizingly close to being able to do the same things ourselves. This includes not only the bodies and minds, but culture and morality—at least from a very high-level, fuzzy point of view.

But by the same token, we don't have to wait for robots to sail in from the stars. We can transform ourselves.

2
First Contact

JOHN R. SHOOK

The mighty Transformers, engaged in yet another episode in the millennia-old conflict between the Autobots and the Decepticons, accidentally encounter Earth and its puny inhabitants. They had no idea we were here, we didn't see them coming, and upon arrival they mask themselves to look like our own machines. A crash landing; a quick disguise. That's all it might take.

First Contact. It's an awe-inspiring question with so many potential answers. How might we humans figure out that we're not alone? First Contact has long been the specialty of science-fiction writers, but real science is now catching up. Admittedly, few science-fiction stories start out the way the Transformers saga begins.

An alien civilization, of machine-intelligence life forms, stumbles across Earth while fixated on fighting its own internal civil war. This is not a typical plot in the science-fiction genre. Maybe it isn't romantic or heroic enough. Don't we prefer story lines that credit us intrepid explorers with penetrating into the galaxy's goings-on? And don't we appreciate aliens more, even the dastardly ones, when they sort of look and think like us? Science-fiction authors know a catchy tale when they write one, because they have a way of knowing us humans really well.

What about scientists? Well, most scientists also seem to prefer some other eventual outcome than the Transformers version of First Contact. Waiting around for aliens to find us is not the sort of hands-on proactive technological solution that keeps scientists employed and busy. Science is about discovery, right? So, let's go out and find them first! And since aliens are probably a lot like us, at least where their vast intelligence and scientific curiosity are concerned, they'd naturally be looking for us too. And while we're on the subject of motivation, muse the scientists, let's infer that superior civilization implies superior virtue. If an advanced alien civilization has survived for so long, it probably has overcome hatreds and wars. These aliens are more like angels!

Tuning In

Neither science fiction nor science fact wants to make a place for seriously considering the strange Transformers scenario. We want to think that we can find them first; or if aliens find us, it's because they were trying to. We want to picture aliens in vaguely anthropomorphic ways, so that they are weird but not *too* weird. We want to hope that advanced civilizations are far more ethically advanced, and not just technologically advanced. Our ideal scenario basically goes like this: Humans seek angels, angels are happy to be found, angels help humans. Does this story line sound familiar (consult nearest religion)?

Nothing about the Transformers plotline seems intuitive or satisfying. All the same, is the saga of the Transformers really so improbable? It might actually turn out to be one of the most likely ways that we finally encounter an alien civilization. Leaving science-fiction writers to their flights of imagination, let's look at some scientific and philosophical reasons why the Transformers story may be wise prophecy. Like the Transformers themselves, the Transformers saga is more than meets the eye.

Let's start with the scientists' search for alien life. Go ahead, pour hundreds of millions of dollars into the highest-tech dish antennas and supercomputers. Analyze the random noise from nearby dense arms of the Milky Way, or from its little nebula clusters, all you want. Yes, we're all curious about whether there's life out there. But do we really know what we're supposed to be watching out for?

It makes sense to suppose that any intergalactic civilization would have incredibly advanced technology. Such advanced technological powers would compare to our civilization's powers, like our human powers compares to that of ants. So which technology are we using for our searches out into space? Oh yes, the Search for Extra-Terrestrial Intelligence (SETI), the pride of so many scientists committed to the goal of detecting ETs, is naturally using—radio. Yes, radio.

Remember radio? Quite the sensation in the late 1800s. The pulsing vibrations of electromagnetic radiation. Photons, essentially, streaming all throughout space. Photons have been around from the beginning, the Big Bang, some fourteen billion years ago. Even 'empty' space has been pretty full of these zippy little things ever since, and the universe's trillions upon trillions of stars, and everything else involving collisions of atoms, keep making more. They can also be artificially generated and controlled with very simple electronics, and that's what Marconi (the radio's inventor, who later won the Nobel Prize for physics in 1909) figured out how to do. Television is just a fancier version of radio transmission, using the same kind of electromagnetic radiation at higher frequencies. Since most AM and FM radio waves get absorbed by Earth's atmosphere, ET's first sight of us might actually be a 1936 TV broadcast of Adolph Hitler. A cause for alarm indeed. But all this earthly information, the good, the bad, and the ugly, boils down to streams of little photons.

Photons are plentiful, cheap, and easy to make. Little surprise, then, that humans invented radio right around the same time that we invented the automobile. Now there's a great technology that we can expect to be using for thousands of years into the future. Oh, no, I guess not. If humans are still relying on petroleum-powered internal combustion vehicles ten thousand years from now, this species has really hit a wall. Will we still be using radio ten thousand years from now? Perhaps, for the simplest of mechanical functions. But if electromagnetic radiation remains our most advanced means of communication for that long, then we won't have progressed very far. We surely will not have dealt with some other major challenges for the spread of the species, such as reaching other star systems for colonization, and communicating in something close to real time across hundreds of light-years of space.

Perhaps advanced extraterrestrial civilizations, as they cruise around galaxies, emit some radio waves in the process. Our antennas might eventually detect them. But would they amount to signals? Would we be able to take notice of them as signs of intelligence? Consider whether the noise produced by a washing machine constitutes a signal, a sign of intelligent communication by humans. Not really. Humans trying to detect alien messages in their cast-off radio waves might be like super-smart ants trying to detect advanced life forms using their high sensitivity to pheromones lingering on the ground.

From the ant perspective, the ants being so proud of their most sophisticated chemical sense, pheromones are obviously the best way to communicate. This assumption wouldn't exactly be wrong. Lots of species use pheromones for all sorts of 'communication'. It can't be the basis for a genuine language, since chemical transmission and reception can't achieve the precision of abstract concepts or the infinite variety of possible meanings that aural or visual interchange can accomplish. Chemical transmission is too crude and clumsy for syntax and grammar. But these super-smart ants might correctly suppose that even highly advanced life-forms will still use pheromones. Humans do, after all. Pheromones can silently but effectively indicate all sorts of interesting things, like sexual arousal or angry aggression. Perhaps human pheromones could be detected down on the ground by super-smart ants. Could they decipher our pheromone signals? Are our smelly odors anything like messages to be decoded? By analogy, radio may not help us decide that we have detected intelligent aliens.

When most people think of First Contact with aliens, what first springs to mind is probably something like either Steven Spielberg's *Close Encounters of the Third Kind* or Carl Sagan's *Contact*. Spielberg borrowed the title of his 1977 movie from J. Allen Hynek. Hynek assisted the U.S. Air Force's Project Bluebook, the government's official investigation into UFOs during the 1950s and 1960s. He proposed a classification system of first, second, and third kinds of alleged alien encounters, from distant sightings of spacecraft to seeing aliens up close. During an era fascinated by numerous accounts of alien sightings and abductions, *Close Encounters of the Third Kind* struck a chord with a public half persuaded that aliens were already hanging around Earth. Good thing none of this hysteria turned out to be verifiable. From 1969 to 1991, U.S. Federal Law criminalized any contact with aliens (no, I didn't make this up).

Sagan's contact scenario starts off with the decoding of alien communications recorded by giant radio antennas and climaxes with human conversations with aliens. Sagan's 1985 book was, of course, a poetic exercise in wish-fulfillment. He lobbied vigorously for the funding of SETI projects, and he frequently predicted success within his own lifetime. Among those scientists who think that it's both possible and important to detect alien civilizations, there is modest support for SETI projects of various sorts. Of course, since our light telescopes haven't come across any evidence of alien activity (sightings of vast solar system-sized construction sites, randomly blown up stars, or suspicious high-energy rays), we don't have much else besides radio to use at the moment. For all we know, broadcasting aliens might be using super advanced lasers, or neutrinos, or who knows what, which still remain out of our technological reach.

SETI projects, until very recently, have only tuned into radio frequencies which are easy to hear on Earth, because neither stars nor our own noise drowns them out. These frequencies wouldn't be too practical for ordinary planetary communications, but they'd be ideal for long-distance beacons saying only "We are Here!" SETI was originally predicated on the notion that an alien civilization would want to clearly announce its presence to the rest of the galaxy. That's why SETI's failure to spot radio or TV signals from neighborhood stellar systems doesn't mean much yet. There still could be plenty of intelligent life around us. Since civilizations as they advance won't be broadcasting using electromagnetic radiation very much or for very long, and since there are probably more efficient ways to draw attention to oneself than photons, SETI would have a low chance of success anyways. If aliens get smarter than us, though, they should figure out that simply shouting across galaxies is pretty dumb in the first place. How are you going to make friends that way? And wouldn't you simply be hanging out a "Come and Eat" sign on your planetary house for bigger, hungrier aliens? The Transformers aren't all angels, remember.

Perhaps in another hundred years, with improved reception capacity to eavesdrop on all planets, at all frequencies, within a sphere of one thousand light years diameter around us, then SETI's results, positive or negative, will really help calculate the distribution of intelligent civilizations in our galaxy. Or so the scientists hope. Not all science-fiction writers have assumed that listening in on alien civilizations will be a simple matter of building an even bigger radio antenna, however.

Some of the most thought-provoking stories about contact explore the exact opposite possibility, that communication with aliens proves to be very difficult or quite impossible. Stanislaw Lem's 1961 novel *Solaris* recounts the discovery of an oceanic-sized organism on a distant planet which is evidently capable of intelligent thought, but no human concepts are adequate for understanding this peculiar life-form. In the Transformers alternate universe, humans don't have a communication problem with the visiting aliens' language, because the Transformers learn ours. In the 2007 *Transformers* movie, Optimus Prime tells Sam that they acquired our language from the World Wide Web. This makes more sense. If the arriving aliens are supposed to be so much more advanced, wouldn't they figure out our languages before we figured out theirs?

For aliens to learn our language to reveal themselves to us, they would have to first find us, of course. Shouldn't that be the more common-sense scenario? Intergalactic civilizations, roaming around at high speeds (maybe even trans-light speeds) for long periods of time (maybe for thousands or millions of years), would presumably get to Earth first. At least they should be able to intercept our primitive signals while passing nearby on some interstellar highway. Even if they stopped using radio for their own communications long ago, they could easily program one of their space sensors to automatically pick up any primitive signals. This still presumes that advanced aliens keep up some curiosity about infant civilizations. We still care about annoying ant infestations.

The nearest extraterrestrial (ET) highway would have to be close to Earth, though; within about eighty light years, in fact, since high-powered broadcasts first escaped the Earth in the 1930s. Since satellites, cables, and Wi-Fi are quickly replacing high-powered antenna broadcasting even now, the Earth will soon go pretty quiet again. Only loud but dumb things like military radars will keep beaming into space, but there's no message in there. Our century-long bright flash of sports, news, and entertainment will keep going further into space, like an expanding shell of exuberant smoke that means the fire of intelligent life to any one still bothering to listen for those frequencies. Perhaps a million years from now, some alien receiver will notice our species's primitive smoke signal and wonder if its senders are still alive. Similarly, we might eventually pick up primitive broadcasts from a long-vanished alien civilization on the other side of the galaxy, if we're patient enough. That's a more likely scenario, actually, than tuning in a nearby civilization. Disappointingly realistic, in fact. We finally hear from them, but not quite in time to have them over for tea.

Dropping In

So far, science and common logic advises us that radio is not a smart means of First Contact. What we really, really want is a Close

Encounter of the Third Kind, anyways. Then they should come to us! Why aren't they here already? Where's ET? That's a very good question. It's such a good question that it has been used in arguments that conclude that no other advanced galactic civilizations exist right now. If they did, then they'd have already gotten here; but they aren't here, so they don't exist.

Now, this knock-down argument against ETs relies on certain additional premises. First, you'd have to assume that ETs would even want to explore this galaxy so thoroughly. Second, you'd have to already think that it would be pretty easy for ETs to get here. Third, you'd have to rule out the possibility that they have already been here, or maybe that they are here right now, IN DISGUISE!! Fourth, you'd have to guess that visiting aliens, if already here, are pretty much benign and unaggressive, since we haven't yet been eaten or enslaved. In other words, we aren't going to get caught up in something like L. Ron Hubbard's *Battleground Earth* or the 1996 movie *Independence Day*. (On the other hand, the incoming aliens might simply be uncaring bureaucrats intent upon demolishing Earth out of the way, like the poetic Vogons in Douglas Adams's *Hichhikers' Guide to the Galaxy*.) Summarizing, it takes four major assumptions to get this argument going against ETs. Success means no ETs at all, and no Transformers scenario for First Contact, ever.

Fortunately for advocates of the Transformers scenario like myself, all four of this argument's premises are probably wrong. We could not possibly rule out ETs in this way. In fact, as we question these four assumptions, the Transformers scenario actually becomes more plausible! Let's start with the silly notion that advanced civilizations earnestly want to reach us. In the Transformers scenario, our heroic ETs have no reason to fool around with such primitive life forms like ourselves. We don't have any impressive technologies or energy sources, and the Transformers don't need lots of oxygen or water-rich planets to inhabit for themselves. Most alien civilizations capable of intergalactic travel are probably far more like the Transformers in this way. For us to think that advanced ETs are vitally interested with planets like Earth is like super-smart ants imagining that we humans are obsessed with finding big anthills so that we can move right in. Pretty silly.

What really troubles our human imaginations is this darker scenario, instead. A slightly more advanced alien civilization, just capable of bumbling around nearby stellar systems, wants to find more Earths for colonization and exploitation. This is the *Star Trek* scenario. For every nice Vulcan civilization in our corner of the galaxy, how many nasty Klingon and Romulan civilizations might there be? In other words, we start envisioning the same basic scenario as European explorers bumping into North America four hundred years ago and wondering how to deal with Native Americans, while the Native Americans wonder how to catch up with European technologies. The ETs that keep us awake at night are really only us in disguise, with greater technologies but the same ethics. Not angels, but devils.

However, unless it's really easy for intelligent life to spring up in lots of kinds of stellar systems, there probably isn't a *slightly* more advanced civilization nearby right now. In fact, we might not currently have any advanced civilizations in our local neighborhood. Even if the Milky Way galaxy has been spawning an advanced civilization capable of galactic travel at the fast rate of once every million years for the last billion years, you're only talking about one thousand civilizations that have had an opportunity to stumble across Earth during that vast stretch of time. Is it really so easy for ETs to discover us? The galaxy is pretty big (one hundred thousand light years across and three thousand light years thick), imposingly big even for aliens with faster-than-light engines. Let's assume that each civilization lasts around a million years before it expires or evolves so far that it transcends petty galactic concerns (that's a pretty optimistic duration, but let's run with it). The precise odds of any of these one thousand civilizations running across Earth now, right when *Homo sapiens* has flashingly exposed itself for all to see, turns out to be pretty small. Just because they aren't here right now, hardly means that they aren't still out there.

Sure, scientists get enthralled by the hypothesis that a fast-growing civilization could pretty much colonize the whole galaxy in a million years, more or less, all by itself. Well, since nobody has already accomplished such encroaching colonization here on Earth, we can rule out that hypothesis, and that does tell us something. It tells us either that it is really hard to colonize a whole galaxy, or that expanding civilizations sooner or later want to do something else, like enjoying the bliss of entering the state of pure energy, or something exalted like that. Just because we humans are obsessively compulsive about reproductive expansion, doesn't mean everybody else is too.

The odds are somewhat larger that aliens or their robotic probes have surveyed Earth in the past, noticing oceans full of fish and trilobites four hundred million years ago, or maybe mapping immense swamps replete with dinosaurs one hundred million years ago. The story line of the 1980s cartoons and comics tell how Transformers crashed into an Earth volcano four million years ago. Only the 2007 movie throws the Transformers First Contact into contemporary times, as the frozen Megatron is discovered by Captain Archibald Witwicky in the Arctic Circle, at the crash site dating from only a few centuries ago. The 2007 movie panders more to audience prejudices, and conforms less to reasonable scientific expectations.

All the same, the Transformers scenario in general does not rashly assume that the Transformers civilization actively searches for Earth-like planets, or cares much about discovering any primitive societies on those planets. In fact, the Transformers scenario also upsets the third common assumption behind all this worry over First Contact: that we could even tell whether aliens have been here. Any alien visitations to the Earth in the deep past probably left no trace, unless artifacts were deliberately left behind to influence evolution or to give us something to discover (this is Stanley Kubrick and Arthur C. Clarke's scenario in their 1968 movie *2001: A Space Odyssey*). And since we don't see any aliens now, any aliens currently on Earth would have to have considerably good disguises, especially if they are trying to pass themselves off as people.

This paranoid fantasy that a friend or neighbor is really an alien has long been fodder for many B-movies and some mediocre TV series (remember *My Favorite Martian* or the reptilian aliens from *V*?) as well as the inspiration for some excellent classics (such as *Invasion of the Body Snatchers* and *Men in Black*). No question about it, aliens smart enough to arrive here could probably figure out how to look like us somehow. But could they just as easily behave and talk like us? Sure, they might be able to learn our languages and even penetrate our minds. But passing the Turing Test is another matter entirely. Building our own computers capable of ordinary conversation under all daily circumstances, so convincing that people can't tell any difference, looks to be tremendously difficult—and we already understand our own psychology, language, and culture. Passing as human would present an enormous challenge to a highly advanced alien race, even if that alien race would want to bother with such effort.

Fitting In

If aliens wanted to watch us up close and personal, without having to actually talk to us (and I could hardly blame aliens if most human conversation would bore them out of their alien exoskeletons), wouldn't it be easier to get some other sort of disguise besides a human body? The best disguise would be complete invisibility, but even invisibility isn't enough, since they'd take up some volume and displace other things anyways. For close contact, hiding out in the open might make more sense. They could be disguised as trees, nice shrubbery, or lovely petunias. If the aliens are made of organic molecules like us, maybe they can shape-shift into other organisms. Actually, if they need to get up close and personal on a regular basis, what about disguises as machines?

Hmmm . . ., there could be serious advantages to a non-organic strategy of disguise. A machine-disguised alien wouldn't have to worry about getting chopped down, or mowed over, or eaten. Scurrying pine trees or flinching dandelions would get noticed after a while. But what about a machine? As long as a machine-disguised alien looked about right and did whatever that machine was supposed to do, it could easily fool us, such as driving around as a Chevy Camaro like the Autobot Bumblebee or playing music as a boombox like the Decepticon Frenzy. A useful machine-form could be as large as an entire apartment building, or as small as a tiny nanobot the size of a flea. Autobots haven't chosen a dumb form by selecting our vehicles, since they can have easy mobility. We hardly pay any attention to cars or planes as they zoom around, as long as conventional traffic patterns are obeyed. All the same, the smaller the better, I'd guess. I keep finding and then losing my watch, come to think of it.

While we're pondering the ideal sort of alien disguise, we should seriously question whether a visiting alien would necessarily be organic in the first place. There are many good reasons to think that if there is life out there in the galaxy, then it evolved from simple organic molecules composed of hydrogen, carbon, oxygen, and nitrogen. But regardless of which organic compounds are the easiest way for life to get started, here we need to ponder a very different question. Would a highly advanced alien civilization, with enough technology and longevity to reach us first, still be mostly organic?

Maybe First Contact will be with hard metallic aliens, not soft and squishy aliens. Seth Shostak has been publicly proclaiming that First Contact will most likely be with a fully robotic civilization possessing computer brains loaded with Artificial Intelligence (AI) programming. Shostak is Senior Astronomer at the SETI Institute in Mountain View, California, and a prominent lecturer on the topics of alien life and First Contact. His prediction is based on the reasonable assumption that very advanced and long-lived civilizations will rely heavily on mechanical and computing technologies to overcome the inherent limitations and frailties of organic bodies and neuron brains. If any civilization approaches immortality, he argues, then it will have transformed itself into AI robots.

Although this reasoning is persuasive but still pretty speculative (are the only alternatives for life just organic or mechanical?), Shostak's view provokes another thought experiment. Perhaps First Contact would not be with an alien race directly, but rather with an alien race's robotic AI emissaries. Sending out robot probes, especially reasoning and self-replicating robots, would provide far more efficient exploring, if what you want is lots of data as fast as possible from all around the galaxy. If a probe reached us, and came equipped with its own AI for smart conversation, then our First Contact would be with an alien race's spokesperson.

Indeed, following out this scenario to its logical conclusion, we might meet a robot probe but never speak with its master. In a way, this possibility still approximately tracks the Transformers scenario, since the Transformers were themselves created, according to the TV series, as robotic slaves to a master race called the Quintessons. If probes take a long while to reach us, especially if the builder race originated in a different quadrant of the galaxy, then there's no assurance that the builders still exist themselves, much less care about communicating directly. Maybe robot probes are programmed for this possibility, announcing messages from the alien master race which could never be personally delivered. A probe's message might amount to, "By the time that you hear this, we will be dead . . ." And a probe might itself have developed its own agenda, perhaps its own autonomy. Could alien probes, originally programmed with good intentions, turn malevolent? Is that so improbable? Ask Captain Kirk, who confronted the mysteriously powerful V'ger invading our solar system only to discover our own Voyager craft at its heart, in the first *Star Trek* movie.

Crashing In

There are very few reasons, if we keep thinking about it, to keep supposing that our First Contact will be directly with a benevolent and peaceful alien race that looks anything like us and is quite happy to meet us. The Transformer scenario, or something fairly similar, is increasing in relative probability against the alternatives. Let's keep going.

We've now reached the fourth necessary assumption, that a disguised alien on Earth would be benign and peaceful, for clinching the grand argument that no ETs really exist. At first, this assumption seems plausible. After all, if they're disguised, then they aren't displaying themselves, which would terrorize or demoralize the human population. Only conquering aliens would display their true, terrifying form. But doesn't this sound like wishful thinking, just another version of "advanced aliens are angels" fantasy? While we're operating on that mythological level, recall some basic religious mythology: it's usually the demons, and not the angels, who are masters of trickery, deceit, and deception.

Let's consider what's going on within the Transformers scenario. The main reason why the Transformers race adopts the disguise of whatever mechanicals happen to be around has little to do with local native species. The point of the transforming disguise is entirely military, to gain an advantage over the enemy. The Autobots and the Decepticons are locked into a terrible civil war that has been going on for many millennia. Ever since the start of the civil war, they have developed their incredibly advanced technologies over that time mostly in order to win this war. In the second TV episode, Spike asks Trailbreaker about why the Autobots transform and Trailbreaker replies, "Simple. Disguise! Besides, it sure beats walking." In a later episode of season three, it's explained that transforming was a technological invention by the Autobots to use against Decepticons, who soon duplicated this ability for themselves.

Not only might alien visitors use disguise for their own purposes rather than for anything having to do with concern for us, we cannot presume that alien visitors are even capable of concern for other species. There's a curious built-in contradiction to the characterization of the Transformers. On the one hand, we have the movie poster for the 1986 cartoon film, *The Transformers: The Movie*, which includes the ominous headline: *Beyond Good.*

Beyond Evil. Beyond Your Wildest Imagination. In what way could the Transformers be beyond good and evil? Maybe because their concerns so completely transcend our own that we couldn't judge them by our human standards of morality. On the other hand, much of the cartoon and comics series is predicated on a degree of goodness attributed to the Autobots. Many Autobots develop positive and even protective relationships with some humans. The 2007 movie goes the farthest in this direction. Optimus Prime pronounces an ethical principle, something akin to *Star Trek*'s Prime Directive, to the effect that each species should be free to develop in its own way. Optimus Prime is even willing to commit suicide if that would end the war on Earth. At the movie's conclusion, the Autobots assume a protective stance over Earth and its human inhabitants. This beneficence is starkly contrasted with the Decepticon's evil disdain towards humans throughout the cartoons, comics, and movies. Taken as a whole, the Transformers race doesn't care about us, although a few Autobots try. This pattern may be common among advanced alien civilizations.

It can nevertheless be disappointing that the Transformers are so militaristic and bent on total war. How realistic is that aspect of the Transformers scenario? To listen to the scientists favoring their hypothesis that highly advanced civilizations roam the galaxy in peace and tranquility, we'd get the idea that war is so primitive and destructive for all species that advancement equals pacification. But this notion is probably wrong, too. It is definitely not consistent with what we know about the cultural evolution of our own species. Quick, name the single greatest source of technological inspiration for humans during the past two hundred thousand years! Okay, the right answer is the quest for enough food. Hunting, agriculture, food processing and storage. Well, then, what's been the second most influential impulse behind technological innovation? That's right—war. Tribes of humans fighting, conquering, and enslaving other humans. How did the pathetic Europeans of the late Dark Ages (say, A.D. 1000), so far behind several other civilizations of that time, accelerate ahead and dominate the entire planet just eight hundred years later? Many historians now credit such amazing success to the intense military competition between European nations during that period.

War's probably also a major driving force behind the evolution of any other civilization. Arnold Toynbee's majestic account of all human civilizations in the ten volumes of *A Study of History*

(1934–1961) even elevates war to supreme status, necessary for explaining the course of a civilization's internal disintegration and its eventual destruction which provides essential materials for successor civilizations. Unless the human species as a whole is peculiarly perverse, rotten at its core, other alien species probably go through considerably long war-like phases, especially in the early millennia. The real question is whether war is compatible with very long term survival. Could war survive across the galaxy?

It's been argued that even if war is important for a while, at some point in any civilization's progress all war must cease. After all, the invention of nuclear weapons, capable of planetary destruction, seems to dictate that a surviving species is a peaceful species. The Vulcans of *Star Trek* renounced violence and even all emotions, to prevent their extinction at their own hands. However, is all this worry over nuclear annihilation simply fostered by the temporary fact that we are presently trapped on just one planet? If our civilization starts colonizing other planets and deep space within the next ten thousand years, no longer will the fate of the entire species rest on a single round ball of rock. Intelligent species like ours, which reach this most dangerous stage, this worrisome bottleneck of development, must pass this test. Can these species resist suicide by war? If so, then the reward is potentially infinite expansion across this galaxy and maybe other galaxies too. After a species successfully passes through the planetary bottleneck, however, it is easy to imagine that war will again arise.

In fact, if war is so devastatingly effective at inspiring fast technological development, we can infer that any very advanced race will probably have followed up its temporarily peaceful phase with even more intense warlike phases. And if there are several advanced civilizations engaged in competitive interaction, they may have every incentive to resort to war. Until a civilization gets so advanced that neither energy nor death is a problem, war is a solution. However, civilizations beyond energy and death are not going to be too interested in us, any more than we'd care to get intimate with bacteria-like organisms on other planets.

Advanced civilizations roaming around the galaxy probably still know all about war. Nor should we suppose that advanced civilizations will have advanced religions that help keep the peace. Human religions are notoriously flexible about war. Even the Transformers have a religion of sorts, according to the comics, but it's not much of a surprise. The primordial gods Unicron and

Primus battle for supremacy over the universe, and Primus creates Cybertron and the Transformers along the way to aid in the fight (recalling the ancient Persian religion of Zoroastrianism). It also seems obvious that a real militaristic civilization would have a really militaristic religion.

We've looked inside a radical argument against ETs, and refuted every premise. We should keep anticipating that First Contact will eventually happen. First Contact will probably be with an expanding civilization farther ahead than us, but not so far as to be completely indifferent to us. They may not be looking for us, and they might be just as surprised by First Contact as we are. They won't be angels, but simply absorbed in their own worries and conflicts. Hopefully, they have enough goodness among them to restrain them from annihilating us. In other words, we are assembling something similar to the Transformers scenario.

When we ponder what First Contact will be like, too often we project our own mythologies, fantasies, worries, and even our own psychologies upon hypothetical alien civilizations. It's understandable that we desperately hope that peaceful and benevolent alien races are just waiting and wanting to be contacted by such primitive species like ours. We gaze out into the vastness of space, feeling vulnerable and scared. We want angels, and dread devils. Sooner or later, the human species will have to realistically deal with whatever, and whoever, is already out there among the stars. Will we continue to play the role of conquerors, until our guilty conscience slows us down? Will we instead end up like the Aztecs, wiped out by superior firepower and deadly disease?

Maybe we secretly fear an even more terrifying future, in which we never meet anyone else and float cold and lonely in the middle of an expanding universe going nowhere. We want, and fear, First Contact. Short of meeting God, this First Contact is now driving humanity's compulsion to gaze skyward. Our imaginations conjure up dreams and nightmares. The Transformers scenario is just one of many, and arguably a prophetic one.

Still, we don't feel ready, and we shouldn't, no matter how long we look up. There's more than meets the eye, out there.

EPISODE TWO

Seeing and Believing

3
Object Lessons

KEVIN S. DECKER, KARL ERBACHER, and
GABRIEL RYE

> Technologically speaking, the closer you get to trying to do something that's really, accurately human, the farther away it's actually going to be.
>
> —GALYN SUSMAN, Technical Director for Pixar's *Toy Story*[1]

In 1984, Autobots and Decepticons invaded western culture and heralded a new phase of America's love affair with Japanese toys and children's culture. For the philosopher, this is a good thing, because philosophers *love* robots. In western philosophy, defining the difference between the human or "natural" and the created or "artificial" has inspired thinkers from Aristotle to Noam Chomsky.

Robots are not only useful conceptual guinea pigs when considering questions in the philosophy of mind. As technology becomes more seamlessly integrated with our daily needs and concerns, our examination of artificial intelligences and humanoid mechanisms allow us to ask questions about what it genuinely means to be human. Happily, the mythology of the Transformers generally gives positive responses to these questions. For example, episodes of the *Transformers* animated series that take place after the events of the 1986 animated movie show the Autobots as key to humanity's achieving its utopian ideals through advanced technology. This seems to confirm J.P. Telotte's view that the positive depiction of robots in media shows "how our technological creations might help us deal with the world we are in the process of

---

[1] Quoted in Michael Mallory, "Creating a New Buzz," *Los Angeles Times* (November 18th, 1999), Weekend Section, pp. 8, 10.

making, help us draw back from the apocalyptic direction in which we seem to be headed, by leading us toward a new and deeper sense of self."[2]

In the Transformers' memorable tag lines, "more than meets the eye" and "robots in disguise," we discover an entry point for a different philosophical approach to these variously benevolent and malevolent visitors from Cybertron. In the universe of the Transformers, human nature is linked to the future of these alien beings—the most recent example of this being the presence of the All Spark on Earth in the movie *Transformers*. Perhaps the most bizarre emergence of this theme is the Japan-only line of "Transformers Kiss Players," the idea behind which is that Transformers are powered by snogging with young girls![3]

Is it possible to learn something of human nature, and specifically about the relationship of the human mind and body, by considering the nature of the Transformers' robotic existence as "more than meets the eye"? Does the fact that the Transformers have capacities hidden from perception have a bearing on the way we envision the objects of our human senses? In providing some answers for these questions, we hope to steal a little fire from Primus, the Transformer god, to further illuminate what it means to be human.

"I bought a car—turned out to be an alien robot! Who knew?"

In the history of philosophy, questions about the relation between mind and body have sometimes been posed as questions about *perception*—that is, questions about the way in which the minds of subjects relate to the objects of the world. The very word 'objectivity'—meaning a neutral way of viewing the world aside from people's idiosyncrasies—is closely tied to the word 'object'. But what is an object? Simple and non-controversial examples of objects would be this book you hold in your hand, the maple tree

---

[2] *Replications: A Robotic History of the Science Fiction Film*, University of Illinois Press, 1995, p. 21. See also the animated episode "Nightmare Planet" in which the innocuous human capability to dream is used as a weapon by the Quintessons; only the intervention of Rodimus Prime can overcome this threat from within.

[3] www.takaratomy.co.jp/products/TF/kiss.

outside, and that battered yellow Chevy Camaro that mysteriously appeared on your lawn last night.

But how do we know that this book *is* a book (and not, say, a book-shaped box for holding valuables), and specifically, a book entitled *Transformers and Philosophy*? How do we know that that is a *tree*, and not a *hedge*; that the Camaro is merely an inanimate vehicle, and isn't a moonlighting robot who saves the world? We know these things because of our perceptive capabilities, which allow us to become aware of something through the use of the senses.

Consider simple, automatic perceptions such as hearing the whine of Starscream's F-22 Raptor missiles or smelling oil and ozone when Ironhide's about. The difference between these perceptions, on the one hand, and visually perceiving *objects* like the book, maple tree, or robot-in-disguise Camaro, on the other, is that three-dimensional objects have *hidden aspects* to them that are not immediately perceptible. What exactly does this mean?

For one thing, no one can both see the facing and the reverse side of something in front of her. So I cannot, unaided by technology, stand directly in front of the hood of Bumblebee's Camaro form and simultaneously view his trunk. But there aren't just *two* perspectives on every object—obverse and reverse, trunk and hood—but actually a large, potentially unlimited, number of perspectives (from beneath, from above, right fender, left fender, and so on). Each of these perspectives reveals a different aspect of the object, making it appear slightly differently to us. From *no single one* of these individual aspects of the thing could we say that we had a comprehensive view of the object, and it's also true that our senses don't allow us to take in *all* the possible perspectives. We could even come up with a down-to-earth definition of the "objectivity" of an object by defining it in terms of this "view from everywhere"—the all-inclusive perspective on it that is greater than any single person's perceptive capabilities can handle.[4] With this limitation, we could conclude that *we can never fully know the appearance of even the simplest object*!

---

[4] As Merleau-Ponty (who we will meet later) puts it, the object "is none of these appearances; it is . . . the flat projection of these perspectives and of all possible perspectives, that is, the perspectiveless position from which all can be derived." *The Phenomenology of Perception*, excerpted in *Maurice Merleau-Ponty: Basic Writings*, Routledge, 2004, p. 79.

But this seems to go against what we normally assume. Let's look at two different attempts in the philosophy of perception to overcome this unexpected and unwelcome result. First, there was the effort by René Descartes (1596–1650) to engineer a solution to the problem of how we see the world "right side up" when our eyes actually function to invert our visual field. Imagine a blind man holding up two sticks crossed in an "X" shape in front of him. The blind man cannot *see* the ends of the sticks, but he knows conclusively that the stick held in his right hand ends near his *left* ear, the stick held in his left hand near his *right*. How is this simple bit of knowledge produced, if not from sense experience? Descartes's explanation was that certain simple rules of geometry are *innate* to the human mind, and can be known *a priori*, or without the benefit of sense perception at all. According to Descartes's way of thinking, both the blind and the sighted need native but unconscious processes to occur in the mind so that we can triangulate objects in the world.

Philosophical empiricists such as George Berkeley (1685–1753) rejected the central belief of Descartes, namely that there were innate ideas that made perception possible. The empiricists believed that *all* our knowledge of objects is gained through sense experience, the information provided by the five senses. They produced detailed and often convincing arguments against the principles Descartes treated as independent of past sense experience, principles vital to comprehending the "hidden" parts of an object.

Empiricists claimed that Descartes's rules of the mind were not innate at all, but instead an accumulation of basic sensory interactions with the world. Like a good empiricist, Berkeley proposed that anything we sense at a distance, which accounts for nearly every experience of seeing, hearing or smelling, is less certain than "close up" tactual experiences, when *touching* things. But there's a problem here: there are many things that we have reliable sensory knowledge about that we *cannot* touch (like the moon) or wouldn't *want* to touch (like the disgusting Scorponok or Tarantulas from *Beast Wars*). Berkeley deals with this conundrum by saying that we "cross-reference" uncertain visual experiences with bodily motions—like the movements of muscles, or the body as a whole—that we experience directly and with certainty. The cognitive scientist Zygmunt Pizlo explains:

> . . . when an observer looks at an object binocularly, the line of sight of each eye is directed toward the object, forming an angle called "ver-

> gence." The observer is aware of the angle by feeling the state of his eye muscles, and when the observer walks toward the object, the angle changes and the sensations associated with change are noticed. The relation between the sensations form the eye muscles and the number of steps required to reach the object is learned, stored, and used later by means of what we would call today a "look-up table" to provide the mechanism underlying the perception of distance. (*3D Shape: Its Unique Place in Visual Perception*, MIT Press, 2008, p. 14)

We might call what is going on in Berkeley's thinking "associative learning," which is very different from doing geometry, as Descartes said. In fact, some Transformers seem to be capable of associative learning: in the animated series episode "Attack of the Autobots," Jazz and Bumblebee must rely on both sensory experience *and* memory to uncover the truth that the other Autobots have been tampered with by Megatron to make them more aggressive (the change to red eyes is always a dead giveaway!).

What's most important for our purposes in Berkeley's advance over Descartes is that it points to the fact that all human experience is made possible by the fact that we have a body. In the history of philosophy, the human body has either been overlooked, or in some cases has gotten a bad rap from thinkers like Plato and Descartes. It's important that we begin to think about how important having a body is to being human, to being a person at all.[5] Beyond this, we mustn't forget that all associative learning based on the senses is gained by *action*, that is through motor experience, testing things out in the world by bumping bits of our body up against things in different ways to produce different sensations for further "cross-referencing." In an excellent recent study called *How the Body Shapes the Mind*, Shaun Gallagher sums up this discovery: "The shape and size of objects are perceived not simply in phenomenal terms (phenomenal size of an object depending on distance from the perceiver), but in pragmatic terms (as something I can grasp or manipulate)."[6]

Yet the importance of this central insight may, like the nature of the Camaro on the lawn, not be immediately intelligible. Clearly,

---

[5] For details on how philosophy has ignored or marginalized the body, and on current approaches that take the body seriously, see Kevin S. Decker, "Knockout! *Killer's Kiss*, the Somatic, and Kubrick," in *The Philosophy of Stanley Kubrick*, edited by Jerold J. Abrams, University Press of Kentucky, 2007.

[6] *How the Body Shapes the Mind*, Clarendon, 2005, p. 8.

more must be said about the relation between mind and body, and accordingly how we know about objects' hidden traits.

"Is it fear or courage that compels you, fleshling?"

Of all the objects we encounter on a daily basis, the human body may be the most remarkably adaptable, certainly more so than the Transformers! Whether dancing or scuba diving, typing or hiding in a tight space from Megatron's latest rampage, the human body is the paradigm of adaptable *usefulness*, next to which all the objects invented to take over our work pale by comparison. But this way of treating the body as "useful" rests on a central presupposition that Descartes and many empiricists shared: that the body and the mind were essentially two different things, related in such a way that the body stands as a tool or instrument for accomplishing the purposes put forth by the mind. Contrast this with what happens to Spike Witwicky in the animated *Transformers* episode "Autobot Spike" when Spike's mind is transferred into an Autobot body, with the result being extraordinary confusion and conflict for this new "hybrid Transformer." This episode implies that the mind and body are so interconnected that it makes no sense to say that they could be separated from each other (yet the reverse phenomena—Autobot "minds" transferred into human bodies in "Only Human" doesn't seem to produce such confusion).

This hierarchy of mind over body has been challenged by the school of thought called *phenomenology*. Phenomenologists concentrate on the study of consciousness and the way things appear to us directly: Edmund Husserl, its founder, described it as the adoption of the "natural attitude" of simply describing objects without applying any philosophical or scientific theories to them.[7] Maurice Merleau-Ponty (1908–1961) even went beyond this, insisting that the body is absolutely essential to "the way things appear to us directly." Merleau-Ponty refused to accept the dualism of mind and body. For him, the problems that concerned Descartes and Berkeley were the direct result of *reducing* what is essentially human to a mere element of scientific theory. Against this idea, Merleau-Ponty declares, "I cannot understand the function of the living body except by enacting it myself, and except in so far as I

---

[7] See Husserl, "The Basic Approach of Phenomenology," in *The Essential Husserl*, edited by Donn Welton, Indiana University Press, 1999, pp. 60–63.

am a body which rises towards the world."[8] For him, there is a more basic science—phenomenology—that deals with the way we "enact" our living on an everyday basis.

Because they attempt to "go behind" current scientific theory to the appearances of objects themselves, phenomenologists like Husserl and Merleau-Ponty try to take nothing for granted. So when I say that I know about an object's hidden qualities—a robot inside a gun, a tank inside a robot—they would not take it for granted that I know what I am talking about. Let's turn to Merleau-Ponty's frankly cryptic response to Descartes and Berkeley about how we know the hidden sides of things. In *The Phenomenology of Perception*, Merleau-Ponty tells us, "To see is to enter a universe of beings which *display themselves*, and they would not do this if they could not be hidden behind each other or behind me. In other words: to look at an object is to inhabit it, and from this habitation to grasp all things in terms of the aspect which they present to it."[9] Transformers can "display themselves," because they are animate, just like us. But what about trees and books? And what does it mean for us to "inhabit" an object?

Without assuming that there is an all-encompassing, "objective" perspective from which all hiddenness of objects is revealed, Merleau-Ponty takes up the challenge of Descartes and Berkeley, agreeing with both that our *perception* of an object is much wider than what we actually *sense* about it. Yet he disagrees with Descartes that geometry provides an explanation for this gap, and with Berkeley that "cross-referencing" what we *do* see with muscular motions allows us to fill in the gap. What we see, for a phenomenologist like Merleau-Ponty, is "determinate," which means we can give a straightforward account of how it appears to us. By contrast, the hidden qualities of objects are "indeterminate," we cannot give a good account of them. When we consider an object *as* an object, and not merely a set of potentially disconnected appearances, "there occurs here an *indeterminate vision*," Merleau-Ponty writes, a "*vision de je ne sais quoi*" (a vision of "I do not know what").[10] This "indeterminate vision" is not guesswork or

---

[8] *Maurice Merleau-Ponty: Basic Writings*, p. 86.

[9] *Maurice Merleau-Ponty: Basic Writings*, p. 81.

[10] Merleau-Ponty, quoted in Sean Dorrance Kelly, "Seeing Things in Merleau-Ponty," *The Cambridge Companion to Merleau-Ponty*, Cambridge University Press, 2005, p. 80.

mere, confusion, however; it is a description of how our visual perception works in terms of 1. a focus of attention and 2. its contrast with a background. Since we are focusing on a particular object or area of our field of vision, the rest of our field (the background) is present, but not the center of our attention. It is indeterminate.

As an illustration of this, consider Sam Witwicky's situation when he first sees Bumblebee in his robotic form in the steelyard in the movie *Transformers*. This is an ideal example, since director Michael Bay clearly filmed this short scene in a way that ambiguously portrays the focus of attention for both Sam and the audience; we are not clear what exactly we are seeing. Clearly, the colossal robot standing far away is the focus of attention; but why does Sam not think that this is a nondescript piece of forge equipment? What allows him to distinguish Bumblebee from the rest of the junk in the steelyard? And more to the point, how is he so sure the next morning that this robot is his Camaro, albeit transformed?

This is plainly a situation in which our perception of an object is much wider than what we actually sense about it. Since we, like Sam, don't see a complete shift from vehicle to robot form, the "hiddenness" of Bumblebee within the Camaro is not something we directly experience. Knowing that the robot casting the Autobot signal to the skies *is* the car requires a kind of logical connecting of the dots. More than this, it requires a process to occur in both Sam and us (the audience) that we are typically unconscious of, and that involves an interplay between focus of attention and background. A situation that illustrates this fact is found in the animated episode "Dark Awakening," when Spike and Daniel Witwicky encounter the cold, lifeless shell of Optimus Prime in a tomb. In this morbid situation, Optimus is no longer the reassuring figure we've come to expect.

For Merleau-Ponty, our sense-perception of an object is not limited to what our attention is focused on. The way the object appears to us is also affected by the other objects and environment that surround it—lights, reflective surfaces, dominant colors, similar objects. In the case of Bumblebee in the steelyard, the lack of good lighting means that Sam's perception of the robot is more ambiguous than, say, his perception of Megatron under the actinic lights of the Hoover Dam bunker. Equally, the inanimate machines in the steelyard make it difficult for Sam to know if he is simply mistaking a crane, for example, for an Autobot. While it isn't right to say that the lighting and the steelyard equipment are part of

Sam's focus of attention (they are, in Merleau-Ponty's words, part of the "indeterminate" background), they aren't *irrelevant* to what he perceives. Instead, as Merleau-Ponty scholar Sean Dorrance Kelly says, in cases such as this, "The lighting context presents itself not as a determinate quality but rather in terms of *how well it enables me to see the thing I'm looking at.*"[11]

The language used here is carefully chosen: by "how well [the background context] enables me to see the thing," Kelly wants to say that our perception of a thing is founded upon an understanding of what the background *would need to be like* for us to have an "optimal" (no pun intended) perceptual experience of it. Sam needs to move closer to the robot, get through the haze of concrete dust between them; this urge is, for Merleau-Ponty, part of the perceptual experience, in the same way that some people feel compelled to touch statues or "kick the tires" of a used car.

Simply by attending a movie called *Transformers*, we know important things that Sam doesn't. Nevertheless, his decision to say that his car "transformed . . . it *stood up*!" is informed by a perceptual value judgment that is at the same time a call to action: "If I had gotten closer, seen the robot in good lighting, perhaps even touched it, I would have known that this amazing machine and my Camaro were, in fact, the same thing."

According to Kelly, the importance of the interplay between focus of attention and background in Merleau-Ponty's view of the perception of hidden traits of objects is *not* that the background provides more information about the object, allowing us to make our understanding of it more determinate (as we have seen, sometimes the background doesn't cooperate). To have seen the object in all its hidden qualities, I would have had to move *this way* or adjust the lighting conditions *up* or *down*. Of course, to do these things, I need a living, acting body. Shaun Gallagher's take on what is going on here is this: "For Merleau-Ponty, motor experience and perceptual experience are . . . reciprocally linked. The mature operation of a body schema [how the body shapes perception] depends on a developed perceptual knowledge of one's own body; and the organized perception of one's own body, and then of the external world, depends on a proper functioning of the body schema."[12]

---

[11] Kelly, "Seeing Things in Merleau-Ponty," p. 84; italics added.

[12] *How the Body Shapes the Mind*, p. 67.

Now let's return, with this understanding, to Merleau-Ponty's unusual statement about perception and hiddenness: "To see is to enter a universe of beings which *display themselves*, and they would not do this if they could not be hidden behind each other or behind me." Now we can say that objects are not at all passively perceived, since they "display themselves" as a function of the interplay between focus of attention and background. He continues: "To look at an object is to inhabit it, and from this habitation to grasp all things in terms of the aspect which they present to it."[13]

This odd notion of "inhabiting" objects is nothing more than our unconscious yet invaluable bodily habit of making subtle value judgments about the optimal conditions for perception, then attempting to act upon them. The limits of our body imply the limits of our perceptions, and so of our knowledge. In short, the more we know about our body, the more we know about what we count as an object and how sure we can be of an object's qualities that may be "in disguise."

"Until that day, till all are one." When Our Reach Exceeds Our Grasp

Would Merleau-Ponty have been a Transformers fan? He was fascinated by the potential for the philosophical study of the visual arts, especially painting. Like many of us, he enjoyed movies. But given this French phenomenologist's "embodied" response to the problems with perception that we started off with, an immediate question arises with regard to the way the Transformers, as special effects, are portrayed on the big screen. That question is, does the status of CGI (computer-generated imagery) creatures and environments as "virtual objects" change the way we must look at perception?

For anyone who hasn't been in stasis lock for the past fifteen years, it's no surprise to hear that the use of eye-popping CGI has mostly replaced the physical spacecraft, matte paintings, stop-motion animations, and puppets that used to populate science-fiction and fantasy films. CGI has become so pervasive that it is changing the way we look at the "real," non-movie world: it has itself become a philosophical problem. In *The Reality Effect*, film studies critic Joel Black pinpoints this problem:

---

[13] *Maurice Merleau-Ponty: Basic Writings*, p. 81.

> It's now common to hear the three-dimensional universe described cinematically, as a thin membrane in which we are trapped like 'characters playing out their lives within the confines of a movie screen'. Unknown to these shallow, two-dimensional players, a larger universe spreads into numerous extra dimensions, like theaters in a multiplex.[14]

Although the use of CGI has a number of different goals, the one that concerns us most directly here and now is the filmmaker's ability, through computer-aided modeling and rendering, to achieve spectacles—armies, vast alien vistas, agile titans of steel—that were previously not possible through the deft manipulation of costumes, props, and other "real" objects. George Lucas, who championed the wholesale use of CGI in the *Star Wars* prequel trilogy, said in its defense, "we can create a photo-realistic, digital character that can look as real as any actor . . ." Digital characters—like the Transformers—have a wider range of expression and action than latex or animated versions would have had.[15]

This greater range of expression and action—the behavioral equivalent of the "hiddenness" of everyday objects—is both the blessing and the curse of CGI. Audiences who enthusiastically pay to see *Transformers* or the *Star Wars* and *The Lord of the Rings* trilogies multiple times obviously know the blessings. The curse is that what is revealed about the "abilities" of virtual characters through CGI—whether this is Yoda bouncing off walls in a lightsaber duel or Brawl and Bumblebee destroying a highway overpass—can seriously overstrain our suspension of disbelief. The savvy cinemagoer knows that since *anything* is possible with computer imagery, no matter how big the payout might be, the original investment was essentially *hollow*.

Through his phenomenological look at our perception of objects, Merleau-Ponty gives us reasons to understand why we might be discontented with grandiose CGI effects even if we enjoy them. If he's right, then beyond the entertainment value of CG imagery, we experience a disconnect with such images at the level

---

[14] *The Reality Effect: Film Culture and the Graphic Imperative*, Routledge, 2002, p. 206; Black is quoting K.C. Cole, "Unseen Dimensions Hold Theory Aloft," *Los Angeles Times* (November 18th, 1999), p. B2.

[15] Quoted in *The Reality Effect*, p. 206. Contrast Lucas's conviction with the often-heard complaint on *Star Wars* blogs that the puppet Yoda, for example, had more "human qualities" when controlled by Frank Oz than the CGI version in Episodes II and III.

of embodied perception because we know that these creations of light and texture have no surfaces to investigate, no unknown aspects to provoke us.

In other words, on a bodily level, we realize that there is literally *nothing to grasp,* no hiddenness of these virtual characters, and our perceptive powers are perhaps the worse for it. Maybe when the next generation of filmmakers "transform and roll out" effects that we can get a grip on, they'll have studied some phenomenology first.[16]

---

[16] Special thanks go out to William Franklin Campbell IV for loaning us his Transformers library and extensive expertise.

4

What Changes when Transformers Transform?

MICHAEL SPICHER

Everybody experiences change. People change from infants to adults. Transformers change from robots to vehicles—Optimus Prime changes from a semi truck to a robot, and back again. Something changes in a person who develops amnesia. Modern surgery even allows people to change their sex.

When a person changes, we still think he or she is the same person after the change. So there has to be something that remains the same throughout all of these transformations. Grown-ups commonly assume that they were infants years ago—that they are the same person as that long-vanished child. But what is it that stays the same when a person changes? Philosophers have investigated this question, which they call Personal Identity, but they have not been able to reach agreement on the answer.

We humans are persons, and Transformers are also persons. Since the Transformers are still in control of their actions when they change to vehicle form (and then back to robot form), it seems evident that something about them has remained the same over the course of their changes through time. These transformations occur in just a few seconds, whereas changes in human being may take several years. But by considering the changes undergone by Transformers, we may come up with some answers about changes in human beings.

A Pile of Parts or a Unified Whole?

Over two thousand years ago, Aristotle observed the distinction between a unity and a heap. In his *Metaphysics*, Aristotle attempted to understand the cause of unity: why is each human considered to be one thing and not just a bunch of things thrown together? Aristotle's answer? He believed that each part of a human needs the whole in order to survive.

What Aristotle meant was that a human is not a random collection of parts, for example hands, feet, a mouth, and so on. Each part of the human being exists for the sake of the whole human being, to perform certain functions. If one of these *parts* were removed, that part would only remain the same in appearance. For example, if my hand were cut off, then it could not perform the functions of a hand anymore. It could not grab things or touch things. Once it's separated from my body, my hand is more similar to a statue of a hand than a real, living hand. A detached hand only looks like a hand; it's no longer a hand in actuality. I would become a man missing a hand, but I would still be a unity.

Similarly for Transformers, if Megatron's leg were severed in the midst of battle, then his leg would no longer be part of his identity. However, the rest of his body would still be a unity. On the other hand, a pile of bricks is considered to be a heap. There is no unity among them. You could remove one brick. It is still a brick, and the pile is still a pile. However, after a builder makes a house from this pile of bricks, then the pile becomes a unity and not a mere heap. A unity continues through change, but a heap, as in the case of the bricks, becomes something different. When bricks are put together to make a house, we call it a house, not a pile of bricks in the shape of a house. When the house was built, the heap of bricks actually became something else, something with a different identity.

Accidental and Substantial Change

Two broad categories of change have been considered in metaphysics: accidental and substantial. In order to understand the transformation of robots into vehicles and back again, it seems necessary to know the nature of the change.

If you paint your red bicycle green, it's still a bicycle. This kind of change is considered accidental because it does not change anything essential to the thing, in this case a bicycle. Examples of common accidental changes among human beings are getting a haircut, growing bigger (in height or weight), or changing clothes. These changes do not add to or subtract from the essence of being a human individual.

A substantial change, however, involves the cessation of one being and the beginning of a new one, at least in a sense. Suppose a tree gets cut down and trimmed into small pieces of wood. The tree cannot function as a tree any longer; therefore, a substantial change has occurred. If the wood, which could be used to make a table and chairs, is burned in a fire, then another substantial change occurs. After the wood is burned up, it does not have the potential to become a table and chairs anymore. When the essence of the thing changes, then a substantial change has taken place.

A Transformer is always in control of his actions, regardless of whether in the shape of a robot or vehicle. Recalling a scene from the movie *Transformers* will be helpful to illustrate this point. The Transformers are able to choose the disguise into which they transform. Bumblebee originally chose to become an old car, which Sam Witwicky purchased as his first car, not realizing it was a robot in disguise. Later on, Mikaelea Banes comments that for such a sophisticated being, the car was a piece of junk. At that comment, Bumblebee, perhaps embarrassed, ejects them from the car, and chooses for his new disguise a cooler car. This scene shows Bumblebee in control of his actions at all times. Their ability to transform is part of their essence, who they are as beings. This ability is comparable to a human putting on a mask to disguise his or her identity. Therefore, the transformation is an accidental change, not a substantial one.

Two Popular Views about Identity through Time

What preserves the identity of beings that change through time? Why is Bumblebee the same Transformer when he's a car as he is when he's a robot?

There are two types of identity which can easily be confused: numerical identity and qualitative identity. If a man had a religious conversion, then we might say that he has become a new or different person. However, this is just a manner of speaking. A religious conversion is a change of qualitative identity, which is an accidental change. In this chapter, we're more interested in numerical identity. Numerical identity concentrates on one thing being the same thing, despite any qualitative changes that may have occurred. Starscream today has the same numerical identity of the Starscream that existed two years ago, even if, for example, he decided to change color.

Identity Means Psychological Continuity?

The main way in which philosophers have attempted to explain personal identity is in terms of people's psychology: the continuity of their minds. Memories, beliefs, consciousness, and so on are each possible candidates for that which preserves one's identity. Basically, a person yesterday that is psychologically continuous with a person today is the same person, regardless of which facet of psychology preserves identity. So a Transformer would need to have some capacity for memory, consciousness, or belief, in order to have his or her identity preserved. John Locke (1632–1704) pioneered the notion that memory is the aspect of psychology that preserves identity.[1]

The memories stored within a person's mind must be causally connected to the events they depict. In other words, it's not sufficient to rely on someone else's claim that they performed a task yesterday. My memory of a particular task must be caused by that task itself. But still, the view that memory is all we need for preserving personal identity has some problems. When someone has lived a long life, it can quite easily happen that the person thinks that events occurred one way, even though they actually happened in a different way. Imagine two ninety-year-old sisters, and each one believes that it was she who did *X* at age ten (when we know that it could only have been one of them who did *X*).

Memory can be mistaken, and so it doesn't seem enough to guarantee continued personal identity. Let's suppose that you have a memory of playing soccer in 2000. An implicit presumption of having this memory is that the current 'you' is identical with the 'you' playing soccer in 2000. Some recent philosophers have tried to find ways to avoid the inadequacies of memory, usually by trying to uncover a different aspect of psychology to posit as the criterion for identity. Consciousness, beliefs, and intentions are some of the other psychological aspects that philosophers have considered as possibly preserving personal identity.

Identity is Equivalent to Bodily Continuity?

The other main way philosophers have attempted to answer the question of personal identity is to relate it to the individual's phys-

---

[1] John Locke, *An Essay Concerning Human Understanding* (Penguin, 2004), pp. 296ff.

ical or bodily existence. The philosopher Judith Jarvis Thomson, for instance, has advocated the view that people *are* their bodies.[2] Wherever the body is, that's where someone's identity also is. When we see someone we know from far away, we often recognize them simply in virtue of their body. Even in those cases where I think I see one of my friends far away and it turns out that I was mistaken, my realization that it was merely someone who resembled my friend is also based on physical appearance. We recognize Optimus Prime as a robot or in his disguise as a truck.

The view that people's continuing identities are to be found in their bodies has become more popular recently, because it is able to handle some of the problems facing the psychological view. One problem is the beginning of human life. If memory or consciousness is required for personal identity, then an embryo, a fetus, or someone's body in a persistent vegetative state (such as a coma) is not part of the continuous existence of a human person. Once memory or consciousness develops, then the embryo or fetus becomes a new being, a human person. However, in the bodily view, persons, in the most basic sense, are identical to their bodies at all phases of bodily development. So there's no problem about me believing I'm the same entity I was when I was a fetus or a newborn baby.

This view has the added advantage that it recognizes the body's importance. The bodily aspect of existence is a necessary component of being human. The bodily view maintains that both the living body and the corpse are the same person, since the person simply is equal to his or her body. This view works well with understanding Transformers because their identity is preserved through changes as long as they have the same body, although the parts of that body can be drastically re-arranged. However, although the bodily approach has some advantages over the psychological approach, it also has some problems of its own.

Some Problems with These Approaches

The psychological perspective suggests the body is either irrelevant or an accidental part of the human being or Transformer. And yet, the first thing we recognize about a person is their physical

---

[2] Judith Jarvis Thomson, "People and their Bodies," in *Reading Parfit*, edited by Jonathan Dancy (Blackwell, 1997).

appearance, their body. So it must be a mistake to assume that the body is irrelevant, even if the body is not the only ingredient to personal identity. Furthermore, a person's psychological existence, his or her mental life, is not continuous.

It's natural to assume that we began as embryos and then became fetuses. These phases of life have no conscious existence. So they can't be psychologically continuous with a conscious human adult. Someone who holds the 'psychological' view of personal identity would have to conclude that once the fetus becomes a conscious infant, then an entirely new being has come into existence. This conclusion follows from the notion of personal identity being preserved solely through a psychological component.

There's another problem resulting from the psychological perspective. If a human being entered into a persistent vegetative state, then this person's identity would no longer be preserved. Once again a new being would come into existence with the loss of consciousness or memory, depending on which psychological component preserves personal identity through time. Furthermore, if Megatron's memory were transplanted into another Transformer's body, then that other body would become Megatron, rendering his body as not essential to him as a person. In other words, it would not matter what body encased his consciousness and memory.

The advantage of the bodily view is its ability to allow for a continuous existence of the human being, regardless of the human's mental states. And yet, if we're identical to our bodies, what happens to our identities when we die? If someone dies in a way that does not destroy their body, does that person still have personal identity since the body continues to exist? If so, then we would continue to exist until the body has fully decomposed or been cremated.

Anyone who has been to a wake or funeral with an open casket can attest that the corpse is no longer identical to the person they knew; the corpse merely resembles the person they knew. What then changed about the human being at death, if the body is still present? Is it merely the fact that the body is no longer moving? We tend to assume that a substantial change has occurred in the human being. If so, then the human must have something beyond just a body to account for its personhood. Aristotle (384–322 B.C.E.) claimed that a corpse is more closely related to a statue than to a person, which jibes with our experience. However, the bodily view gives no reason to assume the identity of a person necessarily ceases at death. Suppose Bonecrusher died, and his body was actually crushed, as an ironic ending. Would the crushed body really still be him, provided all the pieces were there? It seems unlikely. Therefore, the bodily approach is insufficient to account for personal identity.

Each one of these approaches has certain advantages over the other one. However, ultimately each one seems to be insufficient as the primary basis for preserving personal identity through time. Perhaps there's an intermediate position that could encompass the advantages of these positions without their downfalls.

Transformers change from robots to vehicles. Humans change from infants to adults. An acorn changes into an oak tree. Most people will not deny that something is constant in all of these changes, even though clearly something has changed.

Based on human experience, the mind and body seem to have a reciprocal relationship, rather than one controlling or producing the other. If someone worries too much, then that person could develop a physical ailment from this mental or emotional state, such as high blood pressure. Moreover, if someone receives a blow to the head, which is certainly physical, then that person could suffer some mental impairment, such as loss of consciousness or even of memory. A combination of the psychological and bodily views could account for this reciprocal relationship.

Substance as a Compound of Form and Matter

In the *Metaphysics*, Aristotle attempts to unravel precisely what is meant by the term 'substance'. Substances are those things which have independent existence. We know that people, plants, and other animals are considered substances. What makes something a substance?

Aristotle sees substance as a composite, because it has two aspects: form and matter. Form can be defined as what a thing is. For example, what makes a tree *be* a tree is its form. Form should not be confused with shape because it is more of an internal drive toward actuality, rather than how a thing happens to look. Put another way, form organizes the matter in a particular way in order for that thing to be what it is. In living things, Aristotle equates the form with the thing's soul. Soul, in this sense, should not be understood spiritually but metaphysically; it is the principle of configuration for the matter. The form causes the matter to develop in a particular way.

Transformers have something comparable to a soul called the Spark. Each Transformer was created with a Spark, which is the source of life for the Transformer organism. The other component, matter, can be defined as what a thing *could* be. The matter of a thing is the physical aspect of its existence. It is what makes the thing exist in a particular way, while the form is the actuality of the matter. Matter is also the principle of individuation among things. It is matter that differentiates two people, even if they are identical twins. In my understanding of Aristotle, the two aspects, form and matter, are not two separate entities. They are simply two perspectives of the same substance. In this view, living things are neither solely material nor immaterial. Living things are composed of both aspects.

Form Preserves the Identity of Things

Following Aristotle's metaphysical theory, the form of something is what preserves its identity. The form is the metaphysical principle that guides the development of something toward its end or fulfillment. This end refers to the fact that an acorn will develop, provided nothing external hinders it, into an oak tree. Living things develop a certain way toward a final state, unless an external force prevents them.

What differentiates one thing from another is its matter. For example, two oak trees have the same form, even though they probably do not look identical. However, it is the matter that identifies them as separate entities. The form enables us to identify things in reality, since the form is what a thing is. Therefore, the form also preserves the identity of those things. We identify an oak tree as an oak tree because of its form. Suppose someone comes along and chops down the oak tree, makes some wooden planks, and then makes a chest out of the planks. Do we still want to call the chest an oak tree? No. The reason is that the form has been changed. The oak tree can no longer move its matter toward actualization. Hence, it has undergone a substantial change, not a mere accidental change. The principle of life has been removed from the oak tree. Without the form, or principle of life, the oak tree no longer has its identity as an oak tree. It becomes mere wood. Without the Spark, a Transformer would be a mere heap of parts.

The Composite and Personal Identity

I know a tree because of its form. I know a human by its form. And I know a Transformer by its form. But how does all this relate to *personal* identity? Human individuality is an important dimension in personal identity. The emphasis on individuality diminishes as biology becomes simpler. We tend to view human beings and dogs, for example, as possessing a greater individuality than slugs and roaches. However, there are more dimensions to individuality among human beings than even other complex animals like dogs. Humans have diverse personalities, beliefs, imaginations, and many other mental abilities. The form, in the generic sense, may preserve the identity of a human being as such, but it seems there needs to be something more in the case of personal identity through time and change.

The psychological approach to identity emphasizes the role of the immaterial as the sole guiding force. On the other hand, the bodily approach contends that the material aspect is the persistence criterion of the human being. However, these two aspects, the immaterial and material, should not be viewed as wholly isolated from one another, but rather dependent on one another in a reciprocal relationship.

Formal Causality as the Governing Principle

Formal causality governs the way matter becomes configured toward a certain end state, or the thing's actuality. The form causes the matter to develop toward its end or fulfillment. In the Aristotelian approach, there's a direct relationship between the form and matter, between soul and body.

Transformers also require a relationship between the Spark and their material component. As long as people insist on making the soul and body an either/or distinction, then difficulties will plague the discussion. However, if we consider the idea that soul and body—form and matter—might comprise a both/and unity, then it seems we are closer to dissolving this mystery. Form (actuality) and matter (potentiality) are two aspects of the same thing. Trying to uncover what unifies them is already assuming that they are two separate entities.

For Aristotle, form and matter are separable only as concepts, not as actually entities. For Aquinas, the soul can survive the destruction of the body, but it is not complete without the body.

The question concerning how two completely different types of things can influence each other dissolves, since there are not two entirely different types of things. Formal causality is merely the principle of configuration of the matter, guiding it towards actualization. The form will guide the matter provided that nothing external hinders its development. For example, an acorn will become a tree, unless someone cuts it down prematurely or a forest fire consumes it.

Due to the principle of formal causality, there is a unique relationship between the soul and body that is necessary for the preservation of personal identity. The form and matter are one, and they cannot be separated. If this view is correct, then all the ideas about transferring minds from one body to another would become futile. There is a special way that the soul and body are intermingled that cannot be replaced by another body or soul or mind. This view seems to correspond to experience more fully, which I mentioned earlier: a bump on the head can affect one's consciousness, or a person who worries too much could become physically ill.

Personhood Naturally Develops in Human Beings

Personhood is a natural development arising from the composite of form and matter, but it is not the most fundamental aspect of the human organism.[3] If, for some reason, someone fails to develop into a person with consciousness, they still have identity as a human organism. It's part of the normal development of a human organism to become a person. An acorn will become an oak tree, unless it's hindered by external forces. Likewise, a human organism will become a person as long as nothing external prevents it. The form and matter develop in such a way that a conscious mind emerges in the process of the developing human.

The mind emerges not as a separate entity, but as an aspect of the overall human organism. The mind cannot be reduced to the body nor can the body be reduced to the mind. Mind and body are two aspects of the same unified being, which is composed of a material and immaterial aspect. The composite view is able to get

[3] Eric Olson presents a version of this view in his book *The Human Animal* (Oxford University Press, 1997).

around the problem of how the two parts interact because there are not any parts, in that sense. The body and soul compose a unity. Body and soul perform different functions for the human being, but they are one entity, not two. By soul, I mainly wish to imply the immaterial aspect of humans, which could include mind, consciousness, and imagination. The soul and body compose a unity, not a heap. Likewise, Transformers have aspects of their existence that are like the body and soul of human beings.

Are Transformers Composed of Body and Soul?

Transformers have an immaterial aspect along with a material aspect, which we can see from the following facts. First, in *Transformers: The Movie*, both the Autobots and the Decepticons are searching for the All Spark. The All Spark is the source of their existence, which can be used to create more Transformers out of machines. Second, each Transformer has a Spark, which is basically the soul of the Transformer. The Spark ensures that each Transformer has personhood. If the Spark's destroyed, then the Transformer's dead, even though the Transformer's body might still exist in the form of a corpse. Each Transformer is composed of a body and a soul. The unity of the material and the immaterial aspect of Transformers is what preserves their identity through changes in time, including but not limited to transformation. In the sense of existing as a composite, Transformers are similar to human beings. This similarity allows us to assume that the personal identity of a Transformer is preserved in the same way as that of a human being. As it turns out, when a Transformer transforms, it is only his appearance that changes, and not his identity.

Spark and Machine Together

Humans and Transformers both change with the passing of time, and there is something about them that stays the same despite changes, which may have occurred. What exactly stays the same?

The psychological approach claims that something immaterial is what preserves personal identity. This approach is inadequate because it renders the body irrelevant. The bodily approach claims that a person is identical to his or her body. This approach is wrong because seems to equate human beings with machines; it ignores the principle of life in organisms.

As an improvement on either of these approaches, I recommend a composite view. This view has its own set of difficulties, but it pushes the conversation further along by overcoming the problem of the interaction between the soul and body.

In answer to the question of what transforms, identities or appearances, the answer must be that a Transformer only changes in appearance. The Spark and body unity, like the soul and body unity that compose humans, preserves the personal identity of Transformers.[4]

[4] I would like to thank Christopher Tollefsen for providing suggestions concerning the content of an earlier draft of this chapter. I would also like to thank Hannah Spicher for correcting many grammatical incongruities.

5
In the Eye of the Beholder

JOSEF STEIFF

Maybe it's a guy thing. For years, my most meaningful relationship was with my car. I'd like to think that those were my teen years, but even into my 30s (oh, let's be honest, even now), my vehicle has held a very special place in my life. If one day it had kicked some butt and talked to me, I might have had to marry it.

Michael Bay's *Transformers* movie (2007) awakened that adolescent guy in me all over again. Sitting there in the darkened theater awash in projected images, I wondered what would happen if after the movie I discovered my Jeep Wrangler standing up and beaming a bright light into the sky. Would I react any differently than Sam? How would I know the true nature of this four-wheeled vehicle that has been my companion on numerous road trips? Could I trust my perceptions? And if so, what happens when I have two sets of perceptions that seem to contradict each other—would I question the ones that show me a simple car or the ones that seem to suggest an intelligent machine?

Like Sam, I want to believe—and tend to accept—that my perceptions are reliable, that what I see is not an illusion or a hallucination. But in *Transformers*, nothing is as it seems. Perceptual errors abound. By turns, we learn that Mikaela is not just the school's hot chick, but also a jock's savvy disgruntled girlfriend, a skilled mechanic, and a former juvenile car thief. As Sam's backyard is destroyed by the rather clumsy and not-so-adept-at-hiding Autobots, his parents perceive the rumbling vibrations and destruction as an earthquake. The eyeglasses that Sam is so desperate to sell—a keepsake of his grandfather's Arctic expedition—are in fact the equivalent of a treasure map, secretly imprinted with the co-ordinates of the All Spark. And Sam's old beat-up 1976 Camaro is actually a super-advanced intelligent robot who acts more like a big brother than a car and will help Sam navigate the pitfalls of adolescence.

"Because Cars Don't Do That, Because That Would Be Crazy."

When Mr. Witwicky takes Sam to help him buy his first car, Sam is himself a being in transformation, inhabiting that nebulous world between childhood and adulthood. Getting his first car is emblematic of this transition, and in fact, this first car will bring about changes that Sam cannot yet anticipate.

On the way to buy the car, Sam's father has a bit of fun with him by first driving into an upscale dealership. For a brief moment, Sam believes that his father is going to buy him a new expensive Porsche. He infers this from the past promise his father made, the fact that they're driving into the Porsche dealership, and his father's statement that he has a little surprise for him. Of course, Sam quickly finds out that the surprise is that his father is kidding.

Sam's father takes him instead to Bobby B's, a small dump of a used car lot. Though they don't realize it, Bumblebee is following them, and the beat-up yellow vintage Camaro turns into the lot as well, where it will wait for Sam to find it. Unfortunately, Bobby B prices the car at a thousand dollars more than Sam's father is willing to pay.

When Bobby B tries to get Sam interested in the Volkswagen Beetle next to Bumblebee, suddenly the Camaro's passenger door flies open, putting a huge dent in the side of the Volkswagen as Bumblebee pushes the rival car away. The Camaro's radio comes on and we hear a static-laced voice declare "greater than man" before a piercing sound blows out the windows of every other car on the lot. Bobby B drops Bumblebee's price.

Of course, as members of the movie audience, we are in a privileged position to know that what looks like an old beat up yellow Camaro is something else. But why doesn't Sam or his father or Bobby B seem to realize this? Bumblebee is not behaving like a car, and yet they assume that this object in front of them is indeed a car. Okay, Bobby B may have his doubts, otherwise, why drop the price? But neither Witwicky seems to consider the possibility that this old Camaro is more than meets the eye.

Ignoring the fact that *Transformers* is a movie, and that there are certain conventions of movie-going such as suspension of disbelief that are at play in order to create dramatic tension, the fact that Sam and his father do not initially perceive Bumblebee as anything other than what he seems to be—a worse-for-wear 1976 Chevrolet Camaro—may be explained in part by the fact that Sam, like us, is constantly bombarded with sensory information, more than he can possibly process, and therefore he prioritizes this sensory input, often ignoring data that does not support his initial assessment or interpretation of the situation. In other words, Sam sees what he expects to see. Even later, at the lake, when the Camaro's radio once again comes on by itself (blasting The Cars song, "Drive"), Sam doesn't think of Bumblebee as anything more than a car. This is because most of his perceptions support the notion of Bumblebee as a car, and he ignores any data that seems to contradict that perception.

We could also argue that Sam and his father have succumbed to the context of the situation: they are on a used car lot, and Bumblebee looks and feels like a car, surrounded by cars with "for sale" signs and prices stenciled on their windows. This context of the used car lot, the goal of buying a car and the preponderance of sensory information overshadow for the Witwickys the fact that Bumblebee doesn't behave like a car.

Because our context is different, we are able to more quickly understand Bumblebee's true nature. We are after all watching a movie called *Transformers*, and the odds are that we came into the theater with some understanding of the story's basic premise. But also, the film is shot in such a way that we are positioned to see, however quickly, that Bumblebee has been following the Witwickys as well as manipulating the situations with Sam. Here is a case where the car literally does pick the driver, and we as the audience are aware of that fact before Sam is.

"I Can't Be Any Clearer than How Crystal Clear I Am Being."

Sam's initial perceptions that Bumblebee is just a car get challenged when he wakes up in the middle of the night to the sounds of the Camaro starting up and driving away. Sam gives pursuit, calling 911 to report that his car has been stolen. He follows the car into a junkyard industrial area, only to discover that the vehicle has transformed into an erect metal being beaming a light into the night sky. Sam furtively records the event on his cell phone before being apprehended as the car thief, because, well, he's the only one with the Camaro when they find him.

Just because Sam has begun to realize that his initial perceptions are unreliable and that Bumblebee is more than meets the eye doesn't mean that the people around Sam yet see Bumblebee as anything other than a car. In fact, at the police station, the interrogating officer accuses Sam of taking drugs. This seems to be the only explanation for Sam's statements that his car is alive. And drugs are certainly one of the ways we account for the possibility of one's perceptions being unreliable. The police officer's assumption influences his ability to believe Sam's story as well as determines the way he treats Sam, accusing the teenager of wanting to take the officer's gun. Let's face it, if your son came home and told you his car was alive, the possibility of his taking drugs wouldn't be that far of a leap.

Generally we accept that a variety of conditions can affect our perceptions, including not just the influence of drugs but also illness, psychosis, and unusual transient physical states, such as extreme fatigue, sleep deprivation or dehydration. In the *Transformers*' story world, the primary condition that is affecting Sam's perceptions is deliberate deception on the part of the Transformers. In other words, there's nothing about his physical state that suggests his perceptions might be inaccurate.

Other factors that can affect our ability to accurately perceive objects and events include social conditioning. Sam does not live in a world where he is used to seeing cars or other objects as possibly robots. C. Blakemore and G.C. Cooper conducted and reported on a particularly intriguing experiment in 1970 regarding the role of social conditioning on perception. Though their results are cited in a variety of sources, Peter K. Smith, Helen Cowie and Mark Blades' book, *Understanding Children's Development*, provides a succinct but thorough summary of the experiment wherein two groups of kittens were each raised in a different environment, one consisting of only horizontal lines and the other of only vertical lines. After several months, the kittens were brought into a normal room, and the researchers discovered that those kittens that had been raised in the horizontal environment were unable to perceive vertical lines and vice versa. I should point out that their research suggests that this may not be due just to conditioning or learned recognition, but might also have a physiological component. Either way, it does point to the impact of environment and context on perception and perceptual limitations. We often see what we've been conditioned to see and what we expect to see.

This contributes to Sam's confusion about what his senses are telling him. Who expects his car to be lying to him? When he's recording Bumblebee sending a signal to the other Autobots, Sam reports that his car is alive, but then when the Camaro attempts to rescue him from the guard dogs, he talks as if there is a driver—"keep the car"—and later tells the arresting officers that there's someone in the car, that he's not the thief. Both sets of Sam's perceptions are in conflict with each other and don't become fully reconciled for Sam until he is later pursued by a Decepticon masquerading as a patrol car. When Bumblebee comes to rescue Sam and Mikaela from that Decepticon, they witness both vehicles transforming into what we assume are their true forms for what Mikaela describes as a giant droid death match.

"You Know What I Don't Understand? Why if He's Supposed to Be, like, This Super-advanced Robot, Does He Transform Back into This Piece-of-Crap Camaro?"

After their rescue and while being driven home, Mikaela ponders why a super advanced robot would transform into a "piece-of-crap Camaro" (her words, not mine, Bumblebee). Apparently offended, Bumblebee dumps Sam and Mikaela on the side of the road and drives off, only to return moments later as a shiny new 2007 Camaro prototype. But though some of the details have changed, Bumblebee still primarily presents himself as a car.

Much in the way that we can talk about Sam and Mikaela experiencing the illusion of the Transformers as motor vehicles, movies operate in some ways for the audience like an illusion. While watching a film, we can experience physiological changes—increased heart rate, the release of adrenalin in our bloodstream—as well as emotional shifts, such as anxiety or sadness as we engage with the plight of the characters. Many of the techniques and properties by which films affect us have been accidental discoveries. David Bordwell and Kristin Thompson note in their book, *Film Art*, that while filming a bus passing before him at the Place de l'Opera, pioneer filmmaker Georges Melies's camera jammed.

By the time he got it running again, the bus was gone and a hearse was now passing in front of the lens. Upon later screening the film, Melies discovered that the moving bus seemed to transform into the hearse because when watching a film, we tend to perceive the images as continuous. Many of the breaks in time that occur while filming are virtually invisible to our perceptions. This discovery served as the foundation for many of Melies's special effects, which were essentially tricks in perception by starting and stopping the camera during production.

The director of *Transformers*, Michael Bay, is particularly known for his use of special effects, particularly for finding ways to enhance their believability. His goal is to create a more seamless illusion that, in the case of *Transformers*, results for the audience in these robots seeming to be as real as Shia LaBeouf and Megan Fox, the actors who play Sam and Mikaela.

Though there has been some question about whether illusions and hallucinations really are indistinguishable from states of true sensory perception, much has been made of the role of perceptual errors in understanding how we know the world we perceive.

"I Think Direct Contact."

Unlike idealists or skeptics, who would question whether an external world even exists outside our mind, realists argue that indeed there is an external world that we encounter, and that the important area of inquiry is one of how we perceive that world, whether directly or indirectly. A lot of this debate centers on the questions that get raised by the presence of illusions and hallucinations.

Hallucinations are generally understood as perceptions of a real mind-independent object when in fact there is no mind-independent object present to be perceived. The assumption is that hallucinations are subjectively indistinguishable from a veridical perception. However, there is some debate about this assumption, and to paraphrase J.L. Austin, watching a movie about driving a car is nothing like the real experience of driving a car.

An illusion, on the other hand, is the misperception of a mind-independent object that is indeed present but appears other than it really is. Bumblebee does exist, but Sam perceives him as a simple car when in fact he is something more. By these criteria, Sam's perception of his Camaro is not a hallucination but rather an illusion. However, the nature of the Transformers and their motivations introduce that additional aspect of deception, wherein one is deceived into believing that things are other than they are. No matter how you view it, though, Sam and many of the other characters in *Transformers* (even Optimus Prime, in his interpretation that Mojo is "leaking lubricant") are experiencing perceptual errors.

So why make a big deal about this notion of perceptual error? I mean, why can't we just chalk it up to a simple, "Sometimes our senses are wrong?" Most of us can identify experiences where our senses seem to tell us one thing that we later realize is incorrect—just think of seeing someone in the distance who is walking towards you. For a moment you think you know them but as they get closer, you realize they're not who you thought they were.

Epistemologists have theorized that our acquisition of knowledge can occur through two different processes, reason and experience. Sam's knowledge of the Transformers doesn't come from reason, but from his experiences with Bumblebee and the other Autobots and Decepticons. These experiences shape what he knows, via the accumulation of data that comes through his senses. Therefore the reliability of his sensory experiences—and the process by which he experiences the world—becomes an important consideration because it is the way in which he knows the world.

Though there are some refinements and variations on each of these, we can identify two primary realist theories on how we experience the external world. One of these theories, currently called direct realism and closely aligned with what was previously known as naïve realism or sometimes common-sense realism, says that we are in direct contact with the world we perceive, and that our perceptions are correct and unmediated by any representation in our consciousness. In other words, we perceive the world immediately and directly.

On the other hand, indirect realism or representational realism suggests that we are not in direct contact with the world that we perceive. Instead, there is an internal process that mediates our experience, so that what we actually experience is an internal representation. We can know only our ideas or interpretation of objects in the world, not the external objects themselves, which is why this mediation or filter is sometimes described as a veil of perception that exists between the mind and the external world. We might compare it to the difference between seeing Bumblebee in person versus seeing Bumblebee in a movie. Representational realism would argue that when we encounter Bumblebee in the external world, our perceptions are actually of an internal representation (a movie image, in this particular analogy) of Bumblebee. This representation can be called a sense datum (though in variations of this theory, the representations might be known as an idea, appearance, or a percept). These representations, or sense data, not the actual objects themselves, are what we directly encounter and know within our mind during the act of perception.

Going back for a moment to our movie analogy, you and I certainly know the difference between a movie image of a car and a car we encounter as we cross the street. But this ability to distinguish between the two may not be as inherent or as simple as it first seems. After all, when the Lumière Brothers premiered their film "Arrival of a Train at La Ciotat" in 1895, reports indicate that the audience ran out of the theater screening in terror, perceiving the movie's image as an actual train approaching them and potentially about to run them over. This may seem impossible to us today, but for you and I, films have been a part of our entire lives, and we have been trained to perceive the differences between a movie and the world we encounter in three dimensions. The two are clearly distinguishable for us, but for those Parisian moviegoers at the end of the nineteenth century, with no experience watching movies, the train on the screen seemed indistinguishable from a train they would encounter at a station.

"Why Are You So Sweaty and Filthy?"

If we accept that there are perceptual errors, the question becomes whether those can be reconciled with a direct realist view of the world and our knowledge of it, or whether the existence of perceptual errors proves that we experience the world indirectly via representational realism.

Generally, the arguments from illusion and hallucination are seen as evidence that direct realism is not a satisfactory explanation, because it doesn't seem to allow for a consideration of perceptual error. The belief that hallucinations are indistinguishable from actual sensory perceptions of external objects that the perceiver is encountering seems to imply that sensory perception does not require the existence of an external object. Hence what we experience is representations of objects that exist in the external world.

Add to this the fact that recent research in neuroscience suggests that perception, imagination and dreaming activate similar areas of the brain, and we can see why there are those who feel direct realism does not adequately explain our interaction and experience with an external world. On the flip side, critics of indirect realism might retort that once you accept the presence of sense data, how do you prove the existence of an external world? In other words, you may not be that far removed from idealists or skeptics.

Of course, Sam and Mikaela don't really have time to ponder these kinds of questions. There's a battle going on, and they're in the fight for their lives. There's a world to save, after all. Common sense would tell Sam and Mikaela that they are encountering real objects or events in a world that exists outside their minds. And it's these events that bring about Sam's own transformation into a man. When he hands Sam the All Spark, Captain Lennox tells him, "You're a soldier, now," and Sam has responsibilities greater than offering to drive the girl he likes home. The fact that he has experienced perceptual errors is taken for granted and seems without deeper connotations, at least until he has time to slow down a bit and ponder the changes to his world.

By then he might just want to make out with Mikaela on a hilltop, surrounded by his new friends and siblings, the Transformers.

"It's a Mystical Bond between Man and Machine"

It goes without saying that we live in a world of increased technology. Machines appear to surround us. We listen to music that is stored as binary code. We watch movies via machines that project light through celluloid or that translate digital encodings into pixels. We use computers rather than pen and paper. Our iPhones tap into satellites and towers in order to help us determine our GPS coordinates as well as to communicate in various modes with friends and colleagues.

Many of us spend more time with machines than people. Maybe it's not so surprising that we are engaged by a story that describes machines as something other than what they seem, as potential companions rather than tools. Perhaps the idea of Transformers taps into some longing we have for a greater connection with the world we perceive.

That may be why, walking out of the movie theater and into the starry night, I look across the parking lot for my Wrangler, maybe a little disappointed that it just sits there, waiting for me, casually resting on its four tires, still for all appearances just an automobile. But do I know that for sure? I have only my perceptions and experiences, context and introspection, reason and memory upon which to base my knowledge. What's to say that I'm not experiencing my own perceptual error, and that I won't wake up in the middle of the night to the sound of a revving engine, forced to give chase to my car only to discover new realizations about it, myself, and the world I inhabit?

EPISODE THREE

Mind over Matter

6
Can Metal Be Mental?

MATTHEW PIKE

When we think of minds, or of 'events in the mind', such as thoughts or feelings, we think of something ephemeral, something wispy and hard to grasp. And yet as science has continued to march on, our views about what a mind is are now intimately connected with what goes on in the brain—a purely physical part of the body.

Perception, reasoning, and even consciousness are commonly traced to physical goings-on in our central and peripheral nervous systems. Is it possible then that something made not of carbon-based molecules, like our brains, but rather of metal, silicon, or some other non-biological material, could possess what we would call mind?

Even our most powerful computers, despite their amazing capabilities, do not have *minds*. They have microprocessors that can do incredible things, ranging from creating immersive games like *World of Warcraft* to performing state-of-the-art climate modeling and DNA analysis. But they do not think for themselves, feel pain, or reflect on their lives. We might wonder then, whether it's even *possible* for machines to actually have thoughts or feelings.

If we encountered machines, say, from the planet Cybertron, that seemed to be having these kinds of experiences, how could we know that they actually had mental lives, and were not just programmed to act *as if* they did? The Transformers provide an excellent example of what machines with minds might be like. Thinking about the Transformers raises some fascinating questions about what it is to be a person and what it means to have a mind. It may also help prepare us to meet something that looks as if it's intelligent—whether this is something we humans have built or something that shows up one day on our planet, looking for energon cubes or the All-Spark.

What is it about the Transformers that makes us more inclined to believe that they have thoughts and feelings than that our laptops or cell phones do? What evidence could humans have that Transformers actually do have *minds*? For that matter, can you ever be sure that *anyone* besides you has a mind? The problem presented by this last question, known to philosophers as 'the problem of other minds', is that it seems that any action, facial expression, or language use that another person or machine might exhibit *could* be nothing but the programmed response of an unthinking thing. So how do we tell the difference between something that does have a mind and something that doesn't? To answer this question, we need to have a sense of what a mind is, so that we can know what counts as evidence for or against its presence.

One of the first things that comes to mind (no pun intended) is to say that a thing has a mind if and only if it acts in certain ways. René Descartes, for instance, thought that mechanical things (things without souls, or minds) could do everything that things endowed with a mind can do, *except* for using language and solving unexpected or novel problems. Only a special sort of non-physical, God-given thing could do that.

A very different view of the mind became popular among certain philosophers, known as Logical Behaviorists, in the early and mid-twentieth century. These philosophers maintained that mental things (such as thoughts) just *are* doing certain things in certain circumstances, or being inclined to do these things. They argued that being in a certain mental state is nothing except for having a disposition to engage in certain observable behaviors when presented with certain sense input. So, being happy is the same thing as being likely to smile, and saying that you are happy when someone asks how you are doing, and having a certain positive tone in your voice when speaking with other people, and so forth. The behaviors that you engage in when something causes you pain is all that pain is. These behaviors can be very complex though, and, as we know, they can be very unpredictable: different people respond differently, and even the same person responds differently to the same thing in different situations.

According to this theory, you know that your roommate has a mind because your roommate *does* certain things, like talking to you about his or her favorite movie, choosing what to eat for dinner and preparing it, and saying "Ouch!" when stubbing a toe on the coffee table. In the same way, perhaps we can tell that the Transformers have minds because Bumblebee makes grunts and groans when being captured and tormented by the agents of Sector 7, Starscream repeatedly takes actions to try to gain more power and control, and Optimus Prime asks for help from humans in foiling the plots of the Decepticons. These all seem like behaviors that only things with minds can do.

Testing 1—2—3

As a result of the identification of the mind with behaviors, a test was suggested by Alan Turing (which is now unimaginatively called the "Turing Test") that aims at determining what it would take for an objective investigator to make the judgment that a machine was thinking. The test involves a human's asking questions of another human and of a computer, robot, or some other mechanical being, without knowing which is which (so, no peeking—the idea is to judge on verbal responses alone, as Descartes would have us do, not on looking like a person or otherwise observing them). If the human tester cannot reliably tell which is the human and which is the artificial system based on responses to a series of conversational questions, then, according to Turing the system is said to have demonstrated intelligence, that is, real thinking.

The Turing Test works on the assumption that indistinguishable input and output patterns can be safely presumed to indicate roughly indistinguishable degrees of mind. In other words, if a system acts *as if* it has a mind, then it must have a mind. This test is by no means universally accepted as satisfactory, but as a quick justification of its value, we should note two things. First, we all seem to intuitively employ what amounts to a modified version of the Turing Test when determining whether we are dealing with other minds. This seems especially likely during our childhoods, in which we at some point learn to distinguish between objects and persons, and then devise (albeit unconsciously, most of the time) a series of conditions that a thing must meet in order to be identified as a person. These conditions will be relative to a prototypical person (most likely one's mother or father) that then serves as the point of comparison for all future encounters. Granted, by the time that we have performed this evaluation several hundred times, and have noted that each and every "object" we encounter with human shape, appearance, and movement has met the conditions, this process becomes increasingly automatic, but it seems that, at bottom, we are performing something like Turing's test all the time.

Second, Turing competitions are still held annually, because this behavior test is quite a challenge, and the possibility of writing a program that can pass it continues to absorb many an Artificial Intelligence investigator. No machine so far has been able to convince anyone that it is a person, based on its linguistic behavior, although they have come closer over time. Although they have become good at chess, and at other "rational" kinds of thinking, no machine so far has convinced humans set on making the distinction that it is in fact thinking. If we don't consider the Turing Test to be a satisfactory test of whether there's a mind, then we ought to be able to point to some other way of deciding that our fellow humans have minds. It seems unlikely that we will be able to come up with a method that does not depend on observing their behavior.

In earlier eras, the most popular approach which was to judge whether something has a mind based simply on appearance. Only beings of human form, and this very narrowly defined, were believed to possess minds. Famous disputes over "changelings" in the medieval period and indeed into the Enlightenment period were waged over whether babies born with severe deformities were in fact human, and the treatment of individuals with such diseases as neurofibromatosis (Elephant Man's disease) reveals that the pervasive attitude was that individuals who did not look sufficiently like the prototype human surely could not think or feel. Remnants of such views indeed still remain, with many people continuing to maintain that primates other than humans, regardless of their problem solving abilities, tool use, or other complex behaviors (never mind animals such as octopuses, that look so very different from us), cannot really be thinking.

Surely at least part of the reason for our willingness to accept that Transformers are thinking beings is attributable to the fact that they have roughly the same physical shape as us, speak our language, engage in similar interactions, and even appear to have the same emotions as us. Someone even apparently felt the need to give Optimus Prime lips in the 2007 movie so that his facial expressions could more closely resemble ours. Although this is a natural and common association, we can see that physical appearance is the least sophisticated criterion that one might use for determining whether something can think. At least observing a thing's behavior broadens the pool of those who might be considered to have minds; with this approach, even entities who do not resemble human beings could be understood to have minds, if they act as though they do.

The Chinese Room

There seems to be a rather obvious problem, though, with trying to decide whether something has a mind merely by watching the way it behaves. Despite the fact that it hasn't yet been done, can't we conceive that as technology improves, a computer could be specifically programmed to do things that would give every appearance of its having a mind?

If some brilliant and compulsively industrious programmer were to program in every conceivable bit of information, say on a particular topic (this is how the Turing competitions are currently run—the computers being tested are "interviewed" on only a select area of concern, such as baseball, or the stock market, since the more general challenge of attempting to build a machine that can converse intelligently across areas of discourse has been suspended for the time being), and successfully anticipate every question that an examiner might ask it, then the computer would be able to pass the test—but it wouldn't actually be thinking. The reason that we would be inclined to this opinion is that we can see that all this inputting and outputting was being done without the computer understanding what any of it *meant*.

This is the argument made by philosopher John Searle.[1] He illustrated his point by way of a clever thought experiment: he imagined a human being locked in a room where the only opening is a slot through which written messages are passed. The human inside does not speak, read, or understand any components of the Chinese language, and yet is able to successfully process messages passed into the room that are written in Chinese through the use of a collection of Chinese characters (a database) and a rulebook (a program) which, written in a language that the person *does* understand, gives step-by-step instructions for what output to

---

[1] John R. Searle, *Minds, Brains, and Science* (Harvard University Press, 1984), pp. 28–41. Searle had earlier stated this argument in "Minds, Brains, and Programs," *Behavioral and Brain Sciences* 3:3 (1980), pp. 417–457.

send back, given any particular input. The rulebook does not in any way reveal the meanings of any of the Chinese characters; it simply specifies which set of symbols, meaningless to the man inside the room, are to be returned, based on the shapes of the written lines, curves, dots, and squiggles.

Searle points out that the room in this thought experiment may be able to pass the Turing Test *without* the human inside understanding any Chinese, or being aware of any of the content of the "discussion" that has taken place. Searle takes the conceivability of this situation to show that no simple rule-governed manipulation of symbols (as a computer is restricted to doing) is sufficient for *meaning.*

It's the lack of *meaning*, of true *understanding*, in this kind of blind instruction following, that accounts for the failure of the machine to think. As Searle famously put it, "syntax is insufficient for semantics." No computer program, regardless of whom it can fool, Searle insists, is sufficient to give a system the *understanding* that is essential to having a mind. So, even though a Transformer might be able to perform all the actions and provide all the responses we might expect from a minded being, that fact would, according to Searle, be no proof that it actually possessed a mind.

The situation that Searle lays out points to one of the reasons why it's difficult to work with the concepts involved in talk about minds: there are two different perspectives from which we look at minds. First, there's the external, third-person perspective from which we see other people. We see the way they behave, hear them give verbal reports about what they are thinking, feeling, and so forth, and from this we come to the conclusion that they have minds. We don't directly experience their minds. All we actually experience are the external results that would come from their having minds (in other words, evidence *consistent* with their having minds).

Even when we examine state-of-the-art brain scan results, we are only looking at neurons in action—we are not looking at the mind of the subjects. All of this is very different from the way we come to know that we have minds ourselves: we seem to know this directly. We have an internal, first-person perspective on our own mental states. We seem to have direct, privileged access to our own thoughts, feelings, desires, hopes, fears, beliefs, and consciousness, in a way that no other person can have. It seems that I cannot experience what it feels like for you to smell a rose, or enjoy your favorite Transformers episode. I may have very similar experiences, but they are *my* experiences, not yours.

So, since none of us can *be* a Transformer, we are left with the question of whether we can decide if Optimus Prime has a mind based on our own view of him (what philosophers call an epistemological question), or based on his having the right internal experience, regardless of whether we can ever know it or not (which is what philosophers call a metaphysical question).

The Spark Within?

As we have seen, Descartes thought that only beings with minds could perform certain kinds of feats, including using language and solving novel problems. In order to rise above the capabilities that simple mechanical nature accounts for, to the level of language use and reason, Descartes thought that we must have some special element bestowed by God—an immaterial mind, or a soul.

In the opinion of Descartes, Searle, and countless others, it's not enough to behave in certain ways because what makes us willing to say that a human or a Transformer has a mind is the idea that something is going on *inside* of them. When we see someone in pain, we observe their behaviors, such as taking pain medication, or pulling their hand away from a hot stove, and from this we infer that they are *feeling* pain. And we seem to know from our own internal experience that there is a host of internal feelings that go along with our behaviors. When you see someone you are in love with, you do not just automatically start behaving in certain ways; rather, you have thoughts and powerful feelings, and these thoughts and feelings *cause* you to act in the ways that you do.

One of the reasons that Behaviorism became popular is that it seemed to offer an appealing alternative to the view put forth by Descartes, which came to be known as Substance Dualism. The problems with Substance Dualism were many, and were noted from the moment, back in the early seventeenth century, when Descartes published his *Meditations on First Philosophy*. For one thing, there appears to be no way for mind, a completely non-physical thing, to interact with physical things (like one's own body), with which it has absolutely nothing in common. For another, there appears to be no way for one to get a mind other than to have it bestowed on him or her by God. This was objectionable for many thinkers in the scientifically revolutionary late nineteenth and early twentieth centuries, when the theory of evolution, along with developments in mathematics and physics, were becoming popular.

To some philosophers, Behaviorism looked like an improvement over Descartes, but the problem with Behaviorism is that it leaves out altogether the immeasurably important internal mental states that we all recognize in ourselves. By defining mental states as nothing but behaviors and dispositions to behave, it completely failed to recognize the internal thoughts, feelings, and beliefs that many see as central to the nature of mind.

These apparently non-physical elements that we tend to attribute to minds lead many people to think of something very similar to a 'soul', regardless of their enthusiasm for the developments of science. According to this common view, there is something else besides the physical body that composes the individual, and it is that which makes people different from inanimate and mindless things like tables and chairs.

This special internal something is a candidate for what the Transformers have that our current computers do not. The 2007 movie, *Transformers*, seems to portray something similar to this special something. When the All-Spark inexplicably brings cell phones, steering wheels, and vending-machines to life with a single *zap*, something happens. What is it, and how does it happen? Just what does the *zap* do that instills non-living, non-mental gadgets with life and the will to fulfill something like personal desires or goals? Is it some kind of divine magic that gives the Transformers souls and minds, or is it some combination of energy and programmatic information that accomplishes this feat? Whatever it is, the All-Spark obviously imparts something more than being able to perform as the actor in Searle's Chinese Room does. Once hit with that force, machines are able to 'think for themselves'.

Physicalism

Some of us would prefer the explanation that the All-Spark imparts some combination of programmatic information and physical energy to get things started to the idea that it bestows something like a soul on the machines it empowers, because at least with the first option there is some hope of finding an explanation for how minds arise. In the second case, the existence of a mind remains a mystery, something about which no more can be said. For that reason, many of us tend to think that the view known as "Physicalism" makes better sense as an explanation of what minds are than does the Cartesian soul interpretation of mind.

According to Physicalism, having a mind is *nothing but* having the right kind of physical system (which in our case is our brain, together with other parts of our central nervous system, extending to our sensory receptors). This Physicalist view comes in many different forms. For instance, some philosophers who hold this view think that it doesn't matter so much what the physical system is made of, or how it is set up, but rather *that* it is set up so that it performs certain functions. According to these philosophers, it is the function that matters, not the particulars of the physical system. So, whether it is instantiated, or "realized", in organic matter, silicon, or some as-yet-undiscovered substance, as long as it does the jobs that minds do (believing, perceiving, intending), it is a mind.

Others, though, such as John Searle, think that only biological systems could ever develop minds. For those in Searle's camp, it's the organic nature of biological beings (having evolved from and in interaction with their environments), and the very chemistry of the nerve cells themselves, that is necessary for the emergence of mind. So, while on Searle's own view Transformers couldn't have minds, on other views similar to his, it might be possible to say that as long as they were in some sense biological beings, they could have minds. The mere fact that they are not organic, not having evolved on our planet, wouldn't automatically preclude their being biological entities, one might argue. Some physicalists, though, disagree with both these claims, and maintain that neither is there anything magical about biology, nor is function alone sufficient to identify mind. They think that Searle's biological account is too specific (and thus chauvinistic toward other kinds of beings), while functionalism isn't specific enough.

This last group of physicalists, (known as reductive physicalists), think that our scientific research into the way that the brain and nervous system work can eventually provide a complete explanation for our mental life, and that there is nothing else needed, because physical explanations can tell the whole story. They maintain that biology is reducible to physics and chemistry, and functionalism only points to something it could label as mind, but does not explain what makes it function the way that it does. These philosophers lean heavily on developments in the last decade or two in neuroscience, which have been impressive, in the way in which they have come to show how certain processes in the brain allow for perception, memory, association, emotion, and other mental activities.

Perhaps unsurprisingly, though, some philosophers want to have their cake and eat it, too. They think *both* that minds depend upon brains, *and* that mind is irreducible—that it is something purely subjective, something decidedly different from the physical. While there might be neural *correlates* of mental activities, these philosophers say, those correlates are not to be *identified* with mind. Nevertheless, these philosophers maintain, there is no second substance, no soul or mental 'stuff' in addition to the physical stuff of the universe. So they remain physicalists.

What the physicalist philosophers of mind all have in common is their faith in the value of physical explanations and in the achievements of science. Science has proven to be tremendously successful at unraveling apparent mysteries and discovering straightforward (although not always simple) explanations for the things being investigated. Research into the functioning of the brain has provided explanations for innumerable questions about how perceptual processing occurs, about how different kinds of perceptual processing is integrated, and even about how consciousness—or mind—can arise.

If a physicalist view is correct (with the possible exception of the non-reductive physicalists, who will have to determine mind on other grounds), then the question concerning whether Transformers are mental beings is actually just a question concerning the specifics about what constitutes their information systems, how the different mechanisms for perception, self-regulation, and self-movement are organized, how they interact with each other, and how they are tracked by further mechanisms of the same nature. If a 'brain' that is sufficiently functionally similar to ours exists in Transformers, then there's no reason not to credit it with having a mind.

And so, if an entity made out metal, silicon chips, or something completely unknown to us, is hooked up in the right way to whatever perceptual, visceral, and posture and movement systems it has, and if that entity is capable of processing all this information, as well as the information *that* it is doing this processing then we might be willing to accept that this entity had a mind. But would it be a mind *like ours*? Well, that would depend on what you think 'like ours' means.

Many animals on this planet have minds, at least on the views of lots of people, but they differ from our human minds, given, for instance, that they don't encode information into language and use that extensively in their thinking, as we do. But then many people (look at babies!) don't do that, either, and yet we think of their minds as being like ours. So, one might say that Transformers, given the conditions described above, do indeed have minds, both as similar to and as different from our minds as our minds are to each other's, and to those of other animals with which we are familiar.

So if minds are just some kind of physical information processing systems, then why do Transformers have mental lives and our computers (so far) do not? The answer that many physicalists would give is that the difference is just a matter of complexity and function. Our current computers are nowhere near as complex and capable as the human brain, with its average 10^{11} (one hundred billion) neurons, each of which in turn possesses an average seven thousand synaptic connections to other neurons. This means that by some estimates, the average human brain at its peak (our brains begin to degenerate after we are about three years old) has about 10^{15} (1 quadrillion) synapses. Add to that the over four hundred chemical transmitters, peptides, hormones, and large variety of other modulating chemicals that can radically influence the environment in synaptic gaps, and you can see that computers are not even on the same playing field as brains. If we eventually manage to build computers with enough complexity, and with the right kind of structure, they may well turn out to have minds too—according to some of the physicalist views.

Mind—More than Meets the Eye?

If some version of physicalism is right, then there may come a day when our scientific understanding has advanced to the point that we have identified which structures in the human brain are responsible for our mental experiences, and it may be that from this knowledge we can identify which attributes a computer or robot would have to possess in order to have a mind. In this case, definitively identifying whether the Transformers have minds may be as simple as a scan by a hand-held gadget. Until that time, however, or if the most straightforward reductivist version of physicalism is wrong about what constitutes the mind, then we must look for other ways to decide which entities have minds and which don't. So, if you can't know that an entity has a mind by looking at the way it operates (and we can't know that even about human beings, with our current state of knowledge about the brain), how *can* you know whether it does?

It seems that the best candidate for an approach to making this determination may be what philosophers call an abductive inference, or an inference to the best explanation. While this kind of an inference does not provide us with complete confidence that we have reached the truth, it can provide pretty good reason for believing that something is true, and so could justify our belief that the Transformers have minds. This kind of reasoning generally starts from a set of observed facts about the world, and then tries to identify the best theory or explanation of why they occurred. It is a way of reasoning from effects back to causes. Frequently, many different explanations are possible, and so we tend to try and pick the best of them, using several different criteria. We all do this constantly throughout the day, even if we are not consciously aware of it. If you're walking along and encounter a big hole in the ground, you will likely start thinking up possible explanations for it. Maybe this is a construction site, where the hole was made in preparation for a building foundation. Or maybe the hole is a crater that resulted from a Transformer who crash-landed following a journey from Cybertron. Or maybe the hole happened because in exactly this spot, gravity completely ceased to function and the dirt in this specific area all floated into space. All three of these scenarios can explain the observed hole in the ground, but some of them seem less probable than others. We tend to think that the building construction hypothesis is a simpler, less outlandish, explanation that fits better with our other observations in the past, and so is more likely to be true.

Lacking definitive evidence that others have minds, we presumably do something similar to the process illustrated in the example above. If we encounter a robot performing fairly basic tasks, we may formulate several theories about how it does them. We may theorize that the robot is being remote controlled, or that it has been programmed to autonomously perform certain functions, or that it is a robot with a mind. What observations could we make that would lead us to conclude that it actually has a mind? We will have to base our conclusion on the external evidence that we can observe, as well as our past experiences with similar things.

Given that all of our past experiences with mechanical devices have led us to believe that they do not have minds, and being somewhat familiar with the current state of technology available on planet Earth, we would sensibly conclude that the robot was either being controlled by someone, or had been programmed by someone to perform specific actions. But what if it engaged in behaviors that were very different from the other kinds of machines that we had encountered? What if the robot started up a casual conversation about the weather, and started to complain about how stiff its robotic joints were? This could just be a programmed speech, or even a recording. But what if we started to ask it questions on a wide variety of topics? As the robot's behaviors become more and more complex, adaptive, and versatile, it seems that we might become less and less convinced that it was just a preprogrammed machine that was only following the instructions it had been given.

What if there were some reason to think that the robot had originated on a different planet, in which case there might have been a considerably more advanced level of technology available for its construction? This is one of the important differences in encountering a Transformer versus a human-made system, because, if there is good reason to think that the robot is not limited by the present state of our technology, then the possibility that it could be sufficiently complex to have a mind is no longer effectively ruled out. Observing the robot doing very complex things that are sufficiently different from the machines we routinely encounter (such as smoothly transforming from an automobile into a roughly-human shape) will further support this possibility. After an extended period of observing the robot, and seeing it engage in things like learning, attempting to avoid hazards, pursing preferences and goals, making plans to defend against other robots, mourning the loss of its fallen comrades, and making decisions based on what seem to be moral values, we could very easily come to the conclusion that the behaviors it exhibited were too complex to originate from anything without a mind.

It would be nice if the determination of whether something had a mind could be made simply by comparing its actions and characteristics to a check-list of conditions that are both necessary and sufficient for mind. It seems though, that there is a very wide range of characteristics that beings with minds can have, but don't necessarily have. Our understanding of mind is a cluster concept, and some but not all of the characteristics included in that concept belong to anything that we would be willing to call a mind. Persons with certain neurological disorders, for example, can navigate and catch a ball, but they insist that they cannot see; others can function normally in most contexts, but cannot process language. They know what they are doing and show purposive action and even normal intelligence, but they cannot communicate via language. Other kinds of brain damage result in some people's having a complete inability to remember things for more than a minute, while others smell colors or taste sounds. Some people hear music when none is present, while still others can hear individual notes, but cannot put together a melody. In none of these cases do we say that the people in question do not have minds; rather, we say that they have deficiencies or gifts. Identifying the key marks of the mental is thus surprisingly difficult.

While not so many people these days are likely to insist that having a mind is somehow tied to human form, the other proposed criteria seem to also run into problems. We saw already that the Turing Test and its emphasis on language use does not seem to be as good of a criterion as first thought. And as computer programming becomes more advanced, many other suggested test criteria will likely also be met by unthinking robots. This leaves us in the unfortunate position of having to admit that specifying exactly how we decide if other things have minds or not, may not be possible.

Perhaps the best we can do is give a list of things that *some* things with minds do, and if we encounter something that does *enough* of them, then we should be willing to conclude that it does have a mind, although perhaps of a fairly different kind than ours. But having enough of these properties would not guarantee that the thing in question has a mind and can *actually think*. Advanced robots could be programmed to mimic human facial expressions, behaviors and actions, and could *seem* to be thinking, feeling, and acting like humans do, without their ever having minds of their own. Since (at present) we can only observe other people and things "from the outside", there does not seem to be any way to be *sure* that even our friends and family have minds of their own!

It does seem, though, that even if we could never be *completely* sure that a Transformer had a mind, we could have *as much reason* to think that the Transformer had a mind as to believe that any other human being had one.

7
Will We Meet Optimus Prime in Heaven?

M.R. EYESTONE

Is there a chance that, when we die, we'll meet Optimus Prime in heaven? What about Megatron: will he go to hell for all the bad things he's done? Even though Megatron and Optimus Prime have never actually existed, these questions about them raise further thought-provoking questions, such as:

- **Are Transformers and other apparently intelligent machines *alive*?**
- **Do they have *souls*?**
- **Can they *die*, or do they just stop working at some point? (Or are those just two ways of saying the same thing?)**
- **Can we rightly say that they're *virtuous* or morally good?**

No doubt we might say "No" to some or all of these questions. "Transformers," we might say, "are just *machines*, however intelligent and lifelike they might seem. They're certainly not living persons who have souls, like human beings." While I'm somewhat sympathetic to this line of thought, I'm also curious enough to wonder if it might not be oversimplifying things a bit. In particular, it seems to run together a few things that could perhaps be distinguished, namely:

- **Being intelligent**

- **Being alive**
- **Being a person**
- **Having a soul**

These different things are easy to mix up, since they so often go together in our everyday experience of human beings. They don't *always* go together: plants and amoebas are alive, but they don't seem to be persons, and dogs and parrots are fairly intelligent, but it's not easy to say whether or not they have souls. So ask yourself this: when a being possesses all of these features, does that imply that it can *only* be human? Or could there possibly be *nonhuman* beings who are virtuous, intelligent, living persons who have souls?

This is a hard question to answer: the universe is a big place, and the realm of possibility is perhaps bigger still. Or maybe this question isn't as hard as I think. After all, it seems that angels and extraterrestrial spacemen (if they exist) would be intelligent, living persons who'd be capable of virtue, even though they're not human. So we're probably fairly comfortable with the *possibility* of such beings. The question is whether Transformers and other apparently intelligent machines should be counted among these possible beings—whether my childhood hero Optimus Prime can rightly be called a virtuous, intelligent, *living* person who has a soul. Is he just a complex but ultimately lifeless, soulless hunk of metal? Or is there more to him than meets the eye?

To answer this question, we'll have to look beyond our everyday experiences and engage in some deep, philosophical reflection, asking ourselves what a soul is and what it really means to be alive. This isn't quite the old question, "What's the meaning of life?", but it might very well be related to that oldie. Instead, the question is "What does it mean to say that a being is alive, has a soul, and is truly capable of virtue and intelligence, and what are the defining features of such a being?"

My answer is that we have pretty good reason to think that *apparently* intelligent machines like Transformers *actually are* intelligent, living beings who have souls and can be genuinely virtuous. Or at least, we don't have any less reason to think that a Transformer is alive and intelligent than we do any other apparently living, intelligent being. Once we've taken into consideration how a mechanical being *acts* and what it can *do*, I'm not sure that there's anything about its being mechanical that should automatically disqualify it from having a soul and counting as authentically alive, intelligent, and virtuous. So my answer to the question posed in this paper's title is a cautious and qualified "Yes," and not just because (as I'm not ashamed to admit) Optimus Prime is still one of my heroes.

Signs of Life: What the Transformers' Universe Says

Are Transformers alive? Stories about the Transformers certainly *treat* them as living beings. In particular, early issues of the old Marvel comic series often suggest that, while organic life and mechanical life are obviously *different*, one is no more or less a form of life than the other. But we're asking whether Transformers, if they existed, *really would* count as living beings. Our inquiry, to be truly satisfying, has to go beyond just what the story says, meaning that it has to be something deeper than just an examination of what fiction writers have declared to be the case. Still, a look at what Transformers fiction says about its subjects and why they're not merely machines, but *living* machines, will be of some help to us.

Here's a helpful sampling of what's been said about Transformer life:

- **"Many millions of years ago, on the planet Cybertron, life existed—but not life as we know it today: intelligent robots that could *think* and *feel* inhabited the cities."**[1]
- **"Whereas life elsewhere in the cosmos usually evolved through carbon-bonding, here [on Cybertron] it was the interaction of naturally occurring gears, levers and pulleys that miraculously brought forth sentient beings."**[2]

---

[1] "More Than Meets the Eye Part 1," *Transformers*, Season 1 (17th September) 1984, DVD, Rhino Home Video, 2002. Audible emphasis in original. Opening narration.

[2] Bill Mantlo and Ralph Macchio, "The Transformers," *The Transformers*, Volume 1, Number 1 (Marvel Comics Group, September 1984)—henceforth, "*Transformers* #1". Bracketed text mine. Opening narration.

- **"Although a robot, Shockwave is alive, and the pain of the harpoons ripping through his armor plate is real indeed."[3]**
- **"He [Ratchet] is alive, intelligent, possessed of emotions . . . and mechanical . . ."[4]**

Speaking of Ratchet, since he's the Autobot medic and would therefore know more about mechanical life than most, we might be interested in his take on the nature of life. Something he says to the human Buster Witwicky hints at what he thinks: "As you know, I'm certified as a doctor on my native planet. However, the Cybertronic Medical Oath I took makes no distinction between attending to *mechanical* or *organic* life."[5] Like most Autobots, Ratchet shows concern even for life forms very different from himself, as when he's quick to ask Buster if he's "functioning properly" when he appears not to be feeling well.[6] Another revealing (and amusing) exchange between Ratchet and Buster (and a stoplight) runs as follows:

> "Listen, friend traffic signal, we're in a hurry, so if you could please turn green . . ."
>
> "It doesn't hear you, Ratchet. It's only a *machine*."
>
> "*I'm* a machine, and I hear *you*, Buster!"
>
> "Yes, but you're different, you're—"
>
> "Ahh, he changed! Thank you, friend traffic signal. May the rest of the day find you in proper working order. You see, Buster, you have to learn how to *talk* to people."
>
> "I . . . I'll try to keep that in mind, Ratchet."[7]

Buster's comment that there's something that makes Ratchet *different* from a stoplight points directly to what we're after in this

---

[3] Bob Budiansky, "The *Worse* of Two Evils!" *The Transformers*, Volume 1, Number 6 (Marvel Comics Group, July 1985)—henceforth, "*Transformers* #6"—p. 6. Narration.

[4] Bob Budiansky, "Repeat Performance!" *The Transformers*, Volume 1, Number 8 (Marvel Comics Group, September 1985), p. 1. Bracketed text mine. Ellipses in original. Opening narration.

[5] Bob Budiansky, "The New Order," *The Transformers*, Volume 1, Number 5 (Marvel Comics Group, June 1985)—henceforth, "*Transformers* #5"—p. 10. Emphasis in original.

[6] *Transformers* #6, p. 13.

[7] *Transformers* #5, p. 18. Ellipses and emphasis in original.

inquiry. What *is* it, exactly, that makes Ratchet (or any Transformer) a *living* machine, something fundamentally *more than* a stoplight or other *nonliving* machine? And whatever that vital spark is in the case of *mechanical* life, is it the same sort of thing that makes *organic* life different from lifeless matter? Ratchet and the stoplight are different, but are you and a corpse, or you and a statue of you, different for similar reasons?

We'll delve more deeply into the nature of that vital spark later. Leading up to that, we can observe that the Transformers fiction already quoted has given us some signs to look for when we're trying to determine whether something's alive. Living beings, at least *some* of them, and especially the more complex and sophisticated of them, are:

- **Intelligent, or able to think**
- **Sentient, or able to perceive and feel (especially, able to feel pain)**
- **Natural (as opposed to artificial)**
- **Emotional, or able to experience emotions**

We can expand this list of vital qualities without even stepping outside of Transformers fiction. For example, another seemingly plausible addition to the list is being capable of impulse to action, having *will* or *desire*. This, too, comes up in the comic: Megatron, speaking to his fellow Decepticons about human-made vehicles, observes that "Unlike ourselves these machines have no will of their own!"[8] Another important quality of living beings is so basic that it can be easy to miss: motion. Often, one of the first things that makes us suspect that something might be alive is simply its ability to move. Something that the Autobot Prowl says to Cliffjumper is worth pointing out here:

> Look, do you see the movement exhibited by those bizarre-looking objects? . . . It means that the mechanical vehicles we saw were not alive. But those small figures are. That's why the vehicles made no

[8] Bill Mantlo and Jim Salicrup, "Power Play!" *The Transformers*, Volume 1, Number 2 (Marvel Comics Group, November 1984)—henceforth "*Transformers* #2"—p. 3.

> move to defend themselves [from the crossfire when the Decepticons were attacking some Autobots who were investigating a drive-in movie theater]. They are not sentient. When they moved upon the roadway we saw, the small beings were controlling them. What we are seeing is non-machine life, as hard as that may be to accept. That is the only logical explanation.[9]

The "bizarre-looking objects" and "small beings" Prowl mentions here are human beings. Before they'd encountered *organic* life forms capable of self-movement, the Autobots had assumed that all life was mechanical. Since they're mechanical natives of a mechanical planet populated by mechanical beings, that's an understandable mistake. One of the points I'm driving at here is that we organic life forms should be careful not to become prone to making that same sort of overgeneralization. We should try to avoid making the same sort of mistake that Sparkplug Witwicky, a human auto mechanic, makes when he first encounters the injured Bumblebee. Sparkplug is sure that the wounded Autobot is no more than an oddly constructed car, even after Bumblebee speaks to him, until Bumblebee transforms himself into humanoid robot form. Only then, when the little Autobot has changed himself so as to *look* somewhat human, does Sparkplug accept that Bumblebee is, in fact, alive.[10] And as with Sparkplug, so with the rest of us: our expectations about appearance can *inform*, but shouldn't completely *determine*, our view of what can and can't be alive. We should try to keep an open mind about what can be considered alive.

We already know that not all life is human, since we're familiar with other animals, plants, microbes, and so forth. We're also probably comfortable with at least the *possibility* of living, nonhuman beings who have very humanlike qualities, such as intelligence, sentience, emotion, and virtue. Why, then, should we think that all life must be *organic*? If we're willing to be flexible about what can be alive and intelligent (and so forth), it seems a bit strange for us not to be flexible enough to allow for the possibility of sophisticated mechanical life like that of the Transformers. It's true that, like Prowl and Sparkplug, we often expect things to go pretty much as we've gotten used to them going. But while that's understand-

---

[9] *Transformers* #1. Bracketed text mine.

[10] *Transformers* #2, pp. 7–10.

able and even excusable, we should try not to let it limit our thinking too much, especially when we're dealing with something as mysterious as the nature of life.

Life, Soul, and Motion

The vital spark mentioned in the last section, that which makes a living being something more than merely a complex arrangement of inert matter, sounds very much like what the ancient Greeks called the *psukhē* (or, more familiarly, *psychē*). The word can be translated as "breath" or "life" or "spirit" or "soul," which nicely captures the ancients' idea that everything that's alive has a soul; at least for many of them, "soul" pretty much just *means* "life principle" or "whatever it is about a living being that makes it a *living* being."

Not everyone would agree that *every* living being has a soul. In particular, some would say that only *human* beings have souls. Ancient philosophers, though, were more inclined to say that *everything* that lives has a soul, but that there are just different kinds of souls. They might say that plants, animals, human beings, and God (or the gods) all have souls, but maybe human and divine souls are just more complex and in other ways greater and more special than plant and animal souls. Really, this is little more than a difference in terminology: disagreement between someone who says that "soul" refers to something that only human and divine beings possess and someone who says that it refers to something that all living beings possess (though to greater or lesser degree) is more a disagreement about how best to use the word "soul" than a profound disagreement about what the soul really and most properly *is*.

For the sake of this discussion, then, let's agree with the ancients: the soul is whatever it is about any sort of living being that makes it *living* rather than inanimate. If we want to give a good account of the soul, then, we'll want to consider what sorts of activities are most closely associated with living beings. This concern with *activity*, with what living beings can *do*, is central. It's also deeply embedded in how we speak about living and nonliving beings. In this section, I've already used the words "inert" and "inanimate" to describe that which is nonliving. Notice that, besides "nonliving," these words also suggest things like "inactive" and "unmoving." And we've seen that there seems to be a connection between motion and life: seeing that an object is able to move itself is the main thing that persuades both Prowl and Sparkplug that it's not just an *object*, but a living being.

This connection between motion and life/soul is deeply rooted in philosophical history. Thales, one of the very first Western philosophers, allegedly thought that magnets had souls. Why? Because they can make iron objects *move*.[11] Now it's true that Thales was part of a stage of thought that was early even by ancient Greek standards, but this connection between being a source of motion and being alive (that is, having a soul) was enormously influential. In particular, it influenced one of history's finest minds: Aristotle.

For Aristotle, as for Thales (and Prowl and Sparkplug), the capacity for motion is a major defining feature of a natural, living being. "But wait," someone might say, "my car moves, and my computer has moving parts, but they're not natural, living beings." While that's true, cars and computers (of the non-Transformer variety, anyway) don't move *on their own*: they do move, but only when something else (say, a human being) *makes* them move by hitting the gas pedal or switching them on. It is something's being a potential *self-mover*, not its being able to move in just any old way, that points to its being alive. It should also be noted that Aristotle uses the word "motion" for more than just movement in place. For him, a young plant's growing to maturity, an old animal's withering and weakening with age, a leaf or chameleon's changing color, and my walking to the store are all forms of motion. In other words, Aristotle classifies what we'd usually call *changes* as forms of motion.

If we think of motion in this way, we can see that the capacity for self-motion does seem to be a pretty good indicator of life/soul. Most animals, including human beings, can move in place (say, by walking around), and all can move/change themselves in other ways, sometimes voluntarily (deciding to sit or stand, looking at or thinking about something), sometimes automatically (digesting food, healing injuries). Plants, of course, can't move in place, but they *can* move/change in the sense of growing (as when maturing) and shrinking (as when withering from lack of food or water), and some of them change color in the autumn. But now think about Transformers. We're talking about the capacity for self-motion, and

[11] Reported in Aristotle, *On the Soul*, Book I, Chapter 2, 405a19–20.

they certainly have that: like ourselves, they're capable of quite sophisticated self-originated motions, both voluntary (moving around, looking at or thinking about things, talking to allies, attacking enemies) and automatic (processing fuel to continue functioning). It seems to follow, then, that they're alive and that they have souls that are at least somewhat like human souls.

Aristotle on the Soul

But hold on: we might be getting ahead of ourselves. And Aristotle has a good deal more to tell us about the soul, which we'll want to take into account. For Aristotle, the soul is the *form* of the living body.[12] Basically, a thing's form is whatever it is about the thing that makes it a member of its kind, that without which it wouldn't be a member of that kind. Your form, then, is whatever it is about you that makes you a human being, and a *living* human being, rather than a bear or a tree or a baseball or a corpse (or a Transformer). "Form" suggests *shape* or *structure* or *arrangement*, and some complexity of structure is present even in fairly simple living organisms, like amoebas and bacteria. Really, that's just what a living organism *is*: a systematic *arrangement* of functioning bodily organs, sometimes relatively simple, sometimes very complex.

"Organ" comes from the ancient Greek word *organon*, "instrument" or "tool." So when we're talking about the body's organs, we're talking about the "tools" that a living organism uses to keep itself alive and which let it go about the business of living. Living *human* organisms, for example, have stomachs for digestion, lungs for respiration, hearts and blood vessels for circulation, eyes and ears for seeing and hearing, muscles for moving, and so forth. A living organism's form/soul, then, is very closely associated with (and, for Aristotle, largely inseparable from or dependent on[13]) its organ function. It's the things that a living organism's organs let it *do* (and do for it), the vital capacities and faculties that its organs allow it to exercise and the functions they carry out, that really make the organism a member of its kind.

After all, animals can do things that plants can't do, and human beings can do things that plants and other animals can't do; and,

[12] Aristotle, *On the Soul*, Book II, Chapter 1, 412a20–21.

[13] Aristotle, *On the Soul*, Book II, Chapter 1, 413a4–7, and Book III, Chapter 4, 429b4–5.

we might add, Transformers can do things that few (if any) other living organisms can do. So it's not oversimplifying too much to say that, on this view, life and soul pretty much just *are* function. That seems like a sentiment with which any mechanical life form would agree. At one point in the comic, after Shockwave has overcome Megatron and taken over leadership of the Decepticons, he has the other Decepticons swear their allegiance to him, and they do so, saying, "We function for you and you alone!!"[14] And even we organic life forms at least often *speak* in terms of life being closely associated with function. When someone's heart stops, we say that he or she is "clinically dead," nonliving, at least until the heart's *functioning* resumes.

It's important not to associate *form* too much with material *shape* or *structure*, and not just because we're talking about beings who can change their shapes back and forth from humanoid to truck or police car or cassette player or whatever. What are really vital (in every sense) when we're talking about the form/soul of a living being are the *capacities* and *faculties* possessed by the living being.

What is it about you that *really* makes you a human being? Clearly it's more than just your shape and structure: a statue of you would have your shape, and the corpse of your hypothetical long-lost twin would be even more structurally similar to you. But you, a living body, can *do* much more than a statue or a corpse. Your shape and structure in the sense of your systematic arrangement of bodily organs is important: it's what gives you the vital faculties that keep you alive and functioning and let you *do* things. But the idea is that the faculties themselves and the organ function that makes them possible matter much more to life and the presence of a soul than the more *material* side of things, exactly what those functioning organs are made of or shaped like. It's not so much the matter itself but rather what that matter can *do* as a result of its distinctive arrangement (again, its *form*) that's important. We're most familiar with organic beings who use their organic brains to think, but the very faculty-oriented and function-oriented view of life and the soul now under consideration seems to suggest that whether a thinking being uses grey matter or computer chips to think is less relevant to the question of whether it's alive and has a

---

[14] *Transformers* #6, p. 22.

soul than the simple fact that it *can* think, that there's *something* that's functioning so as to produce the capacity for thought. Again, we have to be careful not to let our expectations get in the way here: it's the presence of vital capacities and faculties, not whether they're present in metal or flesh, that matters most.

What are some of these capacities and faculties that are so central to something's being alive and having a soul? Many have already been mentioned, and the fact that humans and Transformers have so many of them in common is interesting. Aristotle mentions many of these same faculties as well. Here's a list of the main vital faculties that he mentions, which I've derived mainly from his book *On the Soul* (*De Anima*) and from a bit of what's said in his *On Memory* and *Nicomachean Ethics*:

- The *nutritive* faculty of the soul is kind of the baseline for what can be called "living" in any sense; all mortal living beings, including plants, possess it. Its most distinctive function is *nourishment*, processing food to maintain the organism's life and health. It's closely associated with those sorts of self-motion (ability to change) that all mortals are capable of and which are the *only* motions/changes that plants are capable of, especially natural growth and shrinkage. It's also associated with something that keeps the organism in existence in a slightly different way: reproduction, which lets the organism sort of continue on in its offspring after its own death.

- The *perceptual* faculty is what distinguishes a life form as an *animal*, as what we'd usually call *sentient*. At its most basic, it's the capacity for *sense perception*, the ability to perceive through touch, sight, hearing, and so forth. It's also associated with *imagination*, the ability to form a "mental picture" even when nothing's being perceived through the senses, and with *memory*, which is basically just imagination of the past. In addition, it's associated with *appetite*, which includes hunger, thirst, passion (simple emotion), and desire more generally, since whatever can perceive can feel pleasure and pain, and whatever can feel pleasure and pain can want what's pleasant and want to avoid what's painful. It's also somewhat related to *locomotion*, the ability to move in place, since animals that can move in place need to be able to perceive where they're going, and when such animals do move, they often do so to pursue what's pleasant or to avoid what's painful.

- The *intellectual* faculty is what separates human (and divine) beings from other life forms. It's associated with higher, distinctly *mental* processes, such as reasoning, abstract thinking, knowing, understanding, and also judging, believing, forming opinions, feeling higher emotions, and deliberating and choosing.

This list seems to work fine for the living beings that we're familiar with, but does it let us say that *Transformers* are alive? Well, Transformers certainly *seem* to possess the perceptual and intellectual faculties of soul and the sub-faculties associated with them. In fact, their intellectual faculties might well be superior to our own, what with their having computers for brains and all. And, remembering that these faculties are supposed to be closely associated with functioning bodily organs, we can observe that Transformers are indeed depicted as having robotic equivalents of our organs: they have limbs (which no doubt contain robotic muscles and nerves) for walking, eyes (optical sensors) for seeing, brains (central processing units) for thinking, and so forth. So far, then, we'd seem to be right in saying that, on this view of life and the soul, Transformers *are* alive and *do* have souls.

The nutritive faculty, though, might present a bit of a problem. Again, Aristotle says that its most distinctive function is processing food[15] and that only living beings feed themselves.[16] And indeed, Transformers do need to ingest and process nourishment in the form of fuel, often the substance called Energon. Megatron confirms this when he says the following to Sparkplug: "Just as you depend on oxygen and food for survival, we require fuel!"[17] But this might not be enough for us to say that Transformers possess the nutritive faculty and so are alive, since the nutritive faculty is also associated with natural growth and shrinkage and with reproduction. This might be a problem, since Transformers don't

[15] Aristotle, *On the Soul*, Book II, Chapter 4, 416a20–21.

[16] Aristotle, *On the Soul*, Book II, Chapter 4, 415b27–28.

[17] Jim Salicrup, "Prisoner of War!" *The Transformers*, Volume 1, Number 3 (Marvel Comics Group, January 1985)—henceforth, "*Transformers #3*".

seem to grow to maturity or wither with age. (Optimus Prime and Megatron, for example, are millions of years old.[18]) They also don't reproduce: they don't mate, and they aren't exactly *born*. Instead, they're designed and created by other Transformers: for example, in the original cartoon series, in the first three Dinobots' debut, the Autobots build them from scratch,[19] and in the Constructicons' debut, Megatron mentions that they were built on Earth.[20] This might make Transformers seem *artificial* rather than *natural*.

The worry is this. The nutritive faculty, again, is what really separates the living from the inanimate. But if Transformers' nutritive faculties differ significantly from those of other beings that are unquestionably living, it seems less clear that Transformers should qualify as living beings. Their apparent perceptual and intellectual faculties *seem* to imply that they're alive. Aristotle himself says something like this: the presence of any one of the faculties of soul mentioned above tells us that a being is alive.[21] Again, though, *all* living beings *must* possess the nutritive faculty, which is associated not just with processing food (which Transformers do), but also with the natural growth and shrinkage that come with aging and with reproduction (which Transformers lack). If Transformers aren't like other living beings in these important ways, we might not be able to say that they really are living beings, regardless of how it might seem based on their other faculties and regardless of how open-minded we are about what can count as alive.

So on the one hand, perception and intellect imply the presence of life and soul no less than does nutrition. But on the other hand, in mortal life forms, though nutrition is sometimes found by itself (as in plants), perception and intellect are never found without nutrition.[22] If Transformers lack a true, full-fledged capacity for nutrition, this might imply that their apparent perception and intellect are no more than *apparent*, in other words, that they're not

---

[18] See, for example, Simon Furman, *Transformers: The Ultimate Guide* (New York: DK Publishing, 2004), p. 15, and "War Dawn," Transformers, Season 2 (25th December) 1985, DVD, Rhino Home Video, 2003.

[19] "S.O.S. Dinobots," *Transformers*, Season 1 (27th October) 1984, DVD, Rhino Home Video, 2002.

[20] "Heavy Metal War," *Transformers*, Season 1 (15th December) 1984, DVD, Rhino Home Video, 2002.

[21] Aristotle, *On the Soul*, Book II, Chapter 2, 413a23–25.

[22] Aristotle, *On the Soul*, Book II, Chapter 2, 413a32–34.

really *perceiving* any more than a video camera is or *thinking* any more than a pocket calculator is.

Solving the Transformers' Nutrition Problems

So if Transformers don't mature and weaken with age and don't reproduce, then they don't really possess the nutritive faculty of soul, which would imply that they don't have souls at all and, despite appearances, aren't *really* alive, sentient, or intelligent. I suspect that this worry comes at least partly from the sort of thinking that misled Prowl and Sparkplug: we're most familiar with life that physically ages and reproduces, and so life that doesn't do those things can seem too alien and abnormal to be called *life* at all. Still, more can be said to lay the worry to rest.

First, let's consider Transformers' lack of physical aging and development over time. It's fairly clear from the fiction that they do *mentally* and *emotionally* and even *morally* develop over time. For example, the recently constructed Aerialbots start out somewhat naive but "grow up" after some experience,[23] and Grimlock only gradually accepts and comes to respect Optimus Prime as his leader.[24] Yet apparently, Transformers are "born" physically mature and don't get old. Though this is unconventional, I think we should ask ourselves why we should think that it *must* imply that they're not really alive. Surely the very idea of a living but physically ageless being isn't too troubling: such extraordinary beings certainly *seem* possible (fiction is full of them), however much their actual existence would challenge our conventional views about life. At least, nothing about being *ageless* clearly implies being *lifeless*.

Regarding Transformers' lack of physical maturation, we can observe that plenty of simple life forms with simple reproductive processes (for example, many single-celled organisms) produce "children" that are essentially mature. "But then," the skeptic asks, "even if Transformers count as *alive*, couldn't they really be just as simple as single-celled organisms and not truly sentient or intelligent?" Apparently not: it seems perfectly obvious from the way they act that they possess the higher faculties of soul. "But," the skeptic

---

23 "War Dawn."

24 "War of the Dinobots," *Transformers*, Season 1 (24th November) 1984, DVD, Rhino Home Video, 2002.

presses, "isn't it *possible* that, though they *seem* to be sophisticated life forms, nevertheless they really *aren't*?"

Well, perhaps that's *possible*, but it seems equally possible that the *apparent* human beings whom I encounter on a daily basis are no more than lifelike robots or even figments of my imagination. But I certainly don't believe *that*. Instead, I set aside skeptical possibilities like these and infer from a human-looking being's humanlike behavior that it is, in fact, a human being, one who possesses the same faculties of soul that I do. Maybe that's a mistaken inference on my part—though I doubt it. Whether it is or not, though, my point here is this: it's not clear that we have any *less* reason for inferring Transformers' life, sentience, and intelligence from their behavior than we have when we (unhesitatingly) draw such inferences in the human case. The mere *possibility* that we might be wrong in making such inferences rarely gives us any real problems (outside of a discussion of philosophical skepticism, anyway).

At some point, it becomes practical and seems reasonable to put aside skepticism and say that an *apparently* living, sentient, intelligent being *actually is* alive, sentient, and intelligent. If we don't allow ourselves to do this, we might have to say that our fellow human beings are no more than *apparently* alive, sentient, and intelligent. But if we make the allowance in the human case, it's not clear why we can't or shouldn't make it in the Transformers' case, too.

It's problematic to suggest that a being's not having physically matured over time implies that it lacks one of the faculties of soul, as simple thought experiments seem to show. Suppose that a being that is to all appearances a male human in the prime of life just suddenly popped into existence somewhere, uncaused by anything. Maybe that couldn't actually happen, but supposing that it *did* happen, I doubt that any of us would think of this person as anything other than that: a living, sentient, intelligent person who has a soul. And we'd think this, I'm sure, in spite of his not having physically matured over time, whether we knew about his unusual origin or not. You can run similar thought experiments with Frankenstein's monster or a clone of yourself or most any non-maturing but apparently living, sentient, intelligent being and you'll get about the same result: the sort of soul that a being possesses seemingly has a lot more to do with what that being is and can do *now* than with how it *came to be* what it is now. So Transformers' not having physically matured doesn't clearly rule out their having any particular faculty of soul.

What about the worry that Transformers don't reproduce? One way of answering it is to observe that there actually *are* unquestionably natural, living, sentient beings that nevertheless can't reproduce. Mules, especially male ones, are examples of this. Another, possibly better answer is as follows. Aristotle emphasizes the importance of natural reproduction because it's a way for mortal beings to approximate immortality by continuing on in their descendants.[25] But Transformers have a kind of natural immortality: they can (presumably) continue functioning forever unless they run out of Energon or are killed or otherwise actively destroyed. Given this fact, we shouldn't be surprised if they're living beings who don't reproduce: if the main reason for reproduction is that it guarantees a kind of immortality, and Transformers are already somewhat immortal and so don't *need* to continue on in their descendants (since they continue on *in themselves*), then they don't *need* to be able to reproduce. Thinking along these lines, we might also note that, for Aristotle, only physically aging *mortal* beings have the nutritive faculty of soul.[26] Again, though, Transformers are no more than semi-mortal and don't physically age, so their differing from true mortals with respect to the nutritive faculty of soul shouldn't be surprising.

Yet another way of answering the reproduction worry is simply to say that Transformers *do* reproduce. As noted in the last section, one Transformer can build another Transformer. But doesn't that make them *artificial* rather than *natural*? Again, I'm not sure that we have all that good of a reason to think so. Maybe designing and building each other is just their natural mode of reproduction. Plenty of people believe that God intelligently designed and created the first human beings in God's own image, but no one seems to think that this implies that the first humans were therefore artificial, nonliving, insentient beings, and many think of human beings as God's children despite this unconventional mode of "reproduction." So perhaps it's just *natural*, in some cases, for reproduction

---

[25] Aristotle, *On the Soul*, Book II, Chapter 4, 415a26–b8.

[26] Aristotle, *On the Soul*, Book II, Chapter 2, 413a32–33, and Book III, Chapter 12, 434a23–26.

to take the form of intelligent design and creation, designing and building. It's also worth noting at this point that (in at least some of the fiction) the first Transformers were created by Primus, the Transformers' version of God.[27] Taking this into consideration, we might say that the Transformers' reproduction reflects their origins more closely and better approximates divine creative activity than that of other life forms, including ourselves. Given Transformers' natural immortality and powerful intellectual faculties, their bearing such resemblance to the divine probably wouldn't surprise Aristotle, anyway, since he thought of God as eternally engaged in intellectual activity.[28]

So much, then, for the problems about Transformers' possession of Aristotle's nutritive faculty of soul. If something as simple as an amoeba or a bacterium counts as alive, it seems strange to deny that a being as complex and lifelike as Optimus Prime or Megatron also counts as alive. Transformers are either alive or so close to it that we might as well call them alive. And, if we think that the Aristotle-inspired, faculty-oriented view of the soul that has been discussed is at least generally accurate, and if we think of the soul as just the life principle, then we seem to have no less reason to think that Transformers have souls than we do anything else that acts alive, sentient, and intelligent.

Transformer Death and Religious Belief

As discussed in the last section, Transformers aren't merely *alive*, but basically *immortal*. Nevertheless, it seems that they can die: they can be damaged and destroyed (or, rather, *injured* and *killed*), and maybe they could starve from lack of Energon. Still, death seems to be a somewhat different thing for them than it is for other living beings. A look back at the fictional account will help confirm these things.

Early in the original Transformers movie,[29] Megatron is badly injured in battle with Optimus Prime. As he lies helpless,

---

[27] Furman, pp. 10–13, 15, 50, and 53.

[28] Aristotle, *Metaphysics*, Book XII (Λ), Chapter 7, 1072b14–30, and *Nicomachean Ethics*, Book X, Chapter 8, 1178b8–23.

[29] *The Transformers: The Movie*, written by Ron Friedman, directed by Nelson Shin, produced by Sunbow and Marvel, 1986, DVD, Sony BMG Music Entertainment, 2006.

Starscream orders the Decepticon retreat, not caring that his leader suffers. Fortunately for Megatron, the loyal Soundwave is nearby, and Megatron pleads, "Don't leave me, Soundwave." Later, as Starscream abandons Megatron again, dumping him out into space, Megatron weakly protests, "Wait, . . . I still function." Clearly, these are the words of a being who's afraid that he might die. We can contrast his attitude with Optimus Prime's stoic calm in the face of death. After the battle with Megatron, as Optimus Prime lies dying, his last words to his friends are, "Do not grieve. Soon I shall be one with the Matrix. . . . Until that day, . . . till all are one . . ."

Perhaps these very different responses to death spring from differences in religious belief or beliefs about the afterlife. Optimus Prime's final words have a certain religious ring to them. Megatron, though, might not believe in an afterlife at all: at one point in the comic series, he threatens Sparkplug, saying "You will cooperate or cease to exist!"[30] (Or maybe he arrogantly thinks that there's no afterlife for insignificant beings like humans.) It is, in any case, fairly clear that Transformers do have some concept of religion. For example, early in the comic series, a group of Autobots who aren't yet familiar with Earth's life forms come across a drive-in movie theater. Having seen the many cars all motionlessly facing the movie screen, and assuming that the cars are life forms like himself, Cliffjumper suggests to Hound that the cars have probably assembled there for "some kind of religious ritual."[31] And even Megatron exclaims "By the divine weld!" to himself at one point,[32] perhaps referring to the Transformers' creation by Primus.

So Transformers display very human sentiments about things like religion, death, and the afterlife. At the very least, they understand what death *is*. This is clear from another scene in the comic, one that also raises questions about exactly what death *is* for a Transformer. At one point, Gears is dashed to pieces in a fall. The other Autobots collect up his remnants, but two of their human friends (Sparkplug and, since it was a Marvel comic, Spider-Man) remark that the Autobots don't seem to care that their comrade has died. At this, Optimus Prime says to himself, "The humans don't understand! Our form of life is vastly different from theirs!" Later, Spider-Man has the following conversation with Optimus Prime:

---

[30] *Transformers* #3.

[31] *Transformers* #1.

[32] *Transformers* #5, p. 16.

> "I'm sorry about what happened to Gears, Optimus! Even the good guys die sometimes!"
> "Die?"
> "You mean he's still alive?"
> "No! But neither is he what you would term 'dead'!"[33]

Here, Optimus Prime doesn't seem to be puzzled by the concept of death. Had it puzzled him, it's not clear why he'd say (correctly, let's assume) that Gears *isn't* dead. Gears is badly injured and unconscious, but he can be (and soon is) repaired and restored to consciousness. Perhaps, rather than being truly, finally dead, he was in something like a comatose state, "dead but able to resume living function if repaired" or something of the sort. It isn't easy to say exactly how badly a Transformer has to be injured before being irrevocably, irreparably dead. Equally, though, it's pretty clear that this *can* happen: for example, several Autobots die in the original movie and never resume functioning. I guess we'd have to ask Ratchet for the final answer on this one, since we're not familiar enough with his form of life to say exactly what has to happen for it to be ended permanently. Still, our lacking specifics on exactly *how* it happens doesn't mean that we can't say that it *does* happen. Until we can get an answer from Ratchet, though, Transformer life, faculties of soul, and death have probably been sufficiently discussed for our purposes. It seems clear enough that Transformers *are* alive, sentient, and intelligent, *do* have souls, and *can* die.

Mechanical Virtue

In an early episode of the original cartoon, Spike, one of the Autobots' human friends, writes the following in his journal shortly after seeing the Autobots in action: "Optimus Prime cares a lot for his fellow robots, and he doesn't want *anything* to happen to them. I think he'd make a neat President!"[34] Optimus Prime is one of the "good guys," good as (unfortunately) only a fictional character can be. And apparently, he's good not because he's been programmed that way, but by his own choice. That Transformers *choose* to be good or evil is suggested by another episode of the cartoon: when

---

33 *Transformers* #3.

34 "More Than Meets the Eye Part 3," *Transformers*, Season 1 (19th September) 1984, DVD, Rhino Home Video, 2002. Audible emphasis in original.

the original Dinobots (who've been misled by Megatron) attack Optimus Prime and are in a position to kill him, Grimlock holds the rest of them back from doing so. Grimlock isn't sure *why* he wants to spare his rightful leader, but Optimus Prime suggests that it's because of his "Autobot training."[35] This at least hints that Transformers aren't *created* good or *programmed* to be evil, but instead become that way much as we ourselves do: through deliberate choice, aided by moral training and advice, and actions taken as a result. The case of the Aerialbots makes this clearer. At first, they're not too impressed with the Autobots or their cause.[36] Later, though, after they've witnessed Megatron's brutality and had a chance to act heroically, they decide for themselves which is the right side to be on.[37]

There's a great deal that could be said about what goes into making people good or evil (beyond "Autobot training," of course). I'll just point out a few things that Aristotle says in the *Nicomachean Ethics* that pretty strongly suggest that Transformers can be considered genuinely good beings (or evil beings, though I'll focus on the good). Ancient ethical thinkers, including Aristotle, talked about being good mainly in terms of being *virtuous*, possessing *virtue*. So what, exactly, is virtue? To understand Aristotle's view of it, it's probably easiest to start by looking at one of the ancients' words, *aretē*. This is usually translated "virtue," but equally good translations might be "excellence" or "effectiveness" or maybe "the state of functioning well." As a concept, this wasn't restricted to discussions of morality: there was the *aretē* of a poet or a shoemaker, too, which implied being good at those occupations. It wasn't even restricted to the realm of human beings, or even of *living* beings: there was the *aretē* of a dog, which might've consisted of barking at strangers and obeying friends, and the *aretē* of a knife, which might've been cutting and taking an edge well. Here, though, we're looking for the *aretē* of humanlike beings, beings like ourselves (and Transformers) who can *choose* and *try* to be good persons. Clearly, it's possible to be good at your job without being a good and virtuous person, and we're looking for what it means to be the latter.

---

35 "War of the Dinobots."

36 "The Key to Vector Sigma Part 2," *Transformers*, Season 2 (26th November) 1985, DVD, Rhino Home Video, 2003, and "War Dawn."

37 "War Dawn."

So what makes for a good, virtuous, excellent, effective person, a person of *aretē*? As we just saw in the cases of occupations and nonhumans, it's basically being able to do a certain job or perform a certain function *well*. But then what's most properly a person's *job*, the function of a person just insofar as he or she is a person and not a member of a particular occupation? For Aristotle, it's closely related to the functions that a person can perform, and most of these appeared on the list of the faculties of the soul that we mentioned earlier. The ones most relevant here for distinctly *personal* excellence or virtue are some of the faculties related to the intellect, like the capacities for thought, choice, deliberation, higher emotion, and basically anything that can guide voluntary action. An excellent, virtuous person, then, is one who thinks, chooses, deliberates, and feels emotions in ways that are appropriate and fitting. Aristotle divides virtue into two types, *moral* and *intellectual*. *Moral* virtue is basically having good emotional habits, training yourself to feel things like desire, fear, confidence, and anger to the right degree, in the correct situations, towards the proper objects, and so forth. When you've done that, you possess traditional moral virtues like moderation, courage, evenness of temper, and so forth. *Intellectual* virtue governs the mental but non-emotional side of a person, including things like making careful and well-reasoned decisions, being knowledgeable, and having practical wisdom and experience.

It would seem, then, that regardless of whether a person is organic or mechanical, so long as he or she has the right faculties of soul, he or she at least has the *potential* to be virtuous. Once again, there's that idea that it's not what you're *made of*, but what you can *do*, that's important. It takes time and training, but apparently any such being who *functions* is capable of functioning *well*. It's important to remember that being a good person (in this sense of being virtuous/excellent with respect to the functions of a person) is distinct from being good *at* something, like being good at an occupation. For example, Megatron is decisive, crafty, tenacious, and rather charismatic, but also savagely cruel and sometimes a bit cowardly. These qualities make him an effective leader: he has the *aretē* of a military leader (of a certain kind, anyway), but he's certainly not *virtuous* in the sense of being a good person, so he lacks the *aretē* of a person. Optimus Prime, on the other hand, is honorable, responsible, brave, and fair-minded, but he's selfless and compassionate almost to a fault. He's at least as effective a leader as Megatron, but he's also a good and virtuous person (if anyone is), so he can be said to have both of these kinds of *aretē*, that of a leader and that of a person.

Why Not?

Finally, we're in a position to come back to the question posed in this chapter's title. What has to be the case for us to meet Optimus Prime in heaven? Clearly, we ourselves have to go to heaven, but let's leave that between ourselves and our consciences. Consider what has to be true of Optimus Prime for him to go to heaven. Presumably, something like the following conditions need to be fulfilled:

1. **He has to live a virtuous life**
2. **He has to have a soul**
3. **He has to die**
4. **His soul has to continue existing after his body dies**

As we've seen, we have at least some reason to think that 1. through 3. can be fulfilled. However, 4. is trickier. We've been working with Aristotle's view of the soul here, and Aristotle implies that (with the possible exception of the intellect) the soul dies along with the body, ceases to exist when the body's organs stop functioning.[38] Of course, that's no less true for human beings than for Transformers: regardless of what a being's organs are made of, when they've finally stopped working, the being has ceased to be. So we can at least say that Transformers have *no worse* a shot at the afterlife than we do.

Frankly, that's enough to satisfy me. There are certainly other theories of the soul out there, ones that might make it easier for us to allow for an afterlife, and we might consider bringing these into our inquiry. However, even if we did, I suspect that the final result of our inquiry would be about the same. That is, I suspect that we'd

---

[38] Aristotle, *On the Soul*, Book II, Chapter I, 413a4–7, and Book III, Chapter 4, 429b4–5.

still end up having no less reason to think that Transformers are alive, have souls, can die, and can be virtuous than we would for anything that acts so lifelike, including ourselves.

So if anything can go to heaven, if we ourselves can, then we seem to have little reason to doubt that Optimus Prime can, as well. To be cautious and precise, though, my answer to the question posed in this chapter's title isn't a definite "Yes." Really, I'm more inclined to answer with: "Why not?"[39]

---

[39] I'd like to thank Liz Stillwaggon Swan for her helpful comments on a draft of this paper, my friend Andrew Happel for also reading a draft, my colleague Matthew Pike for bringing *Transformers and Philosophy* to my attention, and my student Mandy Lyne for asking me whether zombies have souls and so aiding in the genesis of my thinking about unconventional life forms.

Eric Swan says hullo to a non-organic intelligence in Japan.

8
Optimus Prime in Therapy

ERIC SWAN and LIZ STILLWAGGON SWAN

One week has passed since the most recent clash between the Autobots and the Decepticons, a clash that left Megatron extinguished, and Optimus Prime rescued from seemingly ultimate peril thanks to his new human friend, Sam Witwicky.

Since the crisis, Optimus Prime has not shut down for longer than a few moments at a time, having been on continual high-alert, vigilantly protecting Sam, Mikaela, and the whole human race toward whom his loyalty is steadily growing. He has been constantly on the go, ostensibly executing the Autobot plan of providing continuous surveillance of the L.A. metropolitan area in case of a future Decepticon attack.

Privately, our hero Optimus Prime has been harboring a desire to escape the pressures of leading the Autobots and protecting the human race from doom. He has three times in the past week come close to running out of gas on the highway, something he had never done before, has been having difficulty switching gears smoothly, and hasn't been to the carwash in over a week (much to his chagrin, he had noticed someone's idea of a funny joke—the words "WASH ME" written in the thick dirt that had collected on his bumper).

Optimus Prime's keen intelligence has made him aware of the fact that he's going through something he has never before experienced and that, for the first time in his life, he's feeling less than omnipotent. He had always believed himself capable of helping anyone out of any situation no matter what, but now felt that someone was going to have to help *him* to be strong. Optimus Prime decided to tell the rest of the Autobots that he would be visiting the auto body shop regularly over the next few weeks to "have some repair work done," which was believable in light of the recent violent clash with the Decepticons. In truth, he had identified a local therapist, Dr. Sara Sawyer, whom he approached, in search of some professional guidance concerning the new issues he was facing.

Counseling Session 1

Please, take a seat, Optimus. So, what brings you to counseling today?

Well, Doctor . . .

Please, call me Sara.

I think it would be better if I called you "Doctor."

Okay. If that's what you prefer.

Yes. That is what I prefer. I have been operating on overload lately and yesterday there was a . . . situation. I think Sam called it a 'nervous break down' but I do not know what that means. Sounds like something a human would say.

Tell me more about this "situation."

Well, in the middle of my work shift yesterday, the truck I was driving started acting weird, making noises, and then suddenly lost all power. One minute I was cruising down the highway, enjoying the feel of the open road, and the next minute I was stalled there on the side of the road, steam and smoke coming out of my engine. For the first time in my life I felt powerless. I could not go anywhere.

That certainly sounds like a breakdown.

I have never had a situation like that before.

This was a new experience for you.

Yes. I used to have the energy of a truck. I could drive all night, carry any load. At least until yesterday . . .

You said you've been operating on overload lately. That can certainly lead to a breakdown.

I have been under a lot of pressure lately. My job has been very intense. There has been a heightened sense of urgency, people counting on me—some days it seems like the fate of the world depends on me. I have not shut down in as long as I can remember.

It sounds like you've been working extremely hard lately, and you're noticing some changes in yourself.

Yes.

What is it that you do for work?

Well . . . You could say I work in protective services, or law enforcement.

I'll bet that's a demanding field to work in.

It is.

And dangerous too.

Yes. It is a very physical job, it requires a great deal of strength and energy. I am the leader of my squad so I am constantly moving, giving out orders, problem solving. In my career I see a lot of combat, especially recently. These are dangerous times and I have to be on high alert or else.

Or else what?

People get hurt.

Oh, I understand. Given the type of job you have and your sense of responsibility, yesterday's breakdown makes a lot of sense. There's a limit to how far someone can push his body, a limit to how much stress someone can endure before they break down.

But I am Optimus Prime. I am a machine, not an ordinary human. I cannot afford to break down. It is not in my constitution. People are counting on me. The whole world is counting on me. As I speak, you can bet that forces are plotting revenge and preparing for another round of attacks. If I do not take a stand, if I do not stop the Decepticons, who will?

I admire your courage and compassion, your desire to help people, but in doing so, it seems like you are putting a tremendous amount of pressure on yourself.

I just want to make sure that my team and I succeed in our mission.

This mission sounds very important to you . . .

Nothing could be more important.

And yet, I imagine you would like a break from all this stress. This pressure.

Yes. Sometimes I wish I could be doing something else, something less stressful . . . but the truth is the people of Earth are in great danger. It is my duty and that of the Autobots to help and protect them. I cannot fail.

(The counselor nods.)

Believe me, I wish we were living in peaceful times, like how it used to be on Cybertron, before Megatron and the Decepticons. But that is not the case—I will not rest until the threat of the Decepticons is abolished.

This is all very fascinating. I'd like to get clarification on something. You said humankind is in danger because of these Decepticons and that our fate depends on you. Tell me more about that.

The fate of the world does *depend on me, or at least me and my team. I don't think the people of Earth realize how in danger they are. Most of them go about their day without a care, and little do they know that living among them are forces capable of inflicting great harm, fatal harm. As far as I can tell, most humans have no idea about the Decepticons, and they certainly do not have the skills or the power to defeat a war machine like Starscream, who is still unaccounted for. Sam might be an exception, because he defeated Megatron, but that is another story . . .*

Maybe I will get a chance to hear that story at some point.

Yes, I imagine.

The more you share, the more likely I will be able to help you in counseling. You've already shared so much about yourself. So far, I understand that you have a very stressful career and you feel it is your job to protect all of us on Earth from these machines called Decepticons. I'm also getting the sense that this is a tremendous burden to bear since, after all, you just had a breakdown.

I made a promise to myself long ago that I would not stand by while worlds are destroyed. And besides, I made a promise to Sam.

And what promise was that?

I promised him that I, and the rest of the Autobots, would protect him and all humans in case the Decepticons return. I owe it to him for saving my life.

Okay. I understand.

I was hoping you would, Doctor.

With the time that we have left, let's talk about what you hope to get from counseling.

I think for now, I just need someone I can confide in. There are some things that I have not told anyone.

That sounds very reasonable. Counseling is a perfect setting for self-disclosure. While the world outside this office might not feel safe to you, you can allow yourself to feel safe in this room when it comes to sharing your experiences, thoughts, feelings, and anything else for that matter.

That sounds good to me. I cannot say this is going to be easy. This . . . disclosing personal information . . . is new to me.

You're doing great so far, Optimus. For now, maybe we can agree that you're safe in these sessions to share anything you like. Through honest communication, and over the course of a few more sessions, I'm convinced that you will see improvements in your life.

Improvements in my life . . . I like that. (Optimus Prime nods and there appears a faint smile on his lips.)

Things will get better for you, Optimus. I have confidence in you. We'll meet again next week.

Counseling Session 2

Nice to see you, Optimus.

Nice to see you too, Doctor Sawyer.

In our last session, you told me about your breakdown and what brought you to counseling. I'd like to begin today by having you tell me more about yourself. I bet there's more to you than meets the eye . . .

Yes, there is. First, I am an Autobot, a particular kind of Transformer. I come from Cybertron and I have only been here a short while. I have few connections here, mainly to my fellow Autobots—the team I arrived here with.

Tell me again what brought you here.

You could say that we were compelled *to come here. We wanted to prevent the Decepticons from finding the All Spark and gaining power over the universe.*

I've been wanting to ask you about the Decepticons.

Decepticons are Transformers too. They are warmongers, anarchists.

Oh?

We call them Decipticons because they are deceiving; they can take the form of any machine and blend into the environment. They could be right outside this building right now, disguised as vans or sports cars . . . and who knows what else!

That sounds scary.

Some would say.

So, they blend into the environment?

Yes. Lately they have adopted the form of cars, a military jet, a helicopter, but they can look like any machine, and it is extremely difficult to tell the difference between Decepticons and inert machines. I can tell the difference, but I am an expert, this is what I do.

I see. Now I understand why you you're constantly on the lookout.

I have to be. It is my duty.

Tell me more about your comrades.

There is Bumblebee, Ratchet, and Ironhide. There was Jazz, but he is gone now . . .

Gone?

Unlike the Decepticons, we are a peaceful group. We are here to prevent the Decepticons from executing their plan to turn the machines of Earth against people. We are here to prevent worldwide destruction.

That's quite a mission you have. You have quite a strong sense of purpose.

Yes. And that is not my only mission. My mission is also to protect Sam. He is important to me because he saved my life. He is in great danger and I, along with the rest of the Autobots, must protect him against Starscream and all of the other Decepticons.

Sounds like you have a very strong bond with Sam.

I would put my life on the line for him.

Wow. How did that come about?

Long story . . . he courageously stepped in when Megatron was in a position to destroy me.

So, on top of all these stressors you've been telling me about, you also had a recent brush with death . . .

"Brush with death?"

Meaning, you almost died.

Yes. But my difficulties are nothing compared to what happened to Jazz.

Oh? How so?

Jazz was extinguished. He is dead.

(There is a long pause.)

Jazz was killed when I was busy fighting Megatron. He was an admirable Autobot, a real fighter. He gave his life to prevent the Decepticons from getting the All Spark.

He sounds like quite a hero.

He was.

So, in addition to feeling all the pressures of being a leader, of defending the planet, you are also dealing with the loss of your dear friend and comrade.

Yes . . . That is true . . . This talk about my feelings and my life experiences is all new to me. I have never lost a team member before. And Jazz was more than a team member. He was . . . he was a friend.

I understand, Optimus. So much has happened to you recently. With all the stress you've been experiencing, you probably haven't had a chance to process it all. You've been so busy protecting others that you haven't had a chance to look out for yourself and your own needs.

It has been hard, Doctor. That is why I am here in counseling.

I'm curious. What do your friends think about you and counseling?

They do not know about it. I told them that I am getting some body work done, and they believed me because of the injuries I suffered in the recent clash with Megatron.

If they are your friends, why can't you tell them about counseling?

I cannot tell them because I do not want them to think I am weak. If they knew about the breakdown they might question my abilities. I am their leader. I cannot have them doubting my leadership.

I understand. You want to retain your strong exterior, your command over your comrades.

Yes. They already saw me nearly get defeated by Megatron. And I would not blame them if they held me responsible for Jazz's death.

How are you responsible for Jazz's death?

I was his team leader and he was my subordinate.

(The counselor is silent for a moment, letting Optimus Prime brood over this disclosure.)

He was a great soldier and it is my fault that he is no longer with us. He should not have died . . . I should have been there but I was not. I was fighting Megatron. If I were stronger I would have defeated Megatron more swiftly and hurried back to defend Jazz.

How does Jazz's death make you feel? Right now?

I feel . . . I feel . . . I do not know yet. I think I need to get back to my team. I do not want to fail them again. I need to go, Doctor.

(Optimus Prime quickly exits the counseling office.)

Interlude

In Optimus Prime's first two counseling sessions, we have witnessed the beginning of a new kind of transformation happening deep within his wiring. An internal transformation, completely new and strange for Transformers as we know them, has gotten underway. Optimus Prime's breakdown on the side of the road was a pivotal experience for him, one that got him thinking about himself in a new way. Feelings of hopelessness and powerlessness, self-doubt, and even just physical exhaustion were experienced for the first time by this seemingly omnipotent and indestructible machine we know of as Optimus Prime. The untimely death of his friend and comrade, Jazz, caused within Optimus Prime not only a sense of profound and regretful loss—a new experience for him—but also feelings of guilt and moral responsibility. By failing to come to Jazz's defense when he needed it most, Optimus Prime is discovering that actions ought to be driven by a sense of interpersonal loyalty and moral duty, and not merely obligation. In talking about all of these recent major events in his life with Dr. Sara Sawyer, Optimus Prime has recognized just how strong of a bond he feels toward Sam Witwicky and the rest of the humans for whom his affection and sense of loyalty continue to grow. When asked how he feels about the death of his friend Jazz, or the bond with his new human friend Sam, Optimus Prime grows uncomfortable, unable to articulate these very human experiences of *feelings,* and unsure of what they mean to him. The very fact that Optimus Prime has sought out psychological counseling is not lost on him; he is well aware that he is the first Transformer ever to undergo therapy. What Optimus Prime is witnessing in himself is a profound transformation—not in his machine form, which he is accustomed to, but to his internal constitution. He is becoming aware of a richer, more complex *inner* experience that we humans know as emotions or feelings. In essence, Optimus Prime is becoming more human.

Counseling Session 3

Nice to see you again, Optimus. How have things been since your last visit?

Nothing new to report, Doctor. No sign of Starscream or the other Decepticons.

That's good to know. I take comfort knowing that there are individuals like you who are on the lookout.

It is a difficult job but it is my duty. Your planet has so much worth saving and protecting.

I agree. In the last session you were telling me about yourself and some of your friends. I appreciated your honesty, which is essential for a counseling relationship to work. You told me about Jazz and how you felt responsible for his death. I was wondering if you would be willing to spend some more time on this subject.

You are the doctor. If you think it would be good for me, then I will do it.

I do think it would be healthy for you to explore your feelings more deeply. I noticed in the last session when I asked you about your feelings, you appeared uncomfortable. It seemed like you left in a hurry. I was afraid I might have scared you off.

No. It takes a lot to scare me.

You told me that in your job you see a lot of combat. Don't you ever get scared going into battle?

I am Optimus Prime. I am not afraid to go into battle, as long as it is in the interest of peace. I am a soldier and that is what soldiers do.

You said Jazz was a soldier.

And a damned good one.

Right. You said he was a hero.

A great hero.

Let's talk some more about Jazz.

Okay.

I'd like you to think about him for a minute and when you're ready, I'd like to know what *feelings* you notice.

Feelings, doctor?

Yes, *feelings.* Umm . . . feelings are sensations that occur inside of you.

Oh. You mean, like wanting to squash the Decepticon who killed my friend?

Yes. We might call that anger. Or wanting to enact revenge.

(Optimus Prime is silent for one minute.)

I feel mad. I am mad at myself for not being at Jazz's side when he needed me.

Okay. So, you're angry with *yourself.* What else?

I feel sad. I wish he was still with us. I wish I could talk to him. I never got to tell him how proud I was of him. He was a great Autobot. A real warrior.

Optimus, let's try something. It's a technique in counseling we call the 'Empty Chair'.

"The empty chair"?

Yes. The 'empty chair' can be used when we can't otherwise communicate to someone we care about. I think it might help you come to terms with the loss of your friend Jazz.

Sounds a little strange, Doctor.

Maybe, but it can be very powerful. It takes a lot of courage . . .

I am courageous. I can do it.

Okay, then. I'd like you to turn yourself so that you're facing that chair over there, and imagine that Jazz is sitting there in that chair.

(Optimus Prime follows her instruction.)

Okay.

Now, imagine that Jazz is sitting there because he understands that you need to speak with him. Like a good friend, he cares about you. He cares how you are feeling and what you are thinking, and wants to listen to you.

Okay.

At this point, I'd like you to express to him anything you like. Anything you always wanted to tell him.

(Optimus Prime is silent for a minute.)

Jazz, old friend, this is not easy for me. I wish you were still here—that way I could tell you face to face what I am going through. I miss you. I feel responsible for what happened.

(Optimus Prime looks to the counselor, who nods and indicates for him to keep going.)

You were a great warrior, Jazz. A hero. I always felt a special bond with you. I hope you can forgive me for not being there when you needed me. I thought my plan to defeat the Decepticons would work but it did not work as well as I had hoped. If it did, all the Decepticons would be destroyed and you would still be here. I am sorry. I hope you do not blame me. I hope you saw me as a good leader.

(Pause.)

Wow, that was powerful, Optimus. What are you feeling right now?

I am feeling . . . sad. A little better, but mostly just sad. I wish I had talked to Jazz like that before he was killed.

What stopped you?

I do not know. Maybe I was too focused on leading . . . maintaining order . . . making sure every one was doing his part . . . following the mission. Maybe I just thought he would always be there. Maybe I was too busy operating on what you humans call 'autopilot'. And regretfully I never talked to him as . . . as a friend.

All of those reasons certainly make sense.

I would like to believe that he knew those things all along.

Even if you didn't actually communicate those sentiments to Jazz with your words, something tells me that you communicated them with your behavior. Could that be?

I would like to think so. If only I had said those things to him while he was alive, then I would feel better . . . more complete.

Complete?

Yes. That is important to me.

I understand. I'm hoping that, in time, you will feel some sense of completeness, or some sense of *closure* as we say in counseling, now that you've begun to come to terms with what happened to Jazz. We can't expect you to be done missing him, or feeling grief as we say, but I hope you can begin to feel better.

I hope so too, Doctor.

In time, Optimus. One of the things we know about the passage of time is that it can be a great healer. And speaking of time, it looks like we are out of it for today.

Counseling Session 4

Nice to see you today, Optimus. I wasn't expecting you until next week, but my secretary informed me that you just *had* to see me. So, what's on your mind?

Well, Doctor. I mean, Sara, I have been thinking about something you said in the last session. You said honesty is essential for counseling to work, or something like that.

Yes, I remember.

I am afraid I have not been totally honest with you.

Oh?

Well, remember how I told you about my breakdown?

Of course.

Well, there is more to it. Something happened before my truck broke down that day.

I'm listening.

Well, I almost killed somebody. I did not, but I came close.

Tell me about it.

This happened just after Sam saved my life, when I was on constant alert-mode, when I was not shutting down at all. You have to understand, I thought I was doing the right thing, being the best guardian I could be. It all happened so fast . . .

I understand. This was after Jazz died, after your battle with Megatron, when you were fearing another attack.

Yes. I had to be on guard twenty-four hours a day.

Wow. That must have been stressful.

Yes. It was an honest mistake. You know I am not a bad person—or a bad machine, I should say.

I know. Help me understand what happened.

Well, it happened late one night, when I was on guard outside of Sam's house. I was sitting in my truck in case a Decepticon decided to launch a raid and that is when I noticed some movement in a car parked across from me. I thought at the time, that the car had moved, as if it was transforming into some war machine, and that is when I jumped into action. In an instant I suddenly transformed, grabbed the car, and hoisted it into the air. I was just a moment away from smashing it, but when I looked closer—hoping to find a set of eyes to stare into and say "This is for Jazz!"—the only eyes I saw were those of a human. You should have seen the look on this kid's face.

Wow.

I know. There we were, frozen—our eyes locked together for what seemed like an eternity.

This was a really powerful experience for you. And for the kid too, I imagine . . .

It was. I remember thinking, what if I had acted just a second sooner and killed this kid? Then I would be no better than the Decepticons. I would be a murderer.

And how would you have felt?

Terrible.

And why is that?

I would have taken the life of a human!

Okay. And yet, you caught yourself before you hurt this kid, right?

Right. Once I realized there was a person inside the car, just some kid, I lowered the car down to the ground. The kid was in shock. The two of us just looked at each other in total silence and then I slowly drove away.

Did you tell Sam or any of the Autobots what happened that night?

I have not told anyone until now. You are the only one, Sara.

And why's that? What would be the harm in telling Sam or some of the Autobots about this?

I do not know. I guess I just did not want them to doubt my detection skills or worry that I was losing control over my faculties. They have to be able to trust their leader.

I understand. But maybe they could learn something from your mistake. Maybe you could teach them about the importance of getting rest and not overworking.

Hmm . . .

The way I see it, Optimus, is that you're the leader. You're the one who the other Autobots look to for some sense of how to *behave*. How to *respond*—to a crisis, a tragedy, a problem... and even how to respond to a mistake.

(Optimus Prime is nodding.)

I'm sure they would understand if you were honest with them. I bet they would respect you even more. You could teach them that everyone makes mistakes.

(Optimus Prime continues nodding.)

We all make mistakes, Optimus, and it takes courage to admit to them and teach others what you've learned.

I understand, Sara. I like your idea.

I wonder if it's not too late to tell them about your close encounter with this kid that one night.

We have a team meeting later this evening.

That sounds like an opportune time.

Yes. It is perfect! I could tell them everything! I could talk to them about Jazz. I could speak to them about the importance of being careful, being diligent. I could talk to them about the importance of taking care of themselves, shutting down from time to time. I do not want them making the same mistakes that I have made.

Excellent. It sounds like you have a lot to look forward to.

I do.

Is there anything you would like to say before we adjourn for today?

No, that is all, Sara. Thank you.

Counseling Session 5

Good Morning, Optimus. How are you today?

I am great, Sara. How about yourself?

I'm very well. Something . . . looks different about you.

That is what Bumblebee said this morning. It is so good to have him talking again. He has come a long *way. I am so proud of him.*

Have you . . .

I know what you are going to say, and yes, I have *told him. In fact, just yesterday I told him how much growth I have seen in him. He has regained his voice and confidence. He is practically a whole new Transformer.*

Wow. I'm impressed. Bumblebee's not the only one, apparently, who has come a long way.

(Optimus Prime pauses to consider this statement.)

Are you saying that I have come a long way too?

I *am* saying that. And it's true.

That makes me feel better, Sara. I do feel like I have made progress since I first visited you. I bet when you first met me you thought I was just some . . . typical robot. Just another dysfunctional machine. You probably wanted to send me straight to a junkyard.

No, that's not at all the case. I never thought you were ordinary or beyond fixing.

Well, that is good to know. You are not like most human beings.

And you are not like most machines.

Thank you, Sara.

You're very welcome. So where do you want to go today?

I want to go on a long drive. Maybe go to a beach or somewhere and just relax.

No . . . I meant, where do you want to go with today's *counseling session.*

Oh, I get it. That is kind of funny.

It is, but you raise an interesting point. When was the last time you took a break and relaxed?

Hmm . . . I do not know. Recently I got my truck washed. I got it filled up with premium fuel. The good stuff. That felt restorative. My truck runs so much better now. But in terms of a break? It has been a really long time.

What's stopping you?

Well, I would not want to be absent in case the Decepticons returned.

I see. That's very noble of you. By the way, how long has it been since you last saw a Decepticon?

It has been a while.

So maybe now would be a good time to take a break and relax. I know it's your pattern to always be the guardian, but as you've seen, you can't always be on high alert or else you'll burn out.

Or have a breakdown.

Right.

Or mistake somebody for a Decepticon and almost destroy him.

Exactly. It's so important for those in stressful positions to take time off. In the military, this is known as "R and R."

"R and R?"

Yes. It means "rest and relaxation," and is awarded for service and hard work. It's essential for keeping a soldier healthy.

I like the idea of rest and relaxation. I could use a break and so could the Autobots. Hmm . . .

Talk to me. What are you thinking?

I am thinking that I should treat my team and me to some "R and R." It would be good for all of us. I am not the only one who has been overworked. I am not the only one who misses Jazz.

Maybe in the next session, you'd like to talk about how you can make this happen?

I do not think I need another session to make that happen, Sara. I know exactly how to make this happen. Remember I am a leader. I know how to strategize and execute a plan. I have done so before and I will do so again. I am Optimus Prime.

Excellent. I'll leave you to it, then. Anything else you would like to talk about with the rest of your time?

Hmm . . . nothing that I can think of . . .

Let's try something then. In counseling this is known as the 'Miracle Question'.

The Miracle Question?

Yes. It goes like this: suppose you awoke tomorrow and overnight a miracle had happened. As you went about your day, what would you notice about your life that would indicate that a miracle had in fact happened?

Let me think about that. (A long pause follows.) *I guess the first thing I would notice is that I would always be energized.*

Okay. What else would you notice?

I would not always be working. I would have some time to pursue my interests, like my interest in human beings.

Good. What else?

Let me think . . . the world would be peaceful. There would be no more threat from the Decepticons. Planes would be planes and I would not be worrying if Starscream was going to swoop down and attack without warning. Sam and Mikaela would be safe . . .

Anything else?

The Autobots and I would feel proud knowing that the All Spark was safe and that we had done our duty. Our mission would be over and before long we would be returning home to Cybertron.

That's very moving. Now I have a better sense of what would make your life better. Perhaps more complete.

Me too. For all of those changes to occur it sure would take a miracle.

That's the way it seems, doesn't it?

Yes. And yet I feel optimistic. I know those changes will occur in time.

(Optimus Prime pauses to consider a new idea.)

You know, Sara, I want to thank you for helping me over the course of these counseling sessions. I feel transformed in more ways than one.

I'm curious, Optimus. Can you give me an example?

I can give you several. I have learned so much about myself. I have learned how to take better care of myself and those I care for. And I have learned so much about being a good leader; being a good leader requires honest communication, humility, and teamwork in addition to physical strength and commitment. I've learned about feelings and how they affect behavior.

That's wonderful, Optimus. I'm proud of you. You are a noble and courageous individual. A true hero. I am so grateful for having had a chance to get to know you.

Thank you. Likewise, Sara.

Termination of Therapy

And so Optimus Prime's psychological counseling has come to an end. He has straightened out his internal wiring, so to speak, and now feels recharged and ready to resume duty as the powerful leader of the Autobots. With the aid and wisdom of his therapist, Dr. Sara Sawyer, he has learned that it's okay to grieve the death of his comrade, Jazz, without taking on full responsibility for this horrible mishap. Optimus resolves to keep the memory of Jazz alive by talking to the rest of the Autobots about the great courage and sense of duty Jazz had until the very end. Optimus has also learned that it is okay to make mistakes, even grave ones. He will share his experiences from that night when he mistook a regular car for a Decepticon in hopes that his fellow Autobots will learn from his mistakes and be less likely to make the same ones.

The trust and sense of security that grew between Optimus and his therapist over the course of the few weeks they met allowed him to access parts of his Transformer nature that he had never known existed. The series of intense crises Optimus had lived through recently had opened up for him a whole new way of experiencing the world and its people. He had gained a sense of personal duty—to himself, and to others with whom he felt a strong connection. He had been transformed *internally,* a wholly new experience for a Transformer, and now felt better equipped to help the other Autobots if and when they went through a similar transformation. Thanks to his counseling sessions with Sara, he firmly believed he would return to the Autobots a stronger and wiser leader, and felt grateful to her for that.

Our story ends with a final glimpse of the Autobots, reunited as a team. They have driven together to a stretch of beach along the L.A. coastline, under the command of their leader, Optimus Prime. They are parked for the moment, lined up next to one another, facing out over the great expanse of the ocean, watching the orange glow of the evening sun slowly fade into purples and blues. None of them speaks. And just for the moment, there is total silence, and a well-deserved feeling of peace among them.

THE END

EPISODE FOUR

I and Thou

9
Morally Responsible Machines

ROBERT ARP

My daughter, Zoe, has a killer robot. The other day while walking on the sidewalk, Zoe's wind-up toy robot stepped on an ant and . . . SPLAT! Of course, the robot was simply putting one mechanical foot in front of the other, and the ant just happened to be in the wrong place at the wrong time. How unfortune-*ant*!

Now, imagine if Zoe's robot had *planned* to kill the ant and maneuvered its way over to the little guy so as to step on it. Further, imagine a kind of *Twilight Zone* or *Child's Play* "Chucky" scene where the robot actually tells someone that it's going to kill the ant, expresses dissatisfaction when Rob thwarts its plans, and then says it's going to kill every human being, after ridding the planet of all ants. In such an imaginary case, the robot would be treated just like any sinister psychopath who needs to be stopped and then locked away, despite the fact that it's made of plastic and metal. In other words, the robot would be viewed as an evil person who needs to be held morally responsible for its actions. Think of Megatron, that dirty son of a gas truck!

It makes sense to hold adult persons responsible for their actions, but it doesn't make sense to hold a mindless machine responsible for its 'actions'. But what exactly is a person? In this chapter, I argue that Transformers qualify as persons who can be held morally responsible for their actions, despite the fact that they're from another planet and have a machine-like composition. Transformers are like droids in *Star Wars*, Data in *Star Trek*, or Cylons who seem to "have a plan" in the *Battlestar Galactica* universe. In the not-too-distant future it's possible that there will be person-like machines, giving my analysis in this chapter value beyond that of science fiction and fantasy. So, all of you killer robots like Megatron and the Decepticons better prepare—you may be going to the robot jail!

Prelude to Personhood

First, we need to get at the fundamental essence of what it means to be a person. So, what's a person? A person's a being who has the capacity to: (1) be rational and intelligent; (2) have robust mental states like beliefs, desires, emotions, and a general theory of mind; (3) speak a language, rather than simply transmit information; (4) be involved in relationships with those already deemed persons; and (5) be held morally responsible for its actions because such actions are done freely and autonomously (and thus could have been done differently).

Before considering whether Transformers meet these criteria, I need to clarify a couple of points about the definition of a person. The word *capacity* has been used in the definition because we want to make sure that the definition of person is neither too narrow, nor too broad. If we said that persons were beings that *had* traits (1)–(5) in a kind of absolute sense *at all times*, then our definition would be too narrow, and leave out examples of beings we consider to be persons in an obvious and trivial manner. For example, I qualify as a person because traits (1)–(5) are applicable to me (my wife can verify this). However, would I be considered a person if I were in a deep kind of unconscious sleep? Note that when I'm in such a state, I'm out cold and not willfully engaging in any person-like activity; I'm not reasoning, using language, or entering into relationships with other persons. So if we were to say that, as a person, I have traits (1)–(5) *absolutely and at all times,* it would follow that when I'm asleep I'm not a person, and this seems absurd. However, if we say that I *have the capacity for* (1)–(5), then I can be a person, even when I'm sleeping, and not at that moment (while sleeping) actually engaging in (1)–(5).

Also, the word *capacity* is used so as to prevent the definition of 'person' from being too broad. A being can be considered a member of the human race, but still not be considered a person. Let's define a *human being* as any thing that, by virtue of insemination from another set of human parents, has or would have had all of the genetic traits of *Homo sapiens,* as biologists understand these genetic traits.

It's possible that a being could be genetically human, but through some mutation, malformation, or accident, that being could lack the *typical look* of other human beings. I'm a person at the time of writing this essay, but I could get into a serious car accident and lose a limb. If that happened, I would still be considered a person and a human being. However, I could get into a serious accident, lose a limb, *and* be in a persistent vegetative state like Terri Schiavo—meaning I have no reasonable chance of ever engaging in (1)–(5)—at the time this book actually comes out in print. Since I wouldn't even have the capacity to engage in (1)–(5), I would no longer be considered a person. I would be a human being because of my genetic makeup, but I would no longer be a person.

Fetuses, very young children, individuals in a coma, and the severely mentally handicapped are examples of beings who qualify as humans, but not as persons because they don't even have the capacity to engage in (1)–(5). (Though, of course fetuses, young children, and comatose individuals all have the *potential* to become persons.)

Although the severely *mentally* handicapped aren't persons, no one says that the severely *physically* handicapped aren't persons. Again, a limbless Rob Arp is still a person. It's not the physical body that makes a person a person. Mental capacities—say, consciousness or memory—are what make a person a person. Consider someone like my Aunt Jean or the famous scientist Stephen Hawking, who both suffer from Amyotrophic Lateral Sclerosis (ALS or Lou Gehrig's Disease). These are people who are confined to wheelchairs and need machines in order to communicate because their bodies are ravaged by this devastating motor neuron disease. Despite their bodily limitations, we would still consider them persons because they fulfill criteria (1)–(5). They think, reason, have emotions, communicate, and form strong bonds with other persons. In fact, members of my family—who shall remain nameless—have referred to Aunt Jean as a "royal bitch on wheels who needs to be locked away" because of her supposed deceptive and conniving ways.

Further, if Aunt Jean and Hawking lapsed into comas we would likely say that they were not the same persons they were before the coma. In fact, we could argue that they would no longer be persons *at all* while in the coma, but instead vegetable-like bodies of what used to be persons. Even though we called her by her name, did anyone *really* think that Terri Schiavo was the same person—or even a person at all—near the end of her life when she was in a persistent vegetative state? It's arguable that individuals in comas and persistent vegetative states aren't persons because *cognitive capacities* are the real capacities to look to when trying to discern whether a being qualifies as a person, and a normal functioning brain—or something that functions like the brain—is the real material basis of this cognitive capacity. It may be the same *body* of someone you know laying there in the coma, but it *surely* is not the same person, if even a person at all. Why? Because what really makes Terri Schaivo, Aunt Jean, and Stephen Hawking the persons they are—or were—has to do with their cognitive capacities. If cognitive capacities are what really count when considering the fundamental essence or nature of a person—and a body isn't so significant—then Transformers could be considered as persons, provided their cognitive capacities are the same as persons. And I guess a mindless Transformer would simply be scrap metal!

Scientists and Simulations

We automatically think that persons are going to be biologically-based things with brains who metabolize carbohydrates, take in water for nourishment, and breathe air. But consider this thought experiment.

It's possible to simulate various biological functions, and we know there are artificial kidneys that filter urine, artificial hearts that pump blood, and even artificial eyes that process visual stimuli. Suppose, however, that a scientist developed artificial lobes responsible for the sensation of touch out of silicon and metal, and implanted them into the brain of an adult male human being. The artificial lobes perform the same functions that the natural lobes perform, namely, the processing of tactile information from the environment. Next the scientist develops artificial silicon and metallic parts of the brain responsible for memory, and implants these into our male subject's brain. Again, he can store and recall memories with the artificial parts of the brain in the same way he could with his natural parts. Then the scientist develops an artificial silicon and metal brain *in its entirety*, and implants it into our male subject. With this artificial brain, he can do all of the same things he did before the transplant; he touches, thinks, tries tapioca, tells tales, and meets all of the criteria for personhood. Would he actually *be* a person, however, given that his brain is artificial? Finally, say the scientist can simulate all parts of his body with silicon and metal, and replaces his biological body with a robotic body. He now is *fully* a robotic being—in brain and body—with all of the same thoughts, beliefs, desires, responsibilities, and loyalties as any other human being who is a person. Would he actually be a person?

Someone might object that we could never know if a being could meet the set of criteria for personhood because all we can observe are the outward actions of another being, and that it's not possible to draw any conclusions about the *internal mental states* of a being from its *outward behavior*. It seems that all we can ever say we know for sure are *our own mental states*, namely, our own thoughts, beliefs, feelings, fears, perspectives, and the like. To this, I respond that while it's true that we can never come to any *certain conclusions* about one's cognitive capacities just from observing his behavior, we can feel justified in drawing *probabilistic inferences*. In fact, if we didn't feel justified in drawing inference about someone's internal cognitive capacities from their external behavior, then the sciences of psychology, sociology, and neurology would never have been possible. Further, a neurosurgeon would never feel justified in operating on a part of someone's brain for the purposes of, say, adjusting that person's mood swings, because she would think: "Well, I can't know *for sure* what's going on inside that person's head, so I don't know *for sure* if this operation is going to work." But obviously and thankfully, neurosurgeons don't think this way.

Someone could object by noting that the reason why one is able to make these kinds of probabilistic inferences is because other human beings have brains, and that all fully functioning human brains are relevantly similar to one another. However, in the case of a Transformer, one could never make this inference because they lack brains. To this, I respond by pointing out that it seems possible to simulate the internal traits necessary for personhood through mediums other than the brain. To put the point in the form of a question: Why would one need *necessarily* to have a brain in order to think, believe, feel, experience, and the like if such cognitive capacities can be *simulated* by other means? The above thought experiment dealing with our male subject should have made this clear.

Further, think of an android like Data in the *Star Trek* series, replicants in the movie *Blade Runner*, droids like C-3PO and R2-D2 in the *Star Wars* movies, Cylons in *Battlestar Galactica*, or the synthetics like Bishop in the *Alien* movies. Here are examples of beings that act like persons, yet the internal workings of their 'brains' (presumably) consist of a series of silicon and metallic connections; something very different from that of the gray matter of the brain. Also, think of the Martians in the Tim Burton film, *Mars Attacks*. They act just like evil persons since the little bastards begin the process of taking over the world! Yet, they technically don't have brains, but a green plasma-like substance that works, and even looks like, an over-sized human brain. So, it seems that a functioning brain, or something that *functions like* a functioning brain, with all of the cognitive capacities associated with such functioning, becomes what's significant in determining whether something qualifies as a person.

Transformers and the Capacity for Reason

We now can directly address the question of whether Transformers fulfill the various criteria for personhood. The first criterion has to do with the capacity for reason or rationality. In one sense, rationality is the same thing as *intelligence* and has been thought to involve a variety of traits, including (a) calculating, (b) making associations between present stimuli and stored memories, (c) problem solving, and (d) drawing new conclusions or inferences from old information. Can Transformers be said to be rational in the aforementioned senses? In fact, there are countless examples of (a)–(d) in Transformers stories. I'll point out just a few below.

Transformers obviously make calculations, as can be witnessed when Bumblebee sneaks out in the middle of the night to send out a homing signal to the rest of the Autobots in the 2007 film. Part of the process of contacting his Autobot cohorts entails making calculations. In fact, it's arguable that every move a Transformer makes requires the construction of some form of calculation; otherwise, the Transformer wouldn't have made the move in the first place. For example, *if* I want to send out a homing signal, *then* I need to get to a place where I can do it; thus, Bumblebee sneaks out based upon this calculation. Or, *if* I hack Air Force One's computers, *then* I can plant a virus; thus, Frenzy turns himself into a radio and begins the process of infiltrating Air Force One based upon this calculation.

In addition to their calculating capacity, Transformers have memory storage capabilities, and both can store and recall memories based upon present stimuli. Optimus Prime can recall the events surrounding Cybertron's destruction at the hands of Megatron and the Decepticons, and has recounted these events on several occasions. When an Autobot encounters a Decepticon, they both are aware enough of each other to recall that they need to do battle with one another. Further, Transformers can solve problems, as is witnessed when Frenzy solves the problem of releasing Megatron from suspended animation in the 2007 film, or when Vector Prime sets the Autobots on a quest to solve the problem of finding the four Cyber Planet Keys in the *Cybertron* story.

Finally, Transformers are able to reason in the sense of deductively drawing conclusions and making inductive inferences. First, think of the Bumblebee homing signal example above. Bumblebee arrived at his conclusion by a process of deductive reasoning that probably looks something like this:

Premise 1: If I want to send out a homing signal, then I need to get to a place where I can do it.

Premise 2: If I need to get to a place where I can do it, then I need to leave Sam's house.

Conclusion: Thus, if I want to send out a homing signal, then I need to leave Sam's house.

So, Bumblebee sneaks away. Also, Optimus Prime probably reasons inductively like this:

Premise 1: Megatron has been an evil jerk in the past to innocent beings.

Premise 2: Megatron is going to Earth, and Earth is filled with innocent beings.

Conclusion: Thus, Megatron likely will be an evil jerk to Earth's innocent beings.

So, Optimus Prime and the Autobots try to help Earth's innocent beings.

Transformers and Mental States

Now, just because something can reason, this doesn't mean it's a person. A computer can be programmed to reason just like Bumblebee, Frenzy, Megatron, and Optimus Prime—making step-by-step, if-then types of calculations yielding necessary or probable results—yet, we would not consider a computer a person because of this capacity alone. Persons also must have the capacity for mental states. Mental states are definitely a part of a normal functioning, adult human being's psychological life and include such things as holding a belief, having a desire, feeling a pain, or experiencing some event.

The best way to understand what a mental state consists of is to close your eyes and think about experiences where you jumped for joy, felt some pain, or regretted a decision you made. First, think of a time when you jumped for joy over some accomplishment of your own or of someone else's, like winning some award, or your favorite team scoring the winning goal in the last seconds of the game. Recall the experience: how you smiled, relished the moment, and wished that every moment could be like this one. For example, Sam and Mikaela are elated (and relieved) when they realize that they've defeated Megatron at the end of the 2007 film. Now, think about a pain you experienced, like when you touched something that was very hot. Remember how that pain was all-consuming for the duration, how it lingered in your body, and how you thought, "Ow! That HURT!" That was your pain, and no one else's, and only *you* could know what that pain was like. Take, for example, the time Sam fell down when he was being chased by Barricade in the 2007 film. Now, think of a decision you made that you've come to regret. You believe now that you could have made a different, better decision back then and now, having thought about it, it may cause you pain or regret. Sam feels this way after dropping Mikaela off at her house when he wishes he could have sounded more "cool" or "sexy" to her when they were riding together in his car.

These three experiences get at what is meant by a mental state because they entail beliefs, emotions, desires, or intentions. There are plenty of examples of Transformers acting as if they have the exact same kinds of mental states as we human persons. In several stories on film or in print, when a Transformer gets shot, hurt, zapped, or blown up, he/she/it gives an indication that he/she/it is in pain. Or, when Megatron's plans are foiled, he expresses the typical 'curses' of frustration. A typical Autobot will show concern and pity for another Autobot or human, as well as disdain for a Decepticon. The gamut of emotions—sorrow, fear, anger, hope, and joy—are all expressed by Transformers at various times throughout their myriad adventures.

Transformers and Language

Language is a definite mark of personhood, and I assume that you, the reader, are a person. Otherwise, you wouldn't be able to understand the words on this page! Language is a tricky thing to understand, and many people think that each kind of animal has its own language, including apes, dolphins, bees, and ants (to name just a few). However, we can draw a distinction between *transmitting information* and *engaging in a communicative linguistic performance.* I want to equate *language* with engaging in a communicative linguistic performance. All animals, including humans, transmit information in that they relay some useful data back and forth to one another or make mental associations with present or stored stimuli so as to take action. On the other hand, engaging in a communicative linguistic performance entails mental states like the ones spoken about in the previous section, so that only beings with mental states have the capacity for this kind of communication. When engaging in a linguistic performance, more than information or stimuli are being transmitted; beliefs, desires, intentions, hopes, dreams, fears, and the like are communicated from one mental-state-bearer to another. So, a bee is not really *speaking* to another bee when doing his "bee dance" in order to transmit information about where pollen is located outside of the hive. Even apes that have been taught sign language are not speaking—namely, using a language—to their trainers; they are merely associating stimuli with stored memories and transmitting information. As far as we know, no bees or apes have experiences of joy, pain, or regret to communicate. (Of course, what I've said is controversial, but that's okay . . . this is philosophy!)

Now, are Transformers the kinds of beings with capacities for engaging in communicative linguistic performances? I want you, the reader, to understand what I am experiencing, feeling, and thinking when I speak to you in this chapter. So too, Transformers want other Transformers and other beings to understand what it is they are communicating, whether it be "death to Ultra Magnus!" or "we need this supply of energon." Besides engaging in communicative linguistic performances, Transformers also seem to have beliefs about themselves, others, and the world around them. Further, they act on those beliefs, whether to save themselves, aid others, or engage in other kinds of voluntary behavior. Put another way, they appear to be free in their actions precisely because they form beliefs, and can act on those beliefs. Obviously, a typical Autobot believes that a typical Decepticon is forming beliefs about performing underhanded deeds, while a typical Decepticon believes that a typical Autobot is forming beliefs about how to thwart his underhanded deeds.

Transformers and Social Relationships

Do Transformers have the capacity to enter into social relationships with other beings already considered persons? Social relationships can be divided up into: (a) family relationships, or those loving and nurturing relationships found in households; (b) economic relationships, or those relationships people have in the public sphere outside of the home when they conduct business transactions; (c) allegiance relationships, or those relationships that citizens in a society choose to be a part of like churches, interest groups, the Loyal Order of the Moose, and the Shriners; (d) civil relationships, which include the relationships citizens have to one another, as well as the relationship individual citizens have to their governing body as a whole. In each one of these relationships, one finds duties, rights, laws, and obligations that are appropriate to each relationship. For example, in a family a parent has a duty to take care of a child, and one of the fundamental 'laws' in such a relationship is unconditional love. In economic transactions, the fundamental obligation is to the 'bottom line' of staying in the black, and the law may include something like "let the buyer beware." In civil relationships, we see the language of rights and laws being utilized in the most commonly understood way so as to protect citizens from harm, and ensure the prospering of societies as a whole.

Transformers do have the capacity to enter into social relationships. With respect to (d), (c), and (b), Cybertron itself was full of Transformer governing bodies, guilds, and apparent 'interest groups', complete with social and economic rules, as is made clear in many of the stories. What's most important, seemingly, is (a) family relationships, or those loving and nurturing relationships to be found in households. In the 2007 movie, for example, it seems that there are several examples of family-like relationships established between Transformers and humans. At the end of the film, Optimus Prime is cast as a kind of father figure watching over his Earthly children, while Bumblebee is kind of like Sam's brotherly friend. There are countless examples of Transformers acting fatherly and brotherly to each other in the stories, not unlike family members.

The fact that Transformers can autonomously express their desires is significant. Given that Transformers possess mental states, and have the capacity to willfully go about their business in the universe (at least, in terms of acting upon beliefs they have), it would seem that they are exemplars of the kind of being who can be held morally responsible for its actions. Think about how a typical Decepticon utilizes an Earthly piece of technology to hide himself in order to deceive another being, human or otherwise. In fact—and obviously—deception by transforming oneself into a piece of machinery is a typical move for a Decepticon (of course, Autobots do it, too, but for seemingly "good" reasons). If a Transformer can be said to legitimately have deceived, then that Transformer must have mental states. It seems that if some Transformer *can and does* deceive, then that Transformer should be punished as a deceiver.

Disallowing the Decepticons

Transformers communicate, have the capacity for reason, can be involved in complex social relationships, and obviously deceive other Transformers and human beings. More importantly, they express feelings of disillusion, contempt, pain, and suffering, as well as joy, satisfaction, and contentment. As I have tried to show, a being that has these traits has mental states, and such a being is a person, regardless of metallic innards, plasmatic innards, or natural, biological innards. Thus, Transformers can be held responsible for their actions the way persons are. Finally, if some Transformers are like sinister persons with a sinister plan, then their plan should be squelched, and they should be punished accordingly. In short, we should disallow the Decepticons to deceive, destroy, and deprave!

The issue of treating Transformers as persons may seem silly to talk about because, after all, they are fictional. However, as history has proven, science *fiction* has a way of becoming science *fact.* The famous robotics engineer and theorist, Hans Moravec, claims that by 2050 robots actually will surpass humans in intellectual capacity. In the not-so-distant future, there most likely will be advanced forms of machinery that behave much like the Transformers in terms of an artificial intelligence. How then will we, who are already considered persons, react? How then should such beings who seem to behave like full persons be treated?

10
Robots in Love?

JAMIE WATSON and ROBERT ARP

Pussycat, you really know how to tickle my joystick.

—Rattrap, in "Coming of the Fuzors"

In the animated Transformers episode "The Search for Alpha Trion" from the 1980s, two Autobots lock in a loving embrace, as the masculine Ironhide comforts the feminine Chromia with soothing words in her robotic ears. They look just like human lovers, with Chromia laying her head on Ironhide's shoulder. Ah . . ., the sweet sound of metal on metal. What?! Autobots in love? Is it possible for Autobots to experience love the way human persons do?

What exactly is love? Is it simply an erotic passion that one finds in sexual relationships (whether it's flesh on flesh *or* metal on metal)? Is it more of a cosmic force that unites the world? Could love be associated with a general care and concern for the welfare of human and robotic beings? Is it reserved only for our most intimate friendships? Or, is it just a name that we give to processes having to do with blood (or oil and electricity!) rushing to various parts of our bodies?

In this chapter, using examples from various Transformers stories, we take a look at some Western philosophical conceptions of love. First, we discuss reasons why Transformers can be conceptualized as being like human persons. Next, we show how the various relationships between Transformers and humans, and amongst Transformers themselves, embody various conceptions of love. The end result will be a deeper appreciation for the varieties of love spoken about in the history of Western philosophy and—believe it or not—practical applicability for real-life loving relationships.

Are Transformers Capable of Love?

Oh . . ., here comes that sinking feeling.

—Optimus Prime in "Kremzeek!"

Whatever love is, whether in humans or in Transformers, it requires *the capacity for* conscious awareness. "Conscious awareness" requires a mind, and we think it requires some kind of advanced mind, like that found in humans. Saying "the capacity for" lets us keep our belief that someone still loves his wife while he is asleep, yet allows us to be agnostic about whether someone in a coma does. Since we do think people who are asleep or preoccupied with work can be in love, we know that love is more than just a type of behavior. Of course, love does involve *dispositions* to act in certain ways in certain contexts—which is why forgetting your anniversary is a bad thing to do.

So, love is at least a mental state that requires the capacity for conscious awareness and disposes one toward certain behaviors. Now, many animals seem to meet these criteria, but no one would say that animals can *really* love or be in love. Biologists don't think animal minds are advanced enough for that kind of mental state. So there must be something else. But what? And what about computers? Could we design a machine that loves like humans love?

It's easy to imagine that Transformers could in fact love as we do, since stories about Transformers represent them as thinking, feeling, knowing, wishing, hoping, screaming in anger or pain, crying, scheming, lying, and sacrificing just like we human persons do. Consider Sandstorm's very noble, Mel-Gibson-in-*Braveheart*-sounding exclamation: "It's time we fought for what we believe in . . . our planet, our freedom, our lives!" (from "Fight or Flee"). Or, consider Fortress Maximus's Shakespearean diatribe: "Whether I am a hero or a coward is not the issue! I am weary! My joints creak from the corrosion of war without end! I cannot break this ring of hate that surrounds us all. But I can remove myself from it. No matter what you decide, I am leaving" ("Headmaster #1"). If we didn't know this was a Transformer, we might think it was an ancient Roman solider, weary of political unrest.

These expressions do sound like claims made by beings capable of mental states like love. But what would it take to turn a machine into a being that can genuinely love? Let's look at three options philosophers have suggested.

First, imagine we have designed a software program so complicated that it allows Transformers to mimic human expressions of love in every conceivable way. Imagine the software is so good that every affectionate gesture, the slightest body language of attraction, and the slightest loving verbal cues are met with the perfectly appropriate reactions on the part of the robots. In addition, the Transformers could initiate these advances as well. Would running this software on a robot's processors make it a being that loves?

It seems not. We can design machines to tell us what we want to hear. We could program them to tell us they aren't "feeling well" using personal pronouns: "Error! (read: ouch!) I cannot read the device installed in drive E." But these designs are not a sign of love on the part of the machine, they simply represent the way humans have constructed them. We do, however, praise our children when they respond to us the way we've trained them to. What's the difference?

One important difference, as we noted above, is that behaviors alone do not entail mental states with content about those behaviors. Rocks, wind-up toys, and remote-control vehicles respond predictably to a variety of stimuli, but no one would claim that my remote-control replica of Knight Rider has a mind.

Another difference is that one of the virtues of love is that it is given freely. Forced love is not love at all. If we program a computer to exhibit loving behavior, then it only behaves how it is commanded to behave by its program. We would no more praise a computer programmed to love any more than we would blame one programmed to destroy. We would praise or blame the programmers. Therefore, programmed behavior alone is not enough to make a robot that loves.

Second, imagine that an extremely well respected neuroscientist tells you she has discovered a way to implant a soul into a robot. She admits it's difficult to say exactly what a 'soul' is, but assures you it can be done. What's more, though the technology is comprehensible to only a select few, she can find and attach a soul to the computational mechanisms of any computer. Would a soul make a robot a being that loves?

It isn't obvious that it would. What might a soul add? And whatever it might add, would it be the precise element that makes a machine the kind of thing capable of love? And even if a soul could add the right thing, it's not clear that a soul is the only thing that could add it. So, a soul alone just won't do.

Most people would presumably agree that, whatever a thing is that loves, it must be a *person*. To be a person requires at least two properties: intentionality and the power of self-reflection. The "power of self-reflection" is the ability to "know that I know," for instance that I'm hungry or sad or cold. Computers and animals know when there is a problem with their 'operating systems', but it is generally agreed that they don't know that they know there is a problem, that is, they cannot reflect on the problem. "Intentionality" is the ability to "intend," or to act on a variety of reasons despite circumstances or emotions. Computers react solely on the basis of inputs. Their outputs, even their random outputs, are governed by mechanical processes. Persons, on the other hand, can choose to act on a variety of inputs, and no single input can determine what a person will do (unless there is some malfunction).

Some have argued that imbuing a creature with a soul *makes* it a person. But that means that a soul must at least have (or grant) intentionality and the power of self-reflection. But what would it mean for a soul to have these characteristics? Does it make more sense for a *soul* to have these things than a body or brain or processor? If what makes a person a person is intentionality and reflection, then introducing the idea of a soul just seems redundant. Therefore, again, a soul won't help our machine unless it explains how bodies or processors can have intentionality and self-reflection. And the prospects aren't good.

Third, imagine that we come to understand the human brain so well that we can actually 'hard-wire' it into a computer's processing mechanisms. You may have heard philosophical tales of brains in vats, receiving inputs from a computer that causes conscious experiences in the brain. In these cases, though someone feels he is living a life much like yours or mine, he is really the plaything of a mad scientist. Imagine this scenario in reverse. Rather than a computer sending inputs to a brain, imagine a brain sending inputs to a machine, so that whatever conscious state the brain is in, the machine will recognize it and act accordingly. Would a human brain turn a robot into a being that loves?

Again, it's not obvious that it would. Though a human brain is necessary for a thing to be a person who loves, it is not sufficient. We can imagine a human brain-machine combo that produces a creature without intentionality or self-reflection. And we can also imagine a creature without a human brain that does have these features. Recall, for example, the android Data from *Star Trek: The Next Generation,* and of course our ever-emoting Transformers. And even if we were able to transplant a normal, functioning human brain into a machine, making a robot who loves, we are still not sure what it is *about* the human brain that makes a creature capable of love. Perhaps it's simply a gap in our current technology, but we are far from understanding what makes humans capable of love, much less machines! And the answer to this puzzle just might be the same for both.

Does Love Make the World, or Universe, Go Around?

Remember, we're all one with the universe.

—BEACHCOMBER, in "The Secret of Omega Supreme"

The ancient Greek philosopher Empedocles (492–424 B.C.E.) envisioned Strife and Love as polar cosmic principles at work in the universe. Strife is the source of all that's destructive, separate, chaotic, and evil, while Love is the source of all that's generative, unified, harmonious, and good. The universe is held in tension between the forces of Strife and Love, with either one dominant at various times. Here, love is not just something that affects human, Autobot, or Decepticon relationships. Love literally "makes the world go around" as a cosmological principle!

Many people can think that love and hate take on lives of their own, so to speak, leading people to peace, harmony, and respect, or war, chaos, and violence. In fact, there's a bit of this thinking that underlies all Transformers stories, where the Autobots embody the loving principles and the Decepticons embody principles of hate. Consider that the Transformers' universe would likely be destroyed if the Decepticons gained power with the All Spark, whereas several Transformers stories hint that there would be peace and harmony if the Autobots could harness its power. In *Transformers* #76, Grimlock notes: "See, good and evil . . . it's just the way of things. For every yin a yang, for every light a dark, everything balancing . . ."

One Transformers fan echoes this Empedoclean conception of love in a blog posting where he gives his own spin on the origin of the Transformers:

> They were once the Heralds of a being known only as The One, whose existence stretches back to the birth of the Universe. For a time, the twin Heralds of The One sought only knowledge and insight into the myriad wonders of this new Universe. But soon, as they both achieved full sentience, they became polar opposites. One seeking to understand the cosmic harmony of the galaxies, the other seeking only to destroy them.
>
> *They became Creation and Destruction Incarnate*
> *The Avatars of Order and Chaos*
> *The Bringers of Light and Darkness*
> *They are Primus and Unicron.*
>
> And their war has raged for eons, across the almost limitless planes of reality and throughout countless parallel dimensions. Their conflict was eternal and unending . . .[1]

But the Empedoclean view has been attacked as being too vague or inaccurate concerning the nature of love, and this is probably true in Transformers stories as well. The cosmic power of the All Spark in the hands of the Autobots would likely bring peace, harmony, and love. However, love seems to be something *other than* an underlying principle or source of harmony, peace, goodness, or any other positive properties in the Transformers' universe or our own.

Erotic Love

> And what exactly does your do-hickey do?
>
> —Optimus Prime in "The Master Builders"

Most of us associate love with emotions of desiring someone or something with a great deal of passion. This association has a long history in Western philosophy that begins with the ancient Greeks who had one conception of love, understood as *eros*. In Greek mythology, Eros was a god who seemed to have a great power over mortals, causing them to do crazy things like lie, steal, and murder, commonly for some kind of sexual payoff. Hesiod (eighth century B.C.E.) characterizes Eros as the enemy of reason in his

---

[1] From: http://64.233.169.104/search?q=cache:9kZ7a8DoXBYJ:www.allspark.com/forums/index.php%3Fshowtopic%3D12124+transformers+cosmic+harmony&hl=en&ct=clnk&cd=2&gl=us.

Theogony, and this erotic conception of love continued to be influential in the Golden Age of Greek philosophers who envisioned human beings as having (1) a rational, controlled, prudent part of their personality (or soul) that must keep this (2) erotic, irrational, animalistic part of their personality in check. The irrational part of one's personality that is shared with animals often has to do with sex. After all, humans are rational *animals* with basic needs. *Eros* came to be associated with sexual desire, and that's why, today, 'erotic' desire is closely linked with sex and sexual relationships.

There are glimpses of this kind of love in Transformers stories. For example, one of the first female Autobots, Acree, is introduced in the 1980s and is described as having "an attachment to" the male Autobot, Springer, that is laced with double entendre. (In fact, her animated parts are curvy enough to get human men to fantasize what flesh *on metal* would sound like!) We already mentioned Ironhide and Chromia's loving embrace, which has obvious sexual overtones. And an Autobot named Ariel is described as being the girlfriend of a dock-working Autobot named Orion Pax (who later becomes Optimus Prime), and their romantic relationship conjures up racy oil squeaking and gears grinding.

Platonic Love

> Noble Autobots make me wanna puke!
>
> —APEFACE, in "The Rebirth"

In contrast to the irrational and animalistic *eros*, the Greeks had another conception of love that they called *philia*, which can be understood as an appreciation of another's beauty or goodness. This philial form of love is present in Plato's (427–347 B.C.E.) writings—especially in his *Symposium*—where he explains our experience of love as making contact with the abstract 'Form' of Beauty Itself.

Plato believed that reality could be broken up into two basic realms: the changeable, 'visible' world of our sense experiences, and the unchangeable, 'intelligible' world of ideas and concepts, or 'Forms'. There is one, eternal and unchanging Form in the intelligible realm for each kind of object, event, thing, or action that one experiences in the visible realm. A Form is like the ideal essence, core, or fundamental 'nature' of something. So, for example, all of the different cars, trucks, trees, people, and cats—as well as the more or less good actions and beautiful things—that we experience around us in our visible, sensible world have a corresponding ideal Form found in another realm of reality that can only be known or "accessed," ultimately, through our minds.

Further, the highly complex things around us—as well as the various *trans*-formed things—are composed of less complex parts that have corresponding Forms.

Take, for instance, the illustration of the two-dimensional Transformer in Figure 10.1. Here, we can see that the various parts that make up the Transformer can be broken down into basic shapes, like circles, squares, triangles, and the like. The same would go for three dimensional things, in terms of breaking them down into their most basic elemental parts. Plato would say that we can disassemble complex things into their most basic elements in the visible world around us, and those 'basics' have corresponding Forms in the intelligible world.

FIGURE 10.1. *A Two-Dimensional Transformer and Its Parts*

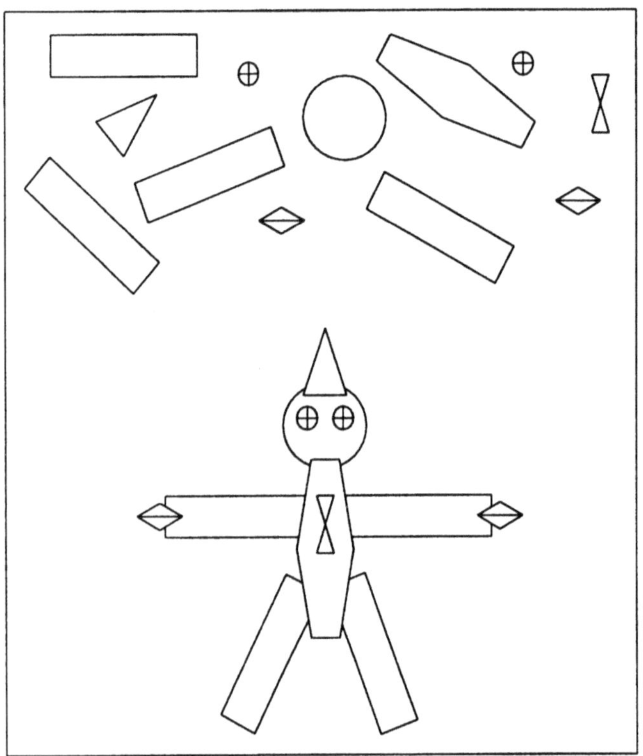

For Plato, the Forms are what humans should be striving to know, as these ideal universals fulfill the twofold purpose of (a) making the things in the visible realm *be known as* what they are as well as (b) making the things in the visible realm actually *be* what they are. Plato expressed this by saying that things in the visible world "participate" in the Forms. So, if you want to be able to recognize and understand objects and events around you in the visible realm of sense experience—as well as be able to explain how it is that these objects and events have come to be—then Plato suggests that you get to know the Forms. After all, to be able to know and understand the essence or fundamental nature of something is good, as it will help you avoid bad reasoning or making decisions based upon too little information that could lead to unwanted consequences in your life.

The idea behind Plato's conception of *philia* is that one will be led from the changeable and imperfectly beautiful (and not-so-beautiful) things of this world to the unchanging and perfect universal Form of Beauty. And unlike any erotic experience, this philial form of love will be satisfying to the mind, rather than the body. In erotic encounters, our bodies make contact with beautiful objects in the visible realm, and physical pleasure ensues. In philial encounters, our minds make contact with the Form of Beauty in the intelligible realm, and mental pleasure ensues. True love, for Plato, is knowing and understanding the ideal Form of Beauty of which beautiful things in the visible world participate. In fact, this kind of satisfaction can be found in the word 'philosophy', a combination of the Greek words for 'love' (philo) and 'wisdom' (sophia). So, 'philosophy' literally means the love of, and also the pursuit of, wisdom; we pursue the things that we love. As contrasted with erotic love, in which sexual or bodily desires are met, philial love is concerned with a desire for the Beauty that underlies persons, places, and things *for Beauty's sake*. We find remnants of this idea today in the term *Platonic relationship*, where two people have a relationship that does not involve sex, but involves more lofty, intellectual-type pursuits.

Now, Plato conceived of love as a contact with an "ideal" or "perfect" Beauty, and there's a sense in which people and Autobots are used as conduits or channels to an ideal or perfect beauty in the Transformers universe. In the original series, as well as the *Beast Wars* and *Beast Machines* series, the All Spark is viewed as an ideal, perfect, and wholly good and beautiful realm where the souls of Transformers—both the good-natured Autobots and the evil Decepticons—have originated, and to where these souls can return one day. (In fact, Plato had a similar understanding of "pre-carnation.") The more positive, caring, loving relationships that Transformers can form, the more likely they will be to share in the ideal beauty of the All Spark. This seems to be at least part of Optimus Prime's motivation for establishing a caring relationship with Sam Witwicky and for protecting the Earth from the Decepticons (see, for example, "The Return of Optimus Prime").

Loving Friendship

> He wasn't just another gun-toting conscript to me, First Aid. He was my friend.
>
> —Ratchet in *Transformers* (#26)

Speaking of Optimus Prime's relationship with Sam Witwicky, one of the reasons why these characters fascinate us is because they do seem to have a friendship, despite the fact that one is a human while the other is a machine. Is love really a friendship, then? This is what Plato's student, Aristotle (384–322 B.C.E.), thought. For Aristotle, love entails an appreciation of the beautiful and good qualities of another person, as well as an interaction between lover and beloved. Thus, love is best understood as a friendship between two people in which mutual awareness of each other's good is kept in mind.

According to Aristotle, there are three types of friendship. *Friendships of utility* are those relationships where mutual benefit is to be gained from each other's services, as in a business relationship. There is a certain sense in which even the Decepticons embody this kind of friendship, as they will establish relationships with one another where mutual benefit is to be had for each as a result of the relationship. So, for example, Megatron and Starscream agree to be 'friendly' enough in this sense so that they can work together to destroy Autobots. Also, Unicron (not a Transformer, but a world-devourer) and Megatron establish this form of friendship when they work together to destroy the Autobot Matrix of Leadership; Unicron benefits because devouring Cybertron becomes easier, and Megatron benefits because Cybertron fits him with a new body and new troops in exchange for his assistance.

Friendships of pleasure are those relationships where pleasure is to be gained from engaging in mutually enjoyable experiences. There are plenty of examples where Autobots seem to be enjoying each other's company, whether it's engaging in some banter, playing a particular sport in the Galactic Olympics, or racing one another through the sky. There's a funny, playful scene in "Fire in the Sky" where Jazz dumps snow on top of Spike and he says, "Oh, thanks Jazz, I get the drift." Or, consider Ratchet's claim in the quotation that heads this section. Interestingly, the Decepticons never seem to enjoy themselves the way Autobots do, probably indicating that their friendships stay at the level of utility, at best.

Friendships of virtue are the best and most noble friendships, and are found between those who are most wise, virtuous, and good. In this kind of friendship, as Aristotle so poetically puts it, the "two bodies share one soul." In friendships of virtue, the two lovers share a desire for one another's good—a good that is concerned with the most true, noble, and virtuous in life. Consider the exchange between Optimus Prime and Scorponok when Scorponok is lying on his death bed after a long struggle with the Decepticons ("Transformers #75") and Optimus Prime comforts Scorponok: "Prime . . . did . . . did I do good?" "Yes, old friend . . . you did good."

Also, in the *Transformers: Armada* series (2002–2004) Optimus Prime and his Mini-Con, Sparkplug, seem to have this kind of relationship of virtue, especially when it comes to thinking about one another's good. They communicate thoughts, aspirations, and emotions in support of one another, and they share the common goal of defeating the Decepticons and obtaining the All Spark. Further, they risk their lives for each other, as when Sparkplug uses the Matrix and assists the other Mini-Cons in the dangerous mission to help resurrect Optimus Prime (Episode #40).

We can contrast Optimus Prime's kind of friendly loving for Sparkplug with the relationship between Megatron and Starscream. Megatron consistently insults and lies to Starscream. Consider Megatron in "Starscream's Brigade": "Starscream is a child! Even with an army of thousands he couldn't lead them in a parade, let alone against us!" And Starscream is treacherous, ambitious, and wants to usurp Megatron's position with his own lies and manipulating. That's why in "Triple Takeover" Blitzwing says, "Starscream's been trying to overthrow Megatron for years." This is hardly a concern for the good of another and, in fact, they would each find relief if the other were not around. By contrast, Optimus Prime and Sparkplug compliment one another's skills, assist one another, and even laugh with one another. They clearly have each other's general welfare in mind.

Equal Love

> Until the day . . . all are one . . .
>
> —Optimus Prime in *Transformers: The Movie* (1986)

> I am sick and tired of being responsible for the entire universe and its outlying suburbs.
>
> —Rodimus Prime in "The Burden Hardest to Bear"

The ancient Greek Stoics, whose founder was Zeno of Citium (344–262 B.C.E.), had a conception of love as a kind of universal respect for all of humankind that we'll call *equal love*. This equal love requires that one should be detached enough from this world and its pleasures to appreciate the beauty and goodness of all of humanity. Such a detachment would bring about a universal harmony and peace, which is the ultimate goal of a happy life. Stoic love treats all humans *equally* as "Citizens of the World," as opposed to being concerned only with one's own family or the citizens in one's own community. The Stoic conception of love is similar to Immanuel Kant's (1724–1804) call for general respect for persons as "ends in themselves." For both the Stoics and Kant, this kind of universal equalizing love is something that needs to be fostered if peace both within communities and among communities is ever to be achieved.

This form of love is a strong underlying theme in all of the Transformers stories. First, the general care and concern Optimus Prime and the other Autobots have for their own Transformers kind, as well as for humankind, is a clear example of this equal love. *All* Transformers and *all* humans—evil or good, young or old, weak or strong—are deserving of basic rights, privileges and respect. The Autobots exhibit this kind of loving to the extent that they will treat their Decepticon enemies with kind, loving, respect, despite the fact that the Decepticons wouldn't think twice about disrespecting the Autobots or enslaving all of Earth: "The conquest of this planet and the enslavement of its people will be a simple task . . . indeed" (Shockwave, *Transformers* #5). There are plenty of instances where a Decepticon gets himself or herself into a dangerous situation that seems fatal, yet gets saved by an Autobot. Often, the Decepticon immediately turns right around and, instead of expressing thanks, tries to kill the Autobot who just saved him!

Family Love

> They made me into a weapon and turned me on all those I loved in life.
>
> —Optimus Prime in "Dark Awakening"

Ultra Magnus and Optimus Prime are often portrayed as brothers with a kind of love only brothers could understand. The same goes for Jazz and Sparkplug. There is a Christian idea of love known as *agape* (pronounced 'agapay') that emphasizes a kind of unconditional love like the one finds in a family. For Christians, God is seen as a kind of father who loves His creation with a deep and profound bond that nothing can ever break. Families stay together through good times and bad times, sometimes treating each other badly and taking each other for granted. There are plenty of instances of this in Transformers stories. We have all heard of family situations where there seems to be nothing that an individual could do that would cause other members of the family to stop loving him or her. Think of the psychopath who is just about to be executed whose family members still claim, "he's still my son" or "he'll always be my brother."

In family dynamics, there is usually someone who is spoiled, someone who takes charge of things, someone who fixes things, someone who lays down the law, someone who gets walked all over, someone who's the youngest trying to compete with older siblings . . . Hey! This sounds just like the characters in Transformers stories!

A Transformation?

As the song goes, "Love stinks!"[2] Or, at least as a philosophical concept, it's difficult to pin down. It's incredibly difficult to know what makes a creature capable of love. We have seen, however, that,

[2] J. Geils Band, 1980.

whatever it would take to make an organic creature (like a human) capable of love would probably work for robots as well. In addition, there are many kinds of loving relationships, and to whatever degree Transformers are capable of love, they will have to bear the responsibility and heartache (error message?) that comes with it.

One of the reasons the Transformers series is so popular is its portrayal of the aspects of our real-life family relationships—*complete* with all kinds of complex loving relationships. The flip-side of those loving relationships are hateful ones, and the Transformers series have no shortage of these kind of relationships either. In fact, we learn how to be loving by witnessing the hate. Hopefully, we can transform hate to love in all we do.

EPISODE FIVE

Good versus Evil

11
Good Robot, Bad Robot, What's the Difference?

NICOLAS MICHAUD

Here's the deal—the Autobots are Good and the Decepticons are Evil. Right? From the first episode's introduction the battle between the Autobots and Decepticons is described as a battle of "good versus evil." The Autobots seem to be clearly good, while the Decepticons seem to be, clearly, very bad. But is it really that easy?

While Optimus Prime is obviously going out of his way to refrain from crushing puny humans under foot, Megatron seems to be doing his best to squish as many humans as he can while fighting for domination of the Universe. But what motivates these intelligent robots to act the way that they do? Is it just as simple as a matter of the Autobots are programmed to be good and the Decepticons are programmed to be evil? What do "good" and "evil" even mean?

We will find that if we look a little deeper, these robots are not motivated so differently from you and me. As a matter of fact, the ethical rules that motivate these gargantuan robots are the rules that govern our own actions. Much like us, these robots don't always understand the ethical rules that they follow. But, due to their size, power, and intelligence, their choices and these rules have a far greater impact than with the average human and provide us with an excellent opportunity to understand what it is that we mean when we say "good" and "evil."

What Motivates a Giant Robot?

So what is it that motivates these machines to do as they do? Even if they're just programmed to be good or bad, what does that mean?

If I program a machine and input the rule "be evil" there would be a great deal of confusion. The machine also needs to know what actions count as evil.

Well, the Transformers are far more complex than any machine we can build. So it's likely that there is more to them then just basic programming. They probably have a whole set of rules that they follow, much the same way that we do. Humans learn all kinds of ethical rules. Some of us follow the "golden rule" and others follow the laws of the land. Some rules are religious, like the Ten Commandments, and some rules are purely selfish like "Look out for Number One." As a matter of fact, when two groups of people have two different sets of rules, there is often a fight—not so different from the Autobots and Decepticons. The question that we need to answer is "What rules do the Autobots follow that make them good and what rules do the Decepticons follow that make them evil?"

Let's consider the actions of the Transformers. Perhaps by observing what they do and how they act, we can figure out the guidelines they follow. Consider the Autobots, specifically Optimus Prime. Although it may be easy just to describe him as someone who is good or does good, what is it that he actually does? Well, we do know that he fights the Decepticons. Just fighting, by itself, is generally not considered a good action. But, the way in which he fights might be an indicator of his goodness. Notice that Prime fights fairly. He is not the kind to attack an unarmed or helpless opponent. Moreover, he is very concerned with collateral damage. Prime goes out of his way to make sure that no humans are hurt in his battles with Megatron.

How Do the Autobots Act?

One of the Autobots' most telling qualities is their desire to help humans. The fight against the Decepticons might be far easier to win if the Autobots did not concern themselves with the welfare of humans. By contrast, the Decepticons are well aware of the fact that they can use human frailty as leverage against the Autobots. Nevertheless, although it makes the battle far more difficult, the Autobots and Optimus Prime continue to try to save human lives.

The Autobots go even further than just preserving human life. They seem even to value human friendship. The Autobots most notably make friends with Spike and Sparkplug with Witwicky.

Spike, who befriends the Autobots very early on, eventually becomes the Human diplomat to Cybertron. Spike's friendship with Bumblebee is perhaps the strongest friendship depicted in the Transformers' Universe.

This brings up a very important quality of the Autobots. Although it may seem perfectly normal to us for one human to make friends with another, it seems rather unusual that a robot would become friends with a human. The Autobots are superior to humans in almost every way. They are smarter, stronger, faster, technologically more advanced, yet Bumblebee befriends Spike not as a pet or object of amusement, but as a true friend. This speaks highly of the quality of the Autobots' character. Their ability to befriend, trust, and respect creatures far inferior to themselves is a moral quality that even many humans lack.

So here we have a few examples which help us determine what motivates the Autobots. They fight fairly, respect their enemies, value innocent life, and befriend others regardless of difference in appearance or ability. We can probably infer a few things from these actions. They are compassionate, loyal, and dutiful. Optimus Prime epitomizes all of these qualities. He always does his duty and shows respect for all life. Regardless of differences in belief, ability or appearance, the Autobots respect those who show basic reasoning capacity and the ability to feel. This is a far cry from the Decepticons who do not even respect those who are superior to them.

Deceit and the Decepticons

So how is it that the Decepticons act? It is clear that they are not interested in friendship with humans. Moreover, they are not concerned with loss of human life. They are not even concerned about the deaths of other Decepticons. Consider the rivalry between Megatron and Starscream. They are only concerned with each other as so far as they find each other useful. Starscream makes no pretense about the fact that he wants to get rid of Megatron and Megatron's distain for Starscream is obvious. Whereas the Autobots are willing to make friends even outside of their own species, the Decepticons cannot seem even to make friends with each other.

Megatron is willing to do whatever is necessary in order to gain control of the universe, as is Starscream. Megatron is simply stronger and so he continues to rule the Decepticons. Whereas the

Autobots follow Optimus Prime out of respect and admiration for who he is, the Decepticons follow Megatron out of fear. Megatron is ruthless and cruel; Starscream is deceptive and conniving. They, and the rest of the Decepticons, murder, cheat, lie, and steal in order to achieve their ends. For example, the Autobots rely on generosity or fair trade to gain the energon cubes they need; the Decepticons simply take them. If anyone tries to stop the Decepticons, the obstacle is simply eliminated.

There's an odd bit of Decepticon behavior that does not fit the norm. It does seem that Megatron has a kind of respect for Optimus Prime. He has even prevented others from killing Prime in the past. The Autobots and Decepticons have even teamed up together. But why would Megatron work with Prime? The reason is very different from the reasons that motivate the Autobots. Whereas Prime always holds out hope for others and the possibility they might choose good, Megatron and the Decepticons are willing to use their enemies when necessary. Megatron has prevented others from killing Prime because he wants the pleasure of killing Prime himself. He will work with Prime to stop a mutual enemy but then has no qualms about betraying Prime as soon as his ends have been achieved. What we come to realize is that the Decepticons are really only motivated by their own self-interests. In virtually every case, the Decepticons' actions are such that they place all others, including other Decepticons, far behind their own interests.

What's So Bad about Being Selfish?

Is it that easy? Are the Decepticons just selfish—end of story? What seems unsatisfying about this answer is that we all seem to be selfish. And in that case, they aren't really all that bad, right? Isn't every action we take one that, in the end, benefits us? In *Leviathan,* Thomas Hobbes argues that we are all, in our hearts, selfish. He claims that our natural state or *state of nature* is one which is "solitary, poor, nasty, brutish, and short." Hobbes's image of humanity seems to be a dark and bleak one, but is there some truth to it? Is everything we do simply motivated by selfishness?

The answer is a matter of perspective. Consider any action that we take, even the most altruistic: why do we do it? Imagine that you save a child from being crushed by Megatron. Do you save the child without any benefit to yourself? Any answer you give can be one which sounds, in the end, selfish. Let's remove all the reasons that are obviously selfish, like saving the child for a reward or for fame. But what if you saved the child because you believe it is something you should do because God tells you to do so? If you are doing it to please God or get into heaven, then isn't it an action that you are really doing to benefit yourself? Or if you commit the act just because it is "the right thing to do" aren't you doing it because doing the right thing makes you feel good? Watching the child drown would have made you feel very bad. So, isn't Hobbes right? Are all of our actions, in the end, selfish ones?

This idea that we are all only able to act from our own self-interests is called psychological egoism. It seems as if it is a matter of perspective. Don't we want people to feel good when they save children and do other good things? Yes, it may be that doing right things because they make you feel good seems selfish, but isn't that better than doing right things and feeling bad about them? Isn't it better that you feel good about saving the child from Megatron than if you feel bad about saving the child? What would you think of someone who saves the child and then says "wow, I really wish I had let Megatron squish this kid." We *want* people to feel good about the good things they do, not regret them! So, perhaps we are all motivated to some degree by our own self-interest and Hobbes is right, but not entirely. But, now there's a new problem: perhaps we can act because we feel good about doing things to help others, but should we?

Why a Good Decepticon Only Worries About Himself

The fact of the matter is that the Decepticons are not just selfish in the sense that we feel good when we do things to help others, but they don't *want* to help others. The Decepticons seem to believe that it's a sign of weakness to put the needs of others before our own. They do whatever's necessary to get ahead, and believe that others are only valuable insofar as they are useful. The Decepticons are what philosophers call "normative egoists." Normative egoists believe that a person should only do what is in his or her long-term self-interest. Whether or not we are naturally selfish, the normative egoist will argue that you should do what is best for yourself, regardless of the consequences for others.

Imagine that you have a conversation with Starscream. You ask him why he does the things he does. Starscream is likely to tell you he acts as he does because he deserves to get what he wants. Starscream would tell you that he should lead the Decepticons because he is best suited to the job. When you ask Starscream why he is willing to do things that most people would consider wrong in order to get what he wants, he would probably say something like, "Well it is survival of the fittest; if they are not smart enough to do what I want, then they deserve what they get." But would Starscream and the normative egoists be correct in saying this? Should we only worry about the things we want regardless of who gets hurt?

There is at least one huge problem with being a normative egoist: if you argue that everyone should do only what's in their best interest then it is probably not in your best interest. Think about Starscream for a moment: he gives Megatron no reason to trust him, nor any of the other Decepticons. The fact that he broadcasts his own egoism results in the fact that he rarely has opportunity to gain the control he seeks. No one trusts him and everyone is aware that he is willing to do anything and hurt anyone to get what he wants. It seems that it makes no sense for the normative egoist to encourage others to be normative egoists. Someone might respond that Egoism is actually a very bad idea as it is not even good for the Egoist. The only way we can really get anywhere or win a war like the battle between the Autobots and the Decepticons is by being able to trust each other. In other words, we want to trust that others will do their duty.

Why the Autobots Do Their Duty

Here, we can see what drives the Autobots: they are motivated by their duty to themselves *and* to each other. This enables them to succeed in ways in which the Decepticons are likely to fail. Optimus Prime does not have to worry about the other Autobots betraying him because he knows they will do their duty. But what guarantee is there that they will do there duty? Why would they follow the rules *all the time*?

An ethical philosophy that is duty-based is called a "deontology." Deontologists argue that right things to do are obligations—once we know the right thing to do we must do it. The foremost Deontologist was a man named Immanuel Kant. Kant provided us with one of the most rigorous ethical systems. When we consider the strict code of duty and loyalty that the Autobots follow, we will see that Kant's theory—Kantianism —effectively describes the ethical system that the Autobots follow.

Kant argued that we should be rational and that we should let logic and rationality guide our ethical beliefs. Kant thought that if we recognize that something is right, then we also recognize our obligation to do that right thing. It made no sense to Kant for us to claim that something is the right thing to do and then decide not to do it. In the same way, it is wholly irrational for a person to recognize something as wrong, and then do it anyway. To say that something is wrong means "this is something that should not be done." So, it is clearly irrational to do that thing that we just said we should not do. It is then, our obligation to do the right thing.

Why Optimus Prime Always Does the Right Thing

Kant argues that if we are going to follow what is right, then we should do so universally—in all cases. Of equal importance is the fact that for a rule to be a rational rule, it must be one which can be applied rationally in all cases. Kant argued that if a rule can only be used sometimes, it makes no sense. So Kant created what's called the "Categorical Imperative." Categorical Imperative simply means "universal rule." It is a rule which can and should be applied in all cases. We should only act on those rules which can be applied rationally in all cases. So Kant has a great respect for rationality and so, anything which has that ability to be rational should be respected according to Kant, even aliens.

Kant tells us that this universal rule can be translated in a few different ways, the most popular of which tells us that we always treat rational beings as ends in themselves, never solely as a means. This just tells us that we should never use a thinking thing just to get what we want. For Kant, this meant that we have to respect people; we could not treat them as mere objects. We can see how, then, the Autobots fit easily into Kant's system. If they simply stole energy from Earth, they would be treating humanity as if it were just a means to an end. In the same way, the Autobots cannot ignore the human casualties that might arise from their fight with the Decepticons because, once again, that would be treating rational beings as if they were just objects. The fact that we are weak and frail compared to the Autobots is irrelevant when considered by the Categorical Imperative because all that matters is that we are thinking things: our differences, and weaknesses are irrelevant.

Who Wins: Autobots or Decepticons?

So the fundamental question presents itself: "Who's right?" Are the Decepticons right in arguing that they should only concern themselves with their own wellbeing or are the Autobots right in arguing that they must do their duty, no matter the cost to themselves? It might seem at first glance that the Autobots must be right, especially given the stake that humanity has in the fight. If the Autobots lose, humanity will be eradicated or enslaved by the Decepticons. But, isn't that just an egoistic concern? Which means the Decepticons might actually be right! Maybe Starscream is just too big-mouthed for his own good. Perhaps Megatron gets egoism right. He seems to be what philosophers call a *Rational* Egoist. Megatron is different from Starscream. He has respect for those who can force him to show it—even sometimes for Prime. Unlike Starscream who just announces his egoism to the world, Megatron actually has the power to back it up.

A famous Rational Egoist, Ayn Rand, argues that we should all be egoists, much like the basic normative egoist, but she argues we should do so because it is rational. Rand thinks that no one else can help you other than yourself. After all, the only person who can get into your own head is you! So she says it's irrational to try to help others as you can't even really know what they actually need anyway. But this is in direct contradiction to Kant's, and Prime's, own rational system. So which system is the most rational?

Rand argues that when we try to help others, we are actually doing them a disservice and showing them disrespect because they can succeed on their own. To assume that they need our help is actually harmful to the needy. Her own rule is almost the exact opposite of Kant's. She sees no reason not to use others to get what you want unless they can demand or force you to do what they want. We might even argue that the reason why this war between the Autobots and the Decepticons continues on and on is only because Prime is unwilling to do what he must to win. He's had the opportunity to kill Megatron, but his own sense of duty stopped him. Might he, then, be responsible for many innocent deaths because of his own weakness?

Megatron tells Prime in the recent Michael Bay film: "You still fight for the weak; that is why you lose." Perhaps he's on to something. Maybe the most rational thing to do is seek your own interests, but play the game wisely. If you can't win, like Starscream, perhaps you should keep your mouth shut. But if you can win, like Megatron, then do what you want. The problem, of course is that this does not seem to lead to a very fulfilling existence for rational beings as a whole. Perhaps a couple of super strong beings who can force others to do their will, like Megatron or Unicron, would do quite well, but what reason would the rest of us have to agree with this? Perhaps Starscream says it best when he says, "I will rule the Universe. Even if I am the only one left in the Universe." It seems that Randian egoism is unlikely to lead to a world of peace or harmony.

In the end, the choice of which system, and who to join, Autobots or Decepticons, is really a question not of which system is best, but which world you most want to live in. Both systems have arguments for and against them. But, they clearly lead to two different places. Kant provides us with a world of peace and loyalty, but a great deal of obligation and responsibility. Rand provides us with power and success. If you want peace, join Prime and likely die with him fighting for those who probably don't deserve your help; if you want power, join the Decepticons—but remember if you do that, you're alone. Either you are the best and first among the Decepticons or you end up like Starscream, dead—and even your fellow Deceptions will be glad when you're gone.

12

Beyond Good? Beyond Evil? Beyond Your Wildest Imagination?

ADAM BARKMAN

"Beyond Good. Beyond Evil. Beyond Your Wildest Imagination" —so reads the promotional poster for the 1986 *Transformers: The Movie*. While, from a marketing perspective, this catchphrase does a good job of promising fans something more than the weekly monotony of Autobots versus Decepticons, it also alludes to German philosopher Friedrich Nietzsche's famous book *Beyond Good and Evil: Prelude to a Philosophy of the Future*.

This raises a few important, interlocking questions. First, in *Transformers: The Movie*, and indeed in the entire 1980s cartoon series, are we supposed to think of good and evil as relative, subjective terms, as Nietzsche does, or are we supposed to think of good and evil with reference to something like an objective, universal moral law, as Plato, for instance, does? Second, if good and evil in *Transformers* does in fact imply a universal moral law that binds all sentient beings, then what other types of universal principles or archetypes might we also find in *Transformers*?

Nietzschean Superman or Platonic Guardian?

According to Nietzsche, morality is relative, meaning that because (so he states, but never argues) there is no universal moral law which speaks with an absolute voice, people have to create their own morality. Nietzsche's story of how morality developed begins with people recognizing that joining together in community is a good way of increasing their chances of survival. However, over the years as people began to work for the greater good of the community, they started to identify "conscience" with the will of the community and obedience to it—shortly after called "virtue"—as the highest good. Eventually, people forgot the subjective origins of their morality and started to speak of it as "universal."

Now such people, says Nietzsche, are typically followers of "slave-morality" or "herd-morality" since, based on "false" universal moral principles, such as mercy, sympathy and humility, they value taking care of the group as the highest moral good. Recognizing the ignorance of the "slaves" or the "herd," the "masters" or the few who subscribe to "master-morality" make no distinction between power, beauty, nobility, and moral goodness and so tend to look down on the "slaves" as weak, ugly, base and despicable. While Nietzsche himself doesn't explicitly identify himself with master-morality, he does envision his ideal man, his "superman," as a person with unbounded freedom, creativity and power to live his own life as he, free from all moral considerations, chooses to live. Thus, when Nietzsche speaks of standing beyond good and evil, what he has in mind is rising above the herd morality, which in his opinion reduces everyone to a common level, favours mediocrity and prevents the development of the superman.

But is it possible to stand beyond good and evil—to transvalue values as the philosophers say? According to the Greek philosopher Plato, it is not. For Plato and for the vast majority of the philosophers up until this century, something like a universal, invisible, immaterial moral law exists that, *contra* Nietzsche, is not created by people, but rather is discovered by the mind upon introspection. Principles of this law, such as it is always wrong to murder for profit, are the basic axioms or foundations of all moral thinking and consequently should provide us (via our conscience) with general guidance as to how we should live our lives. Since this law and its principles are invisible, immaterial, and universal, they in no way depend on space and time and are absolutely binding to all beings who can comprehend them—to gods, men and even, if they exist, rational robots.

So does *The Transformers*' universe support Nietzsche's assertion that there can be something beyond good and evil, or was that just movie marketing? In order for Nietzschean philosophy to be the favoured philosophy of *The Transformers*, we would have to see evidence that morality is constructed, that the amoral or immoral superman is admired, and that followers of herd morality—those who value mercy and self-sacrifice—are fearful and ignorant. On the other hand, in order for Platonic-style philosophy to be the favored philosophy of the transformers, we would have to see evidence that certain moral statements can be universally agreed upon, that the Nietzschean superman is a villain, and that followers of the universal moral law—those who value mercy, self-sacrifice and so on—are wise and admirable.

"Thrones Are for Decepticons"

In the episode "Fire in the Sky," the Decepticons unearth the transformer Skyfire, an old friend of Starscream who had crashed to the Earth before the civil war between the Autobots and Decepticons had broken out. Being an old friend of Starscream, Skyfire naturally trusted his friend when he said that the Autobots were evil and the Decepticons were good. However, shortly thereafter, Starscream ordered Skyfire to hurt some innocent human beings and kill a few captured Autobots. Because Skyfire knew that hurting innocent beings was immoral—not just relatively, but objectively—he refused, saying simply, "It is wrong." Plato would have applauded, and so, I hope, would all of us.

In another episode entitled "War Dawn," we are told of a young robot named Orion Pax, who admired Megatron for his immense power. However, once Megatron revealed himself to be a greedy robot who steals Energon and kills and injures those who get in his way, Orion Pax, who is later rebuilt as Optimus Prime, tells us, "I was wrong, my friends. I admired Megatron merely because he was powerful; I failed to see how he used that power." The point is clear: Megatron, like the Nietzschean superman, is a villain because he does not feel bound by regular morality and simply covets and uses power to satisfy his own "hunger" ("More than Meets the Eye, Part 2"). Optimus Prime, on the other hand, is shown to be the universally admired one, for it is he who "cares a lot for his fellow robots" ("More than Meets the Eye, Part 3"); it is he who tries to stop the Decepticons "before they destroy the world" ("More than Meets the Eye, Part 2"); it is he who keeps his promise, even to his enemies ("Heavy Metal War"); it is he who is willing to save another even if it means sacrificing himself ("The Search for Alpha Trion"); and it is he who, like the ethical guardians of Plato's *Republic*, does not covet power, but accepts the burden of leadership with great humility, declaring, "Thrones are for Decepticons" ("Triple Takeover").

But What about Unicron and the Quintessons?

Now some might object and say that universal morality may apply to the Decepticons and the Autobots, but not to others. However, such an objection is quite ridiculous, for if there is a universal moral law, then it must be *universal*. Hence, neither Unicron, whom the 1986 movie poster declares to be beyond good and evil, and the Quintessons, who say that the good of the Autobots and the evil of the Decepticons make "no difference at all" to them ("The Killing Jar"), are free from the universal moral law. Both may *talk* as though they were, both may *act* as though they were, but they are not. Hence, the Quintessons are quite clearly shown to be evil in simply a different mode than the Decepticons, and the writer of *Transformers: The Movie*, Flint Dille, says that Unicron is not beyond good and evil but is simply "so evil" that even Galvatron and Hot Rod are willing to join forces to defeat him ("*Transformers: The Movie*; Twentieth Anniversary Special Edition, Movie Commentary").

But Didn't Optimus Prime Support a Kind of Relativism When He Asked, "In This Vast Universe Is Anything Truly Forever?"

Another objection that people might have to my strong division of Decepticons-relativists-villains and Autobots-universalists heroes is from Optimus Prime himself, who, in the episode "Heavy Metal War," asks, "In this vast universe is anything truly forever?" While I will address the specifics of this quotation a little later, perhaps one of the things we could see this question asking is whether morality is something that should be judged, not specific to the individual, as a moral relativist like Nietzsche sees it, or universal to all rational beings, as Plato sees it, but rather specific to a given culture—where a culture is a semi-stable, but not universally stable, entity. In other words, should the rightness or wrongness of a given being's beliefs and actions be evaluated *solely* in terms of his own culture?

This objection is an objection from what is known as cultural relativism. According to cultural relativism, the problem that we all face is that of ethnocentrism, which is when a given individual feels that his group is at the center of everything, entailing, among other things, the belief that his group's morality is truer and better than anyone else's. Ultimately, what lies at, or near, the heart of cultural relativism is the denial that any culture or sub-culture can know any principle as self-evident, such as those who support universal morality pretend to do. To a cultural relativist, the claim by any culture to have access to universal, self-evident knowledge is misguided and dangerous, for this claim often turns into a form of imperialism, where the group in question tries to impose its view of morality on other cultures. Hence, the cultural relativist advocates tolerance through ethnography, the process of living among other cultures to better understand them, and ethnology, the process of comparing and contrasting a wide range of cultures in a fair way.

However, while both ethnography and ethnology are important methods of increasing our knowledge of the world, which, in turn, usually makes people more sympathetic and just, cultural relativism as a whole has two serious flaws, both of which, as we shall see, Optimus Prime and the Autobots seem to recognize.

The first flaw in cultural relativism is this: if the cultural relativist denies that people can know self-evident truths that can be universally and cross-culturally applied, then how can the cultural relativist advocate *universal* toleration? The cultural relativist has no defense against the charge of self-contradiction, for it is easy to see that the cultural relativist himself is intolerant of any society that lacks the cultural relativist's particular—twentieth century, western, secular—view of tolerance. The cultural relativist, in other words, becomes an agent of imperialism by the very philosophy that he created to stop it. Thus, the cultural relativist is like the pacifist Autobot First Aid, who, through the belief that true peace can never be achieved by fighting, refused to help the Autobots in a crucial battle against the Decepticons, the ultimate result of which was less peace than before, not more ("The Ultimate Weapon"). However, unlike the cultural relativist, who sticks by his guns, First Aid later came to see the self-defeating nature of his philosophy through the recognition that mere peace is not the goal, but the right kind of peace—peace achieved and maintained by the universal principles of justice and mercy.

And this leads to the second flaw of cultural relativism, which is that the principle of tolerating all cultures will ultimately tolerate the intolerable. In order to illustrate this, let's consider the cultural history of the transformers by means of a *reductio ad absurdum*. A *reductio ad absurdum* ('reduction to absurdity') is a special type of logical argument which begins by assuming the truth of the thing it wants to disprove in order to show how absurd it would be if the thing were true. So, let's assume that cultural relativism is true and now turn our attention to the cultural history of the transformers.

By piecing together various episodes, we know that in the beginning, the Quintessons brought the supercomputer Vector Sigma to the planet Cybertron, which the five-faced creatures converted into a massive factory for producing robots ("The Key to Vector Sigma, Part 1" and "The Five Faces of Darkness, Part 5"). Although we don't have all the details, we know that the Quintessons produced two general types of robot: consumer robots and military robots. However, when these two types of robot developed a high enough level of intelligence, they overthrew their Quintesson masters and established a "Cybertron Law" ("Heavy Metal War"). Yet eventually the military robots, who became known as the Decepticons, became ambitious for power like their former Quintesson masters, and so attempted to enslave the consumer robots or Autobots. This resulted in the Cybertronian civil war that finally ended with the destruction of Unicron.

While the cultural relativist could argue that under the common culture of the Decepticons and Autobots, the Decepticons are usually immoral; for instance, when Megatron appropriated the power of all his Decepticons in his one-on-one battle with Optimus Prime, he violated the law while Optimus Prime did not ("Heavy Metal War"). In this respect, the Decepticons' evil is culturally-specific evil. But what about when the Decepticons invaded the Earth and Megatron declared the Decepticons' goal to be "total domination" ("More than Meets the Eye, Part 1")?

Speaking within the context of universal human culture, the cultural relativist could try to say that total domination of the universe is wrong; however, is the cultural relativist justified in declaring human culture so universally unified? Even if we grant that this were the case, human culture, while not agreeing with Decepticon aggression, would have to be tolerant of the particular goals of the Decepticon sub-culture. To be fair, it would not mean letting the Decepticons do as they like, but it would mean that humans would be in no position to declare the Decepticons' plans for mass slavery and genocide absolutely morally wrong. While most of us recognize that conflict is rarely black and white (hence most of us cringed when George W. Bush declared Iraq, Iran, and North Korea "the Axis of Evil"), I think it is absurd to say that some things, such as mass slavery and genocide, are only immoral for some, but not all, cultures. In the end, therefore, cultural relativism isn't much more than glorified moral relativism—something that Optimus Prime and the Autobots rejected.

So if morality can't be culture-specific and Optimus Prime and the Autobots are supporters of the universal moral law, then why does Prime ask, "In this vast universe is anything truly forever?" When we see this quotation in context, we know that Prime was not asking whether everything is relative, but rather was answering Spike, who had asked him if they have seen the end of the Decepticons. While everything belonging to space and time may be relative, the universal moral law, among other things, does not belong to space and time and hence is truly forever. And it is with this idea of forever—the forever of the universal moral law—in mind, Optimus Prime and the Autobots constantly declared their sincere hope "till all are one"—not 'one with the Autobots' particular idea of morality' but rather 'one under the universal moral law, which makes possible true peace, freedom and justice' (*Transformers: The Movie*).

"Sometimes Even the Wisest of Man and Machines Can Be in Error"

With the objection from cultural relativism aside, it should be clear both that Megatron and the Decepticons are moral (or cultural) relativists—and villains—and that Optimus Prime and the Autobots are supporters of universal morality—and heroes. This argument can be further strengthened by considering the contrasting views of Megatron and Optimus Prime in regard to moral knowledge.

As a creator of his own morality, Megatron wants others to either leave him to his own devices or follow him and his moral ideas with blind faith; thus, like Hitler, Megatron thinks that "a warrior doesn't need a head, just a good strong body" ("War Dawn") and his Decepticons have no qualms about manipulating people's religious beliefs in order to achieve their selfish goals ("The God Gambit"). Nevertheless, the price of moral relativism, which, as we know, is distantly related to cultural relativism, is that Megatron has to constantly fight off those who, like Starscream, equally—either personally or culturally—disregard universal moral commands, such as it is wrong to covet what is not yours. Consequently, in a Nietzschean world or in a particular culture where rational fidelity and honor are ignored, Megatron is right when he tells Starscream, "If you dispose of me, there will always be someone to dispose of you later" ("More Than Meets the Eye, Part 3").

In contrast, as a follower of the universal moral law, Optimus Prime wants to be surrounded by those who think freely and discover the moral law within; hence, he tells Blaster that he himself "must decide when it is the right time and the wrong time" to use his power ("Blaster Blues") and asks Vector Sigma to let the Aerialbots "think for themselves, to grow in knowledge and wisdom; and . . . always value freedom and life wherever they find it" ("The Key to Vector Sigma, Part 2").

And so while rational obedience to one's superior—for instance, a child's obedience to his father when his father makes a rule in keeping with the universal moral law—is in fact a principle of the universal moral law and should be admired (meaning that Hoist and Grapple were wrong to disobey Optimus Prime in "The Master Builder" episode), blind obedience will certainly lead to trouble, even when it is blind obedience to a person whom you know to be good. It is for this reason that although Optimus Prime told Bumblebee and Wheeljack not to re-activate the Dinobots, they still re-activated the Dinobots in order to save Optimus Prime and the others, eventually prompting Optimus Prime to admit that "Sometimes even the wisest of man and machine can be in error" ("S.O.S. Dinobots").

We may take Optimus Prime's point to be that although the universal moral law reveals basic axioms for how one should live one's life, the application of the universal moral law to the particular circumstances of life is far from easy and, due to weakness of will and limited knowledge, all rational beings can make mistakes in particular situations (again, was Optimus Prime right in sacrificing Earth for the sake of Cybertron in "The Ultimate Doom, Part 1"?). Consequently, the wise being is he who, like Optimus Prime, boldly claims some universality and certainty in ethics and yet is humble enough to realize his limitations.

"You Were Never Programmed for Self-Sacrifice"

If a universal moral law exists and rational obedience to it is praiseworthy, then we should also expect that such rational obedience to the moral law is a matter not of any predisposition or programming, but of free choice. While I doubt any man-made robot could ever achieve the ability to make free moral choices, the transformers seem to be different than man-made robots. The very fact that the transformers are able to discern the moral law and are held accountable to it implies that they are able to make free moral choices.

While the 1980 cartoon series speaks with an uncertain voice in regard to what constitutes the personal identity of a transformer, sometimes appearing to reduce transformers to mere physical machines (for instance "Attack of the Autobots") and sometimes unashamedly showing them to have rational souls ("The Ghost in the Machine"), it is fairly clear that moral choice is a matter of training, not programming. For instance, in the episode "War of the Dinobots," we are told that the reason the Dinobots didn't destroy Optimus Prime is because they had "traces of Autobot training," and in "The Five Faces of Darkness, Part 3," one of the Quintessons, shocked upon witnessing Rodimus Prime saving the others from a janitorial ship, declares with the authority that comes from being the creator of the transformers, "You were never programmed for self-sacrifice." Indeed, even the zombie Optimus Prime is somehow able to bypass his deadened state and make the heroic choice to save the Autobots from a Quintesson trap ("Dark Awakening").

"Everything I Ever Needed to Know about Ethics and Morality I Learned from Optimus Prime!"

So far, I have argued that *The Transformers*' universe is bound by a universal moral law, which can be comprehended and freely chosen by all rational beings. The significance of this is both historical, insofar as it illuminates the internal workings of the transformers' universe, and also didactic, in that many children (and adults) have had their stock responses to good and evil strengthened by this show; for instance, on the internet one person wrote, "Everything I ever needed to know about ethics and morality I learned from Optimus Prime!" (http://lordcoyote.deviantart.com). And this leads to the topic of universal archetypes and their significance in *The Transformers*.

Why *GoBots* Have Not Endured

While many mythologists, such as Carl Jung, C.S. Lewis, and Joseph Campbell, agree that people share a kind of collective unconscious, in which universal archetypes, such as "the virgin birth" and "the orphan hero," exist, most do not agree on how these archetypes got into our minds and what their significance is. I generally agree with C.S. Lewis, who sees mythical archetypes as irreducible, divinely-originated images of some mysterious truth which is consistent with, though not reducible to, general moral commands (*An Experiment in Criticism*, pp. 43–44). For instance, while a universal moral command *states* that a good leader should be revered, an archetype of the good king doesn't state anything but rather presents us with an image or vision of a noble king, such as King Arthur or Aragorn, which in turn carries deep meaning and points to something important, mysterious and true about higher reality.

Yes, the archetype of the good king teaches us the important moral principle that it's right to revere noble leaders, but, no, the significance of this archetype is not *simply* that it teaches us moral commands; that is, besides its clear didactic purpose, this archetype, for instance, gives us quasi-revelatory knowledge about something deep and elevated.

And this is why *The Transformers*, with its universal ethics and its profound mythical archetypes, has endured, while *GoBots*, for instance, have not. What's my evidence for this? One name: Optimus Prime.

"We Didn't Know that Optimus Prime Was an Icon. We Just Thought We Were Getting Rid of the '84 Product Line."

According to Flint Dille, before *Transformers: The Movie* was released, he and all those working on *The Transformers* didn't know that Optimus Prime was "an icon." Dille went on to say that he and the others had simply viewed the show as "a toy show," which, "in the business sense," demanded the elimination of the old, and the introduction of the new, product line (*Transformers: The Movie*, Twentieth Anniversary Edition, "The Death of Optimus Prime"). Of course, to every fan of the show, this is blasphemy which only confirms C.S. Lewis's belief that sometimes the author is not the best judge of the mythical elements in his art (*The Personal Heresy*, p. 16). Why? Because Optimus Prime is *more* than a mere product to be bought and sold. He is one of the finest examples of the archetypal noble leader that this generation, and perhaps any generation, has ever seen.

In *Transformers: The Movie*, myriads of people were deeply moved when Prime declared, "Megatron must be stopped, no matter the cost" and then slowly transformed to the inspiring music of Stan Bush's "The Touch," and these same people could not hold back the tears when the heroic leader's lights were finally extinguished after his epic battle with Megatron. People were affected in both cases, not simply because Optimus Prime was a deeply moral being—though he was certainly that and this, as I have said, adds to the love people had for him—but more importantly, Optimus Prime was also an archetype who gave us a glimpse of something grand in weight and scope: in short, he is the hero who died saving the world; he is a powerful Christ-type, through whom many of us could feel almost religious awe and *numinous* in addition to proper ethical admiration.

13
Optimus Prime: Hero for Our Time

COREY NEIL

This chapter is for anyone who shed a tear when the Autobot leader Optimus Prime died after his heroic battle with the evil Megatron in the 1986 animated film, *Transformers: The Movie*. Something about the character Optimus Prime was powerful enough, inspiring enough and lovable enough to break the heart of any youngster who was mildly interested in the Transformers story line, upon seeing his death.

What was it about this animated robot that was so emotionally moving for so many fans? What was it about this artificial being that inspired a large part of a generation to do good and stand for justice and honor? There are surprising ways to answer these vital questions.

Where Did He Come From?

Lets start with a little bit of history. As seen in the episode "War Dawn," Optimus Prime began his life as a robot named Orion Pax, a mostly defenseless dock worker during the Golden Age of Cybertron (the Transformers' home planet) nine million years ago. At the time, a new breed of robot had recently appeared on the planet with new flight capabilities that led Orion to idolize them.

Unfortunately for Orion, when Megatron, the leader of the new group of robots, approached him with inquiries about using one of the dock warehouses, Orion was swayed by Megatron. Orion was severely wounded when Megatron and his forces then attacked in order to claim the energy stored there. Searching for someone to help them, Orion's friends took him to the ancient Autobot, Alpha

Trion, who used Orion as his first subject for a new reconstruction process, thus rebuilding the frail Autobot frame into a battle-hardy configuration.

With this reconstruction, Orion Pax became Optimus Prime, the first of the Autobot warriors. Optimus Prime took the mantle of leadership as a civil war against the Decepticons erupted, and would remain in that position for the next four million years.

In the first episode of the Generation 1 TV cartoon, both groups find themselves marooned on the energy rich and teeming-with-life world called Earth after having been out of commission for four million years due to a crash landing of both of their space ships. As the Transformers are woken up, the stage is set for the struggle between the two groups to find enough energy to fuel their forces to victory over their opposition.

In the early episodes of this series, you quickly learn that the Decepticons are perfectly willing to exploit the planet Earth and any living species on it, to retrieve enough energy to fuel their troops. This is in stark contrast to the Autobots, largely because of the example set by Optimus Prime, who are only willing to utilize energy sources without causing harm or disruption to the human species already inhabiting the planet. There are countless examples where the Decepticons are trying to exploit energy sources such as the kinetic energy of running water, solar energy, or the heat of the Earth's core—much to the peril of the planet—and the Autobots step in to stop them. Most, if not all of the time, this effort to stop the Decepticons is made primarily with the goal of protecting the human species and all other forms of life on Earth.

Why Is He a Hero?

Based on extensive research into world mythology, the popular writer and college professor Joseph Campbell uncovered a pattern in many of the mythological stories about great leaders from around the world. Campbell called this pattern the "myth of the hero" and published his great book *The Hero with a Thousand Faces* in 1949. This pattern can be seen in legends about many great religious leaders, such as Osiris, Moses, Jesus, and Buddha, and also in stories about demi-gods and kings such as Prometheus and King Arthur. Once you get this pattern, you begin the see it everywhere. Intentionally or unconsciously, storytellers from Shakespeare and J.R.R. Tolkien to Walt Disney and

George Lucas have re-told the hero myth in their own heroic characters.

Campbell describes the classic journey of the archetypal "hero" in four basic stages. First, the potential hero undergoes a reluctant separation and departure from his homeland. Second, he enters a strange new realm where he undergoes severe trials and victories of initiation against dark and evil forces. Third, some magical or even supernatural power shows up to strengthen the emerging hero. Fourth, having been transformed in this strange realm, he then returns to his homeland with helpful wisdom and power for leadership. Campbell's careful analysis of hero myths reveals more details found across most legends. However, we don't need such details to make good use of this four-stage pattern to take a second look at Optimus Prime.

Using Campbell's model, we can analyze the origins of Optimus Prime to support the idea that he is a classic example of a hero. The essentials of the story go as follows. A group of Autobots are sent back in time seven million years to Cybertron, the home planet of the transformers, during the golden age of their civilization. At the time, Autobots did not yet exist, and the Decepticons had just recently been created. The character named Orion Pax, who would become Optimus Prime, is introduced as having lived on Cybertron as a young, friendly, and happy Transformer. Living the simple life of a dock worker, Orion admires the Decepticons until one day he is deceived and betrayed by Megatron, the leader of the Decepticons, and Orion is left for dead. The Autobots, witnessing these events, intervene to take the dying Orion Pax to a wise elder transformer named Primus for repairs. Primus rebuilds Orion Pax into the first Autobot and names him Optimus Prime, who then takes the leadership role for the Autobots.

Campbell's model of the hero does apply fittingly to Optimus Prime. The first stage of Optimus Prime's journey from being just a peaceful Transformer, Orion Pax, shows him to be a young and relatively naive character, living as simple member of the community. As he is drawn towards the Decepticons and then directly encounters Megatron, he embarks on the separation-departure stage.

During the second stage of conflict and trial, Orion Pax is beaten up so badly by Megatron that he is close to death. With the hero's fate in doubt, the third stage arrives on the scene. First he receives "supernatural" aid from the group of Autobots who traveled back in time. Then the powerful Primus rebuilds Orion Pax into Optimus Prime as the first Autobot. Now ready for the climactic battle over dark forces, Optimus Prime daringly confronts Megatron and the Decepticons in their first battle with the Autobots. By representing the dangers of this journey, the story of this battle can be viewed as the victorious climax of the trials of the initiation stage. The fourth stage then finds Optimus Prime successfully taking up the mantle of leadership in the war against the tyrannical Decepticons. All four stages of Campbell's hero model are fulfilled in the story of Optimus Prime. We have seen a true hero emerge, who is more than capable of leading his community.

More than Just a Hero?

Heroes can inspire people to admire, imitate, and follow them. We grasp the rather obvious point that we expect heroes to be "good" or "virtuous" in some sense or another. But we haven't really explained Optimus Prime's ability to inspire. What makes a hero more than just a hero, but a character so compelling that so many children would get emotionally attached to Optimus Prime?

Optimus Prime is a special character who displays not only heroic conduct but also the important virtues of wise leadership and ethical commitment. Optimus Prime is able to effectively inspire and guide his community of soldiers in an ethically principled way. This all sounds great, but why would these virtues appeal to us, and especially to young people?

Perhaps evolutionary psychology can suggest an answer. Starting from the concept of "group-fitness" in evolutionary psychology, it makes sense that individuals who know how to survive and thrive in the natural environment, who are good at teaching others in their community, and who are devoted to the survival and happiness of their clan, tribe, or community, are adaptive individuals for a community to encourage and support. It can also make sense, from this group-fitness perspective, that an instinct or genetic propensity for children to seek out role models that exemplify these types of personality traits would be selected for in our environment of evolutionary adaptivity. It's therefore likely that our desire to take close notice of the narratives of "heroic" characters originates in this natural evolution of psychological adaptations. We not only need good leaders; we also must be willing to follow them. Special individuals who not only have a valuable knowledge of what is good for the community, but who also know how to draw adaptive strengths out of other individuals in the group, and inspire those individuals to utilize those strengths for the benefit of the group, are noticeably special for human beings. This inherited psychological mechanism, passed down from thousands of generations, survived because communities who followed and emulated good leaders were more likely to survive.

Special traits of Optimus Prime that make him a great leader come together into what could be labeled as his particular coaching style of interacting with the other Autobots. In his book *Successful Coaching* Rainer Martens describes how the co-operative coaching style is exemplified by a coach who listens to his athletes, but provides enough discipline to create an ideal atmosphere of healthy competitiveness and motivation. A coach who is too passive is seen as counterproductive, while a coach who is too commanding is seen as destructive. A co-operative coach, by contrast, leads with a winning combination of empathy and discipline. Optimus Prime repeatedly exemplifies this co-operative coaching style.

Optimus Prime is assertive and stern in a number of instances with his Autobot soldiers. In Episode 21 he firmly asserts to one Autobot who is accusing another Autobot of treason, that no punitive action will be taken until adequate evidence is presented. Another example of firm structure and discipline is when Optimus Prime, in Episode 16, insists that the Autobots honor their agreement with the Decepticons after Optimus loses a duel with Megatron requiring the Autobots to leave the planet Earth.

An example of the sensitive or compassionate side of Optimus Prime, also a trait of the co-operative coaching style, is seen in Episode 27 when Optimus tells their human friend Chip to "hold on to your dreams." Another example of the leadership trait of empathy is in Episode 45 when Optimus must convince Omega Supreme to give up his desire for revenge in order to save San Fransisco from an alien invasion, he is only able to do this by appealing to Omega Supreme's inner emotional turmoil, helping Omega overcome his obsession with revenge.

Optimus Prime's leadership style is also highly principled. For a robot, Optimus Prime knows ethics. Let's take a look at some specific instances of ethical valor on the part of the character Optimus Prime. In Transformers Generation 1, Episode 16, Megatron challenges Optimus Prime to a one-on-one duel—and the stakes are high, because the loser has to leave Earth with his army, forever. The Cybertronian code of battle calls for a fair fight, which Optimus points out to other Autobots who express their concerns about the potential outcome of the fight. Optimus Prime states that under the terms of the code, he is confident that he can beat Megatron. At this point in the challenge, Optimus Prime has every intention of honoring the code, and Megatron obviously has every intention of cheating in order to win this battle. Specifically, Megatron arranges to have the other Decepticons contribute parts of their central processing units to Megatron's mainframe which will give him the special abilities of each of the Decepticons.

When the duel takes place, Megatron actually beats Optimus Prime (although Optimus puts up a valiant fight). When this happens, the rest of the Autobots want to attack the Decepticons and avenge Optimus Prime. However, Optimus, being the righteous leader that he is, insists that the Autobots keep their word, lest they "destroy their honor" by breaking Cybertronian law. From a pragmatic perspective, it's in the best interest of the human species, and of all other transformers who fear the ruthless oppression of the Decepticons, for the Autobots to disregard the code, and "kick the Decepticons' tails all the way back to Cybertron." BUT, Optimus Prime, in his wisdom, believes that keeping their word, and maintaining their honor, even in the face of such discouraging circumstances, in some way is in the best interest of all parties involved. He believes that even in the face of such circumstances, it's better for the well being of the cosmic community for all sentient beings to hold themselves to the highest standards of honesty and fairness. At the end of the episode, Optimus Prime's honorable behavior is vindicated when the Autobots discover that Megatron cheated anyway, and they go back to their old battle over planet Earth and Cybertron.

Leadership Ethics for Robots and Humans

In Episode 21, an Autobot by the name of Mirage is accused by another Autobot, Cliff Jumper, of treason. Cliff Jumper seems to have good reason for believing that Mirage is a traitor, and states his case firmly to Optimus Prime and the rest of the Autobots. Optimus Prime is careful to point out a lack of evidence in his case and the negative impact of "bad feelings" resulting from unfounded accusations. At this point, Cliff Jumper's suspicions are set aside, however begrudgingly. As events unfold further into the episode, evidence surfaces that supports Cliff Jumper's case against Mirage. Upon presenting this evidence to Optimus Prime, and insisting that Mirage be charged with treason, Prime makes the assertion that Mirage's side of the story must be heard before any judgment is passed. This reflects the wisdom of an ethical leader who does not jump to conclusions, but compassionately includes the perspectives of all involved and relies on all relevant evidence before making punitive decisions that effect the well being of others. In the end it turns out that Mirage is *not* a traitor, and once again, Optimus Prime's principles are vindicated.

In Episode 26 Megatron succeeds in building a clone of Optumus Prime. His plan is to fool the Autobots into believing that the clone is the real Prime and then use the clone to lead the Autobots to their doom. The Autobots struggle to distinguish the real Optimus Prime from the fake one, and not until the end of the episode can they figure out who the real Prime is. At one point in the episode, the human friend of the Autobots, Spike, is captured by the Decepticons. The fake Optumus Prime orders the Autobots to follow him into a battle with the Decepticons. One of the Autobots then points out that they should probably rescue Spike first. The clone of Optimus Prime dismisses the value of rescuing Spike. This surprising lack of concern for Spike causes the Autobots to clearly perceive that he is not the real Optimus Prime. The Autobots knew their leader: the real Optimus Prime would value the life of a human over winning one battle with the Decepticons. This episode once again reflects the compassionate nature of the true leader Optimus Prime. Ever since their arrival on Earth, the Autobots consistently give great consideration to the impact of their operations on the human beings around them. This consideration is most exemplified by Optimus Prime.

In Episode 27, another human friend of the Autobots named Chip exhibits great regret that circumstances did not turn out as he had hoped. In a consoling tone, Optimus Prime tells Chip "hang on to your dreams, Chip. The future is built on dreams." This moment is striking if one is able to recognize the significance of this exchange. For a robotic being with "artificial" intelligence to speak in this way about such cognitive-emotional phenomena as hopes and dreams has many philosophical implications. First, this shows a sense of empathy and compassion on the part of Optimus Prime for the emotional state of hopelessness that a human being was experiencing. At the very least, this reveals the remarkable level of intelligence that the Transformers possess. Secondly, this implies that the Transformers are able to identify with having hopes and dreams, because they experience these phenomena themselves. It's stated many times in different episodes that Transformers have "feelings" in an emotional sense. This fits well if one makes the argument that they also have what could be considered "hopes and dreams." This kind of behavior is likely one of the parts of the character Optimus Prime that generates affection for him by the audience.

There are many instances throughout the storyline of the Transformers where Optimus Prime's honor and his commitment to justice end up contributing to a victory for the Autobots. The sense of fairness and honesty that Optimus Prime exhibits is by no means hard to see and is made clear time and time again by his actions. Although this ethical "righteousness" has played an important role in the success of the Autobots in many of their missions, at times Optimus Prime has led them to victory simply because he had knowledge that was relevant to the circumstances. The best leader carefully integrates ethical virtue with reliable wisdom. There were many times when Prime's knowledge of Cybertronian history or his knowledge of the Decepticons in general contributed to him knowing what to do in order for the Autobots to win a battle. This gave the impression of a wise and knowledgeable leader. In many scenarios where an individual is successfully leading a group, often times their sheer knowledge of the circumstances provides critical instruction on what is the best course of action for a group to follow, similar to an athletic coach having a vast amount of knowledge about a particular sport.

In Episode 32 the value of this kind of knowledge is exhibited once again by Optimus Prime. When the Autobot Red Alert's thought circuits are damaged, he begins to experience a state of paranoia. Optimus Prime is quick to realize that the damage to his circuits is causing the disruption in Red Alert's thinking and that he needs repairs. This kind of familiarity with the normal behavior of an Autobot gave Optimus Prime the knowledge that Red Alert simply needed repairs and had not descended into becoming an evil-minded Transformer. The statement made by Optimus Prime to Red Alert that "you need help" is also another good example of Prime's compassion.

In this same episode, someone must volunteer to enter an exploding facility in order to rescue two Autobots, one of which is Red Alert. Optimus Prime sees the danger in entering, and insists that he be the one to go in. This is heroic for two reasons. One, Optimus Prime is the strongest of the Autobots present on the scene and the most likely to succeed in rescuing the two stranded Autobots. Second, he's willing to be the one to take the risk of entering into the exploding facility so that others will not have to. This is a typical gesture by Optimus Prime, and is a classic example of the good natured heroics his character exhibits throughout the Transformers storyline. In the end, Red Alert is rescued by an Autobot other than Optimus Prime and both are given special recognition for their bravery. During this ceremonial recognition there is also the acknowledgment by Optimus that the original injury sustained by Red Alert causing his malfunctioning was a result of a choice Optimus himself had made, and Optimus takes responsibility for the misdirection that occurred. Once again, Optimus Prime displays his maturity and integrity by taking this responsibility.

And Justice for All

In Episode 34, the Autobots encounter another one of Megatron's schemes when he tries to turn the human race against the Autobots. Megatron has some of his Decepticon troops dress up in Autobot disguises and steal energy from a human power plant. This is caught on film, and the film is used as evidence to the human race that the Autobots are the evil robots and the Decepticons are the good robots who have been trying to protect the humans all along. The human race buys it, and holds a trial for the Autobots. When being taken into custody, Optimus Prime instructs the Autobots to offer no resistance and to co-operate with the humans. Upon receiving the orders to not resist, the Autobot Iron Hide make the statement: "I sure hope Prime knows what he's doing." This is one of the rare instances when an Autobot actually expresses some doubt about Optimus Prime's judgment. To me this indicates that however revered the leadership of Optimus Prime may be, he is still perceived to be imperfect by his followers.

Although this may seem to be something that would count against Optimus Prime, it can also be interpreted as a testament to his good judgment. While the Autobots know that Optimus is not perfect and that he is able to make mistakes, nevertheless they still follow him with an enormous degree of loyalty. In other words, Optimus is held to the high standards of a kind of merit system of evaluation by his followers. Evidenced by the Autobots' willingness to follow him into any situation, regardless of his imperfections, Optimus Prime must meet their standards to an exceedingly high degree. This is another sign of a great leader.

This episode also speaks to the fairness and honor that Optimus Prime espouses. It would have been very easy for the Autobots to resist the law enforcement officials sent by the humans to take the Autobots into custody. The technology of the Transformers is far superior to that of the humans in terms of weaponry and mobility. However, once again we see that at the core of Optimus Prime's beliefs is his perception that the best course of action, with consideration to all involved, is to respect the wishes of the human governments and to follow the legal guidelines of the world they are inhabiting. This sense of justice is another essential part of Optimus Prime's character that wins the hearts of the Transformers audience.

In one of the most interesting episodes, Optimus Prime solicits the help of the mammoth Transformer Omega Supreme. The size of a rocket base, Omega Supreme is one of the mightiest Transformers in the universe. He's also one of the only Autobots who can reach "escape velocity" or fly into outer-space by means of his own propulsion system. Optimus Prime asks him for his help defeating the Constructicons who have inhabited a near-by asteroid with strange and valuable ore. Omega Supreme grants Optimus's request but only because Omega Supreme has a vendetta against the Constructicons. As Optimus has a heart-to-heart with Omega Supreme we learn that the Constructicons and Omega were once friends long ago, while still inhabiting the planet Cybertron. Unbeknownst at the time to Omega Supreme, the evil Megatron had kidnapped and re-programmed the Constructicons in order to turn them into his slaves. They eventually fought and defeated Omega Supreme and destroyed the ancient Cybertronian city he was sworn to protect. In the story, it is further explained that Omega incurred some damage to his programming and lost his ability to express himself emotionally, thanks to the Constructicons. This leaves Omega psychologically isolated from the rest of the Transformers, and with a strong sense of hatred for the Constructicons that is left to fester for a very long time. Optimus is very careful to acknowledge these feelings in the context of asking him for his help. Once again we see a compassionate and understanding leader reaching out to his fellow Autobot on both an intellectual and an emotional level. This is an effective strategy for any leader who is tasked with rallying a group for a cause that carries the weight of the destinies of entire worlds.

Close to the end of the episode, during the final confrontation between Omega Supreme and the Constructicons, the city of San Francisco is about to be destroyed. Optimus Prime points out to Omega Supreme that he is the only one who can stop the destruction of the city. In order to do this, Omega Supreme has to disengage from battle with the Constructicons and lose his chance for revenge. At this point Omega is so obsessed with exacting vengeance, that he is willing to allow San Francisco to perish so that he can finish his battle with the Constructicons. Optimus confronts him and appeals to his better judgment by pointing out that the prevention of something as atrocious as the destruction of a city is more important than vengeance. In an emotional confrontation, Optimus convinces Omega to disengage the Constructicons and rush to the city's aid. At the end of the episode Optimus Prime thanks Omega Supreme for saving the city of San Francisco and suggests that in spite of the hurt that the Constructicons caused him in the past, perhaps one day he'll see that there are "more important things in life than revenge." This is a sentiment commonly upheld by wise men and strong father figures in many cultures. It indicates the impressive depth of Optimus Prime's understanding and concern about the meaning of life, for the Transformers and for the human species alike.

The Ultimate Sacrifice

When the 1986 animated film *Transformers: The Movie* was released after three years of cartoon episodes, the story line of the Transformers had reached a terrible crisis. Cybertron had been overrun by the Decepticons, and the Autobots were evidently losing the war. Optimus Prime fully realized what the ramifications could be if the Decepticons ended up ruling the universe. It would mean the exploitation of all worlds where the Transformers could harvest resources and energy. This would mean the destruction of the human race and potentially any other life forms that the Decepticons would come into contact with. This was not acceptable, and the

Decepticons had to be stopped by the Autobots at all costs, even if it meant making the ultimate sacrifice.

Early on in the film, a battle breaks out between the Autobots and the Decepticons, and the Decepticons clearly have the advantage. The defenses of the Autobots' base on Earth had been compromised and the Decepticons, following the lead of Megatron, were very close to wiping out all the Autobots. At this time, Optimus Prime showed up and engaged Megatron in a historic final battle between these two titans. In the end, Optimus Prime defeated Megatron, but not without receiving fatal wounds himself. In a scene long to be remembered by those who adored the leader for his good and wise leadership, Optimus Prime passed the "Matrix of Leadership" on to the next leader of the Autobots, and died.

Let's examine the actions of Optimus Prime throughout this sequence of the movie, keeping in mind what it really means to be a hero. We already know that Optimus stood for justice, peace, fairness, honesty and just about anything we can think of that falls in the category of "goodness." Optimus knew that the Decepticons had no regard for these principles, and he also knew that if the Decepticons succeeded in ruling the universe, a time of tyranny, oppression, and exploitation would be at hand. This had been the motivation for fighting the Decepticons all along. This fight is no longer merely about the protection of the Autobots and the rest of the Transformers throughout the universe, but also for all other life forms, such as the human race, as well. This consideration for the well being and survival of others on the part of the Autobots and Optimus Prime as their leader, entitles Optimus to the status of "hero" to any individual or species that he would protect.

When Optimus Prime enters the battle that had been raging from the beginning of the movie, he knew there was a chance that he may not survive his fight with Megatron. This is indicated by his line just before entering the fight: "Megatron must be stopped, no matter the cost" and his famous line just before his one-on-one combat with Megatron commences: "One shall stand, one shall fall." Given the seriousness of what was at stake for the well-being of so many other life forms, Optimus clearly saw beyond the value of his own life, and he did what needed to be done in order to stop the Decepticons. This self-sacrifice is a classic example of heroic behavior throughout the ages.

On his death bed, Optimus hands over the Matrix of Leadership (a powerful and mysterious object containing all the wisdom of the leaders that have come before him) to the Autobot character Ultra Magnus. When Optimus hands him the Matrix, Ultra Magnus declares that he is not worthy of receiving it. Optimus immediate responds by proclaiming that he was not worthy either. This candid acknowledgment of his own limitations illustrates Optimus Prime's humble nature. Optimus also predicts that the Matrix will one day be used to "light our darkest hour." This reflects the passionate dedication Optimus has to his fellow transformers, even as he is nearing his own end.

Optimus Prime's dying words while handing the Matrix on to Ultra Magnus were "Until that day, when all are one." Based on the actions and words of Optimus Prime throughout the storyline of the Transformers saga, I interpret Optimus Prime to be referring to the day when all sentient beings can set aside their differences and join each other in the spirit of good will, justice, and peace. Until that day, all Transformers must continue to try, using all the power available, including the wisdom and power of the Autobot Matrix, to defeat those who would govern with tyranny and violent oppression. This is the heroic spirit at its core. It is the beauty of this vision that places Optimus Prime in the mythological history of the good.

EPISODE SIX

War and Peace

14
Megatron, Fascist Philosopher

JOHN R. SHOOK

No one could mistake Megatron for a philosopher. But it would be an equally big mistake to overlook his intellect. And his principles. Yes, Megatron lives and acts according to principles. Except when he doesn't, of course, like when he bursts into a violent rage.

Still, there may be a method to his madness. His personality, his character, is twisted and dark. But if we shine a little light into Megatron's soul, what could we find? I think that we'd find a philosophy engraved into his circuits. Megatron exemplifies a philosophical outlook on life. His behavior, all of it, is consistent with a decisive stance towards the whole universe. His leadership role with the Decepticons gives Megatron plenty of opportunity to express, and inflict, his philosophy.

Sure, Megatron seems like pure evil on first (and second, and third) acquaintance. But we might just discover that Megatron has been badly misunderstood. Let's try to have some sympathy for this devil. He does command respect, after all. You don't rise up the ranks to become one of the most impressive and feared villains of all time by just being really evil. It's way more complicated than that!

Megatron's Evil Behavior

Megatron's behavior is notoriously evil. It goes way beyond bad manners. The rudeness, the sarcasm, the temper tantrums, the screaming. Lots of screaming. No, Megatron does not play nice with others. His conduct has bigger faults than mere rudeness, though. Let's catalogue some examples. Its always about what

Megatron wants. Never caring about what others need, too. Always having to be in charge. Ordering other Transformers around like they have no feelings. Trying to start fights. Abandoning comrades at any convenient moment.

Megatron's bad attitude is not only rude and inconsiderate, but it tends towards downright nastiness. There's no getting around the nastiness. Megatron can be terribly nasty. To anyone. At any time. And just because he feels like it. Once he decides upon a brutal plan of terror, he is completely ruthless and unforgiving.

But it's really all about the way Megatron goes about killing.

Now, let's slow down here. We can't pass judgment on Megatron just for killing. Lots of ordinary soldiers and even heroes sometimes kill, after all. Try to understand Megatron by starting with who he truly is. His essence is not hard to describe. Megatron is first and foremost a soldier. A trained fighting and killing machine. Literally. And he has the mind and soul of a soldier. If the basic mentality of a pure soldier could be hardwired into a robot, Megatron would perfectly exemplify this military mind-set. But he's way more than just a soldier.

How can this be put delicately? Yes, Megatron kills. Okay, he kills a lot. Extravagant killing. It's safe to say that Megatron really enjoys murder and mayhem. All his victims, piled up together, would make a heap big enough to fill a lunar crater or two. Megatron has had his enemies, millions of years' worth. Lost in that pile would be some of his friends, too. Well, probably not "friends," exactly. Hard to recall if Megatron ever had any friends. Maybe way back when he started out as just one of many Transformers, before the wars began. By the time we see him as Megatron, leader of the Decepticons, he only has comrades, not friends.

Well, maybe not comrades, exactly, either. Calling guys like Starscream and Frenzy his "comrades" doesn't quite fit. You have a serious bond with a comrade, a caring relationship that goes beyond just happening to working together. Decepticons are definitely not comrades in arms. Megatron doesn't even really work with his, um, colleagues. He tells them what to do all the time, that's for sure. And we can't forget that he frequently tells them to kill.

Megatron is happy to let other Decepticons do the killing. He is forever hatching new plots and schemes and strategies for fighting, using them as his tools. Sure, Megatron will take pleasure in a kill himself when the opportunity strikes. But he really is focused on one particular killing opportunity. Maybe we needn't mention who.

Megatron's arch-nemesis, that goody-goody robot, has become an obsession. Megatron won't let anybody else kill that guy. A battle with Optimus Prime (did you guess?) is enough to make Megatron's day. What would a hero be without an anti-hero? Megatron is so fixated on Optimus that he even believes that the entire universe would be his, if it weren't for Optimus. Only Optimus has ever earned Megatron's respect. Sometimes they even talk to each other in almost brotherly terms. The kind of brothers who are pretty sick of each other, and just want to kill each other and be done with it.

If you happen to take Optimus Prime's side, it is easy for you to hate Megatron. Optimus is so kind and good and righteous and heroic, blah, blah, blah. Whatever. To anyone filled with admiration for Optimus, Megatron would seem pretty one-dimensional. He's just evil. Pretty predictably evil, in fact. You just know that Megatron's up to something evil. It's always the same. Megatron plots evil; Optimus Prime and the Autobots have to put a stop to it. After a while, Megatron's character looks so thinly drawn, that you'd take him to be just a cartoon figure. But look again!

Megatron's Evil Character

Selfishness. Egotism. Megalomania. Words fail after a while. Megatron's pretty into himself, you know? If Megatron can think about things other than his own personal goals, it's hard to tell. There's more to this character than just a big ego, though. Megatron has an ego so big that there's no room for anything else.

Megalomania. Psychologists had to make up a new word for the sort of ego that a guy like Megatron has. Selfish people put themselves first, to be sure. But there are lots of selfish people in the world who are happy enough doing their own thing. Megatron's not like that. We can't imagine Megatron simply going off by himself to do whatever he wants to do. A megalomaniac is a special kind of maniac. An ordinary maniac is single-mindedly focused on himself and whatever he's doing at that time, to the exclusion of everyone and everything around him. By placing "megalo" before "maniac," you can invent a new label for a mega-sized maniac. This sort of supersized maniac inflates his ego, his own self, beyond his own person to encompass everything around himself.

William James, the founder of psychology in the United States, explained how we think of our selves in terms of what we possess. In his greatest work, *The Principles of Psychology*, James explained that one's conception of one's self is way more than just one's own mind or consciousness. That's a narrow philosophical view that has little to do with the way ordinary people have always thought of themselves. A psychologist has to deal with real people, and their real selves. You can tell how people think of themselves, James explains, by their concern for things. People feel concern for, and ownership of, their minds and bodies, but it doesn't stop there. What about our clothes, the furniture of our intimate lives, and our treasured homes? When these things are damaged or violated or stolen, we feel personally violated. It's all about control, ultimately. Our most precious possessions are a part of us. What we possess, what we control, what we need to live our lives—these things are a part of us, part of our person. That's the only way to fully explain why we feel so personally violated or harmed when anything happens to these external things. By extension, our loved ones, our families, are also a part of ourselves. It's very hard to understand human psychology without properly recognizing this wider self that extends beyond the inner self.

Healthy psychological attitudes rest on our feelings of safety, security, and control over all the dearest things around us that we care about so deeply. Unhealthy psychological states emerge when a person either has too little security and control, or seeks excessive security and control, over this wider self. People who care little for anyone around them, or care so much that they try to obsessively control them, will have serious psychological problems. Now, imagine someone whose personality combines two quite unhealthy characteristics: this person thinks that their self encompasses *everything*, and this person is so insecure that he has become obsessed with *controlling* everything. There's your megalomaniac. As the Oxford English Dictionary puts it, a megalomaniac suffers from "the delusion that one has great power or importance" and has an "obsession with the exercise of power."

Before we hastily diagnose Megatron as a megalomaniac, let's try to consider the evidence carefully. Megatron's own words must be heard. What sorts of things do we typically hear our of that big metal mouth? We certainly hear some bragging.

> We are indestructible! Power to the Decepticons forever!

Megatron not only brags about his power, but he is also proud of his wits.

> Power flows to the one who knows how. Desire alone is not enough.

Megatron certainly likes power. The more power for him, the better. He just can't feel inferior or indebted to anyone else.

> I belong to nobody!

Megatron is quite sure about the proper use of power. Power is for domination.

> Decepticons do not cower behind gun batteries! Our destiny is to go where we please on this wretched world—to conquer!

Megatron is proud of himself. He even gladly admits his megalomania.

> **Optimus Prime:** You destroy everything you touch, Megatron!
>
> **Megatron:** That's because everything I touch is food for my hunger. My hunger for power!

Yes, I think that we can safely conclude that Megatron is a paradigm example of a megalomaniac. We are dealing with a seriously deranged character. But there are greater depths to Megatron than just his psychotic delusions of grandeur.

Megatron's Evil Leadership

Megalomaniacs may like to feel in command and in control all of the time. Yet few of them actually rise to any level of authority, and very few could actually be any good at authority. Perhaps fortunately for Megatron, few other Decepticons are anywhere near as maniacal as he is. They sure take a beating from him every once in a while. Megatron maintains his authority over the other Decepticons mostly by beating back every challenge to his command. The Decepticons evidently regard the right to command as rightfully belonging to the strongest and wiliest of them all. That's been Megatron.

Megatron never suffers from any shortage of strategies. He tries all sorts of deceptive tricks, surprise attacks, and forthright confrontations to achieve his evils aims. An evil genius, Megatron is not. But at least Megatron stays focused, and you've got to give him credit for stubborness. The prime object is, of course, control of the home planet of Cybertron itself. After that, the universe! But Megatron finds it so frustrating that the present stage for this cosmic drama is ridiculously limited to an irrelevant planet, the planet Earth. All the same, with his impressive intellect, Megatron knows exactly what the master plan must be:

> My plan is to conquer this mud-ball of a planet, and suck it dry of energy!

Smarts *and* strength. Admirable, but is it enough? Admittedly, Megatron's a leader only in the most basic of senses. Many things that we might expect from a good leader are things that Megatron could never do. It's just not in his nature. For example, a real leader would be concerned for the good of whole team. No, that's not Megatron. He'd gladly sacrifice any of his followers for his own sake. As another example, a good leader would take responsibility for his contribution to any failure, as well as any success. No again, that's not Megatron. Megatron won't ever take any blame for failure. How many millions of years of failure to defeat the Autobots? And never once was it Megatron to blame? Here's yet another quotation straight from his mouth:

> We've failed before through no fault of mine! But this time, I shall not be denied. This device will enable me to strike at the Autobots through Optimus Prime's only weakness: his over-developed sense of honor.

A good leader would understand what's he's up against. Megatron knows Optimus Prime through and through. He at least can credit Optimus Prime for his strengths. Megatron is usually gracious enough to state the obvious: they are a fair match. They possess roughly equal technological powers and constitutions. After all, it's still a tie after so many battles. But there's one things that makes them very different. Megatron picks out Optimus Prime's honor. That's the Autobot leader's reputation, of course. That shining coat of virtue he wears all the time. But that makes Optimus Prime predictable, and weak. Quite unlike Megatron—there's no ethical principle slowing *him* down.

STARSCREAM: You wouldn't want to cheat, would you, Megatron?

MEGATRON: I will win by any means, at any cost! Even if it means terminating you, Starscream!

No, no ethical principles at all, in any reasonable sense of "ethics." Not even anything resembling military ethics. Both the Autobots and the Decepticons are analogous to military organizations, of course. Any military organization will operate by minimal rules of authority and obedience. A military ethics goes beyond the command structure to encourage the virtues of honor, loyalty, courage, cohesion, and other virtues essential to any successful military organization. Megatron is barely capable of registering when Autobots display these virtues. He will have none of that for himself. Under Megatron's leadership, it's probably an insult to the military to ascribe that label to the Decepticons.

Megatron is all about victory, absolute and utter victory. For Megatron, victory is the complete annihilation of anything that stands in his way. Nothing makes him giddy with glee like a battle going his way.

Their defenses are down, let the slaughter begin!

There can be no mercy. Megatron despises the weak, enslaves the useful, and destroys the rest. If you were to ask him whether it really is necessary to kill everything, he'd laugh in your face and say something like,

Compassion is for fools!

Megatron is not merely a homicidal megalomaniac, but also a manipulative paranoid who consistently abuses his reckless power just to make others suffer. Just what you want in a leader.

Of course, you'd want the right leader for the right situation. Megatron clings to power not merely because he lusts for more and more control. He really believes that he is the best leader for the Decepticons. His exemplification of all that the Decepticons must stand for fully entitles him to his leadership status. Without Megatron, the Decepticons probably would have been defeated long ago (regardless of what Starscream may think). He really is the heart and soul of the Decepticons, representing everything that they truly are. And the Decepticons do stand for something, something more than just serving Megatron and his grand schemes.

Just exactly what the Decepticons might stand for is a matter that mostly eludes the other Decepticons. You won't hear anything too sophisticated from that bunch. Occasionally Starscream will let loose with complaints against Megatron, indicating how he sees things. It's mostly about whether the Decepticons are currently winning or losing, and who's to blame when things go wrong, and what Starscream would do differently. No, Starscream is no philosopher. If you want to hear about the big picture, about how it is more than survival and victory at stake, you have to listen carefully to Megatron.

Megatron's Evil Philosophy

Like Optimus Prime, Megatron is not above enunciating the core principles animating their perpetual struggle. Good and evil don't mix, to be sure. But good and evil don't bother fighting for all eternity unless there are contrasting visions, competing philosophies, trying to gain supremacy. Sure, sure, good must try to defeat evil. But it's never really that simple. The really interesting devils of religions, devils with developed characters and important roles to play in the cosmic drama, have unique perspectives on the play worth hearing out. Consider the way that Angra Mainyu plays counterpoint to Zoroastrianism's Ahura Mazda, or how Satan just can't help teasing Christianity's Yahweh. Lex Luthor didn't find his purpose in life until Superman came along. And the Joker finds his alter-ego in Batman.

Myth and legend agree with art and literature. Evil, true evil, has just a much a right to a fully articulated version of things, its own valid (if regrettable) perspective from which to make a stand. This is as true about evil as it is about good. That's just the reality of evil. It's not right, it's not just, it's not fair. And sometimes it just doesn't make any sense. But that's just the way it is. Unless evil is just as real as good—unless evil is a serious philosophy of life that could really tempt and sway and infect and pervert—goodness and righteousness just wouldn't make any sense either. They are the cosmic yin and yang, the universe's balancing act.

Somehow, Megatron is dimly aware of this. It's in the way that he takes special pleasure taunting and goading the Autobots. Megatron feels compelled to thwart the Autobots, as if he senses that he and the Decepticons really are crucially important to the universe. This attitude goes way beyond mere megalomania. It's one thing to *follow* the devil; it's quite another to think that you *are* the devil. Now there's a cosmic role worthy of Megatron.

Megatron flamboyantly plays the satanic role to the hilt, and not just in his evil deeds. Megatron shows nothing but utter contempt for the Autobots' self-righteous moralizing. Their concern for each other. Their code of honor. Their rules. While these things deeply annoy and bemuse Megatron, he sees more deeply into the Autobots than that. If you had to put your finger on precisely what disgusts Megatron the most about the Autobots, it would probably be the way that the Autobots care for humans. He just can't wrap his circuitry around that bizarre relationship. Why would any mighty transformer go out of his way to protect the puny life forms infesting Earth? In Megatron's words,

> Humans don't deserve to live!

In Megatron's evil philosophy, Might makes Right. The Strong not only rule, but it is Right that they rule. By implication, the weak must die. If the weak are allowed to live and proliferate, then everything around them becomes weaker as well, by Megatron's logic. A strange logic, to be sure. You have to see how Strength only remains strong through continual struggle. Only the constant repetitive exercise of strength can maintain it. And the best way to exercise strength is battle. Not exercise, not practice, not games. Only real battle, when everything is on the line, supplies enough motivation to the winner and enough penalty to the loser. If the weak aren't attacked, if they aren't getting eliminated, then the strong aren't staying strong. In Megatron's words,

> Strike! Strike! With all the might at our command! Death to the Autobots and the decay that they stand for!

By the strange logic of Strength, the only alternative to growth is decay: there can be no compromise, no toleration of the weak. Megatron tries over and over to get this through the Autobots' thick metal skulls.

> **Optimus Prime:** It's you and me, Megatron . . .
>
> **Megatron:** No, it's just *me*, Prime!

Optimus Prime: At the end of this day, one shall stand, one shall fall!

Megatron: You still fight for the weak! That is why you lose!

In a war, only true Strength can prevail. The eventual outcome of the titanic battle between the Autobots and the Decepticons remains in doubt. But there's no doubt in Megatron's mind what the glorious utopian outcome will be. The Decepticons will control Cybertron and spread throughout all the galaxy and beyond, with Megatron in supreme command forever.

In Megatron's electronic dreams, with the transformers wars over and only domination of the weak to look forward to, the Deceptions will enter a final glorious stage of peaceful existence. Only in Megatron's delusional fantasies could this make good sense, but by the logic of Strength, continual war against the weak by those in supreme power is exactly the final peaceful solution to all the struggles of existence. As Megatron puts it, in his witty manner of cybernetic brevity,

Peace though tyranny.

Fascism

"Peace through tyranny." That's sounds an awful lot like those paradoxical slogans of George Orwell's novel *Nineteen Eighty-Four*: "War is Peace; Freedom is Slavery; Ignorance is Strength." Like Orwell's fictional Party holding totalitarian domination over everything, the Decepticons would hold the universe in absolute control. Paradoxes express seeming contradictions. Could peace be achieved through tyranny?

Megatron's philosophy of Strength could only work under conditions of continual war. If war is not immediately available, it must be sought out or it must be artificially created. The struggle for survival can never end, for if struggle ceases, so does Strength. Peace cannot really be any sort of goal for the philosophy of Strength.

The only way to make any sense of the phrase "Peace through tyranny" is to take "peace" to mean that one supreme power dominates everything. It can't mean "peace" in the ordinary sense, when there is no conflict. Rather, the "peace" that a tyranny enjoys is the peace of knowing that nothing will overthrow the dictators, and that the dictators control all the violence. The peace enforced by the tyranny has ended all significant wars between groups of the weak. There really is only one struggle anymore: the Weak versus the Strong.

For more insight into this philosophy of Strength, we can turn to another megalomaniac who also rose to great power. Let's hear from this deranged lunatic. Does this quotation sound familiar?

> Those who want to live, let them fight, and those who do not want to fight in this world of eternal struggle do not deserve to live.

Yes, those words came from a real twentieth-century tyrant—Adolf Hitler. Here's another quotation from Hitler:

> Only force rules. Force is the first law.

Hitler's philosophy of evil was a philosophy of Strength. No one would mistake Hitler for a philosopher. But he could understand and express the philosophical principles behind the philosophy of Strength. These principles resound throughout all his writings, speeches, and proclamations.

Hitler had a vision of leadership to match his philosophy of Strength. Not surprisingly, it again sounds a lot like Megatron's:

> The efficiency of the truly national leader consists primarily in preventing the division of the attention of a people, and always in concentrating it on a single enemy.

During the twentieth century, this philosophy of Strength suddenly erupted in central and southern Europe at a time when the nineteenth century options of Communism and Democracy were facing off against each other. It's new label was Fascism, but it was an old philosophy. The Spartans perfected Fascism. The empire of Imperial Rome took Fascism to new heights of world domination. Military dictatorships every since have experimented with Fascism.

During the twentieth century, these three political philosophies of Communism, Democracy, and Fascism fought for control of western civilization for about thirty years. Unlike the others, Fascism alone was designed for war. As we know, Fascism is all about war. Another Fascist, the Italian dictator Benito Mussolini, explained Fascism in this way:

> Fascism, the more it considers and observes the future and the development of humanity quite apart from political considerations of the moment, believes neither in the possibility nor the utility of perpetual peace. It thus repudiates the doctrine of Pacifism—born of a renunciation of the struggle and an act of cowardice in the face of sacrifice. War alone brings up to its highest tension all human energy and puts the stamp of nobility upon the peoples who have courage to meet it.

Fascism is a philosophy of Strength, and therefore it develops into a political philosophy about Perpetual War. If your first assumption about humans is that Strength is the supreme meaning of life and the highest excellence to achieve, you can draw some conclusions about politics.

A political philosophy explains why humans need government, and argues for one form of government as the best. According to Fascism, humans need government because humans ought to be in a perpetual state of war, and only a strong government can sufficiently bind the people together for the immense effort required. Therefore, the best form of government would be the best at unifying and commanding the people in a time of war. That government is a Fascism: a military dictatorship designed to fight wars.

The basic principles of Fascism are something like the following:

1. **Government must identify and fight the enemy (there's always an enemy).**
2. **Government must be a military organization with a supreme commander.**
3. **The best rulers possess the military knowledge and skills to wage wars.**
4. **The best rulers must also know how to manage society for increasing its strength.**

From these basic principles of good government, everything else so characteristic of Fascism necessarily follows. Government demands absolute and unquestioning obedience; government completely controls all social institutions and all ways of thinking; government silences any dissent and destroys any differences among the people; and government indoctrinates complete loyalty and devotion from the people towards the government and especially to its supreme leader.

Megatron's Fascism

Megatron has a philosophy about the meaning of life, his philosophy of Strength. Combined with his severe megalomania and his capacity for leadership (such as it is), Megatron develops his own diminutive version of an imposing political philosophy: political Fascism.

By contrast, the Autobots don't stand for any political philosophy. We can't get much of an idea of what life would like under the rule of the Autobots. But that notion strikes us as odd. Autobots as rulers? No, that doesn't seem part of their plan at all. The Autobots do exemplify a contrasting philosophy of life, based on compassion, honor, freedom, and peace. "Til all are One," as Optimus Prime so touchingly puts it. But the co-operative "One" envisioned by Optimus is hardly anything like the commanded "One" dreamed by Megatron. If it needs a label, we might fittingly use Community for Optimus Prime's vision for life in the universe. The Autobots are fighting against the Decepticons to save the universe from Fascism. But the Autobots have no way of imposing Community on us, either. Optimus Prime is not designed to become a benevolent monarch. Rather, Optimus represents an ethical ideal, that only we the people would have to try to put into practice.

In the meantime, as we struggle for community (the true meaning of pacifism, by the way), we can stay motivated and on course by conjuring up the devil and his temptations. We can imagine more Megatrons, waiting for any opportunity. When we feel weak and scared, when we feel frustrated, when we wish for fast action and quick victory—that's when a fresh Megatron sets aside the disguise and stands up among us. Announces he's recruiting followers. Promises revenge and pride, glory and riches. Sounds tempting, no?

Which are you, deep down inside? Are you an Autobot, or a Decepticon? Megatron's waiting for an answer, and you really don't want to keep him waiting!

15
Are Ethical War-Bots Possible?

DAVID R. KOEPSELL

I was in the midst of my teenage years when the first Transformers series aired in the United States. While it was clearly primarily a means of peddling Hasbro's toys, which admittedly stoked the lust of any young boy (they're trucks, they're robots, what more could a boy want?), there was a more-or-less consistent and sustained story line that held the series together, and could even be compelling.

As with most non-comic cartoons of the era, there were obvious heroes and outrageous villains. I had grown up with the first wave of Japanese animation which aired as reruns in my early childhood. Prince Planet (also known as Astroboy) battled Warlock throughout most of the run of its fifty-two episodes. Prince Planet, like the Transformers, came from another planet as some sort of savior, and chose to help humans whenever and wherever he could.

Prince Planet, while aided by technology (his amulet of power, which needed occasional re-charging) was biological, and so his motivations to do good were not in doubt. He had come to determine whether Earth was ready to attain status in the Galactic Union of Worlds, and became sympathetic to humanity, assisting it where he could, serving as a moral example of how advanced interplanetary people could behave. There's a theme here. The Transformer plight, and the moral context of their appearance on Earth, are similar to that of Prince Planet.

In both the TV series and the recent Transformers movie, we're offered a vision of robots as "life forms," some of whom are clearly intended to be models of moral behavior, and others of whom are clearly evil. In the TV show, the Transformers came to Earth quite by accident, and unfortunately both the good and evil factions crashed and became intertwined with the fate of the Earth. In the movie, both good and evil Transformers come in search of the "All-spark" but for different reasons. These conflicting reasons and the ongoing battle between good and evil Transformers in both the TV series and the movie are more-or-less identical.

Optimus Prime and his nemesis Megatron are the quintessence of good and evil, locked forever in battle, with the fate of the Earth in the balance. In the TV episodes, and for much of the movie, it's up to Optimus Prime and his cohorts to subdue the unbridled will to power and destruction of Megatron, and to save the people of Earth in the process. Optimus Prime and his friends are larger-than-life embodiments of selfless sacrifice and honor, exhibiting virtues that are mirrored by their human compatriots.

Megatron and his minions are the polar opposites, driven by nothing more than desires, hatred, and greed, threatening the futures of both Earth and Cybertron. The morality of the Autobots, headed by Optimus Prime, and the immorality of the Decepticons, headed by Megatron, are clear. No one can doubt their moral status. (Or can they? See Chapters 11 and 12 in this volume.) Before examining what this means, and the question of whether and in what manner robots could possibly be "moral," let's look at some classic examples, from both the TV show and the movie, that illustrate the virtues of the Autobots, and the evilness of the Decepticons.

Automated Evil

In the TV series, Megatron and the other Decepticons first go to war with the Autobots in order to take over the planet Cybertron, and eventually secure domination of the universe (the only worthy desire of any arch-villain). The battle between the Autobots and the Decepticons comes to a pitch as Cybertron is running out of energy, and both the good and bad robots try to venture into the galaxy to find new sources of energy. In the ensuing space battle, the ships become intertwined, and crash-land on Earth, where four million years later, when all the robots are revived automatically, they find themselves in the midst of present-day humanity.

For the Decepticons, twentieth-century human technology offers vast reserves of power which can finally help ensure total domination of the universe, and for the Autobots, their mission becomes to save humanity from the Decepticons. The plotline in the movie is sufficiently similar, and exposes the dual natures of the robots from Cybertron. Examples of Decepticon evilness and Autobot virtue abound in both the movie and the series.

Megatron's only motivation for action is his desire for power, and in the series, he has among his minions a challenger, Starscream, who is constantly vying for power. The raw, brute, and unbridled quest for power and domination that compels the Decepticons is at the heart of their lack of virtue. They are often cowardly, with the possible exception of Megatron, but even he looks out only for himself, never for his minions. They are impelled by vanity and pride to vanquish not just the Autobots, but the whole universe.

Their greed and desire lead them always to their temporary defeats at the hands of the Autobots, all of whom exhibit the Aristotelian virtues, and serve as moral models for their human friends. Or if we wish to be Kantians, they act only according to their duties, impelled by the categorical imperative. The Autobots' duties often conflict with their desires, preventing them sometimes from leaving earth, and requiring them to sacrifice their own goods for the sake of the earthlings' needs. Or finally, if we are utilitarians, then we can see the good of the Autobots in attempting to maximize the pleasure of all, including humanity, by thwarting the Decepticons who seek to increase their pleasure at the expense of that of the rest of the universe.

In the movie, Optimus Prime and the other Autobots attempt to help not just themselves, but humanity. Their selfless sacrifices can be seen in their frequent confrontations with the Deceptions. They preserve and save human lives wherever possible, often injuring themselves in the process. Although their war with the Decepticons predates their entanglement with Earth, they view Earth's inhabitants as ends in themselves, worthy of life and autonomy, whereas the Decepticons seek to use Earth and its resources as means to their own ends, humanity be damned.

The Autobots, having defeated the Decepticons (apparently) at the end of the Transformer movie, remain on Earth, forgoing their return to their home-world of Cybertron, to help keep humanity safe from harm. Throughout, the Autobots not only co-operate and sacrifice for humans, but with and among themselves. They struggle together, unlike the sniping and contriving Starscream (in the

TV show, at least—he appears in the movie, but his bitter rivalry with Megatron is not shown) and exhibiting the valor of a team working together, rather than self-interested individuals, unconnected to one another. The valor and virtue of the Autobots is clear, the cowardice and contrivance of the Decepticons equally so.

In the movie as in the TV show, Bumblebee bonds with his human compatriot, in a way that even seems like affection. In both media, Bumblebee is both transportation for, and protector of his favorite human. Thus, his sacrifice is more particular at times, aimed not only at protecting humanity, but also a particular human, whom we could even surmise he loves. Here, the virtue of Bumblebee is less abstract, and appears to be like that of the best of people, guided by the most supreme form of self-sacrifice, that which is made for the objects of our affections, for our families, and friends. Indeed, even among the Autobots, there is a clear friendship. They joke and play like good-natured colleagues, while the Decepticons bicker and vie for power, their rivalry with one another only overshadowed by the desire to conquer Earth and beyond.

The Decepticons, by any ethical measure, are meant to be bad, and the Autobots are models of good. In this chapter, I'm not going to investigate the very real problem of determining how, theoretically, we are to distinguish among theories of morals or ethics. Nor will I decide here which acts, qualities, or modes of behavior are good or evil. Instead, I'll just accept that the Autobots are highly moral and the Decepticons highly immoral, and consider the question: How can robots be judged moral or immoral? This question is fascinating, not just as a philosophical problem, but also as an issue relevant to the design of modern machines, and their uses in our present world.

Auto-Morality

While it's clear that the Autobots are meant to represent good and the Decepticons evil, it remains unclear whether this is even a metaphysical possibility. And this question—whether it's possible to *model* moral behavior—is important for us right now, because a concerted and well-funded effort is under-way to automate warfare, and in so doing, take some of the decision-making out of the hands of humans and give it to machines.

War is dangerous, too dangerous for humans. The machines of modern warfare have developed historically along two lines: 1) giving humans the means to be more deadly, and 2) protecting soldiers in the battlefield. Many of these technologies have resulted in creating distance between soldiers and the enemy. Artillery and armor have enabled a longer and more deadly reach across the battlefield, and more safety from counter-attack. The ability to conduct airstrikes to launch missiles has, in some cases, totally removed soldiers from the battlefield, but until recently, the trigger was always pulled by a human, and at the behest of human decision-makers. Now, the military is interested in being able to create some autonomy on the part of our war-machines, allowing for some of the tactical decision-making to be made by the machines themselves. Humans suffer from warfare in ways other than the obvious, and human decision-makers suffer frailties due to the stresses of battle that can make their opponents and innocents suffer in "unnecessary" ways as well. To combat these tendencies, the various militaries of the world are attempting to create automated and autonomous war-fighters.

While Predators and other human-operated drones are robots, or sorts, capable of extending the reach of humans beyond a certain distance, and enabling precision delivery of deadly force without endangering the human controller, these tools still leave open the very real possibility of human error. Moments of uncertainty, emotionally-charged motivations such as vengeance or retribution, and battle-induced stress, can all lead human soldiers, even aided by sophisticated machines, to lash out at both innocents and enemies in tragic ways.

In both the Afghanistan and Iraq wars, there have been numerous incidents of civilian "collateral" damage and excessive or illegal treatment of enemy combatants by overly-stressed or otherwise impaired NATO and Coalition soldiers. War is inherently stressful, so there's little that can be done to reduce its impacts on humans, but by taking the humans out of the battlefield, and replacing them and their decision-making with autonomous artificial agents, unnecessary injuries and deaths could, theoretically, be avoided.

This vision is fraught with significant technical and moral problems. Supposing we could devise machines capable of making decisions on the battlefield, and preventing collateral damage in the process, is it right to cede both technical and moral responsibility for the deaths of enemies to machines? Would doing so ever really occur, or does it just create further distance between humans and their wartime opponents? Will robots on the battlefield be able to be held morally responsible for their mistakes, just as human soldiers are? Would such a change be simply another step in the evolution from cross-bow to H-bomb to autonomous fighting robot, or would it represent a paradigm shift in the morality of warfare itself? Can machines be "bad" or "good," and does this matter? These questions matter quite a bit, both for those who are developing new autonomous fighting machines, and for some philosophers and ethicists.

In their new book, *Moral Machines: Teaching Robots Right from Wrong*, Wendell Wallach and Colin Allen consider some of the practical and philosophical issues of designing robots that can make ""ethical"" decisions. Their inquiry looks to the very real potential consequences that increased automation has for human relationships with machines. It isn't just robots that will be used on battlefields, but also artificial agents used in monitoring and sometimes conducting financial transactions, robots used in assisting the disabled and the elderly, and other potentially beneficial, but autonomous machines meant to improve our lives.

Countless science-fiction scenarios have considered, as long as robots have been envisioned, the practical and ethical implications of conflicts between humans and their creations. Isaac Asimov's *I Robot* contains the first fictional attempt at a robot ethical code. It has three simple rules. Asimov's rules of robotics state:

1. A robot may not injure a human being or, through inaction, allow a human being to come to harm.

2. A robot must obey orders given to it by human beings, except where such orders would conflict with the First Law.

3. A robot must protect its own existence as long as such protection does not conflict with the First or Second Law.

These rules embody a simple preference for human life over robots, and weigh actions rather than intentions. In some ways, they might be argued to be the basis for the actions of the Autobots in Transformer. In both the movie and TV show, the Autobots repeatedly sacrifice their own safety in an apparent attempt to save humanity from the Decepticons. But is this enough to say that the Autobots are moral? Suppose they followed all the Law of Robotics, would this make them praiseworthy? Would violating the Laws make them blameworthy? Let's consider some of the arguments regarding this fundamental question of robot ethics.

Good Design, or Designed for Good?

Humans design machines with inherent safeguards—this is just a matter of good design. Good chainsaws have guards that prevent the chain from flying back and decapitating you if the chains break. Cars have airbags to help prevent drivers and passengers from flying head first into the dashboard on impact. Elevator doors don't open in between floors. All of these are matters of good design. Machines ought to be made to avoid harming humans. Why aren't the Laws of Robotics, or any code that becomes part of a machine's algorithms, simply analogous to airbags and elevators? I think that, at least where robots are made by humans, "ethical" codes that become part of an intentionally-created robot or other artificially-created intelligent agent, are little more than expressions of the intention of the designer, and not truly responsible for "moral" machines.

Suppose we designed guns that would not fire upon a non-enemy or civilian. The gun has some sort of detector in it that can determine whether the target is a friendly force or a civilian, and can thus prevent firing upon illegal targets (illegal under the conventions of warfare, and "immoral" or unethical under the codes of conduct for most militaries). Is this a moral or ethical machine because it has sophisticated detection equipment? The machine "decides" autonomously from its human user, and so it is in some sense intelligent, overriding decisions of a human for its more-perfect artificial detection and decision-making capacity. In a simpler way, guns with safeties also protect humans by preventing accidents, and forcing more decision-making by their human users. In our "smart-gun" scenario, however, the gun takes decisions away from a human. Is this enough to make the gun moral, even where it may be acting automatically?

Elevators make decisions too. They're programmed to decide in what order they "ought" to go to floors, not based merely on a first-come-first serve button-press order, but based on complex algorithms meant to keep people waiting a minimal period of time while fulfilling the linear efficiency necessitated by vertically stacked floors and limited numbers of available elevators. Their programming is made to assist humans, keep them happy, and move them safely. Both the smart gun and elevators appear to be making decisions. Their programming makes them capable of action apart from a human user.

But all of that decision-making is according to some algorithm created by a human programmer. In what sense, then, are elevators and fictional smart-guns truly autonomous? Is it enough that a machine is given a set of instructions and tools for detecting its environment, and then acts without further input although according to those rules? I think we'd say that such behavior, while "intelligent" to some degree, escapes both moral praiseworthiness or blameworthiness.

If I program a washing machine not to run if it detects a kitten in it (by sensing a heartbeat, or hearing a "meow" coming from within it, and that washing machine then fails to drown a kitten, I haven't created a moral washing machine. I have projected my morals onto a machine and designed it to act according to those morals, even where it now has the physical autonomy to turn itself on and off. The values it acts according to are designed into it. Similarly, in *A Clockwork Orange*, when Alex is unable to commit crimes because his brain has been programmed to make him sick if he tries, he is not acting morally by failing to commit the crimes he once delighted in. He is simply blocked by programming from carrying out a certain range of actions.

These two examples point to the critical missing element that makes the Laws of Robotics just as suspect as a safety-gun or airbags. In none of these cases is there any real "choice" on the part of the machine. Of course, in *I, Robot*, the robot does make a choice, and in other Asimov tales, not to mention the *Terminator* movie franchise, robots become truly autonomous, over-riding their programming, and making dubious decisions that cause harms to humans. This is where things become interesting, and it leads us into the realm of the Transformers.

In both the TV series and the movie it is apparent that the Transformers are meant to be not *merely* automatons, carrying out pre-set instructions, but rather are intended to be *autonomous*, thinking and feeling beings. Their actions are supposed to be self-guided, and so they are the results of choices of someone other than a programmer. Thus, we are meant to view their actions as either morally good or blameworthy, rather than the mere mechanical results of some predetermined scheme of behavior. Of course, this raises a number of tricky problems that, should we choose to dwell on them, throw into doubt not only the moral value of robot decisions, but our own as well. Let's take as the starting point for this discussion the example of the kitten-protecting washing machine, and reconsider whether it might be acting autonomously after all.

The Autonomy Straw-Man

It is perhaps too quick a move to argue that a kitten-sensing washing machine does not truly make a choice. It is based upon our self-assured sense that when we refuse to kill a kitten, we too are exercising a choice, just as those who choose to kill kittens also makes choices.

It's true that before the kitten is dead, we *seem* to be able to choose to kill it or to save it, but this seeming is no more assuredly true than that a kitten-sensing washing machine, programmed to not kill kittens *chooses* to save the kitten. In other words, we have a pragmatic sense that our choices are indeed ours, and that our actions reflect free choices, but we cannot substantiate this in any convincing way. We can only point out that at some time we did the thing we did, and that it was preceded by some mental state that appeared to us to be decision-making.

This is essentially the problem outlined by John Searle's "Chinese Room" criticism of the Turing Test. The Turing Test was proposed by Alan Turing as a means of testing whether an artificial agent is truly intelligent. In Turing's article entitled "Computing Machinery and Intelligence," published in 1950, he proposed that the way to test whether a machine really was intelligent would be to carry on a conversation with the machine (for instance by sending text messages). If the machine's contributions to the conversation would be indistinguishable from those of an intelligent human, in other words if no one could tell that the machine was not a human, then the machine would have to be judged intelligent. The conversation would have to be open to any subject, and the machine taking part in the test (or game, as Turing preferred to call it) would be programmed to convince the judge only that it is human.

John Searle challenges the use of the Turing Test by proposing what has come to be called either the Chinese Room or Chinese Box. In a 1980 article, "Minds, Brains, and Programs," Searle argues that the Turing Test fails to verify *understanding* on the part of the computer. Even if the machine gives appropriate answers, this does not show the machine really knows what's going on. Searle asks us to consider whether a person in a room, given a Chinese dictionary and the grammar and syntax for the Chinese language, when asked to decipher and respond to incoming Chinese messages with Chinese responses, truly understands Chinese. According to Searle, while to an outside observer it would appear that the man in the Chinese Box understands Chinese, he has merely learned the rules for manipulating symbols which are meaningless to him.

While Searle believes that this "Chinese Box" thought experiment shows that robots or other allegedly intelligent machines are not truly intelligent, it poses another problem for us in the context of our discussion of Transformer ethics: Who's to say that we or other humans exhibit true "choice" in ethical dilemmas? We have no external evidence that any other human, much less a robot, makes a truly autonomous choice when confronted with an ethical dilemma. The internal evidence of our own choices is similarly suspect. Could we be simply providing post hoc justification for our actions? Might our own decision-making be guided by algorithms that are beyond our own control, but designed to appear to us to be the result of what we have come to call "free will?"

It's a legitimate conclusion of the Chinese Box thought experiment—though not a conclusion drawn by Searle—to doubt that any other mind, or even our own mind, is doing anything more than manipulating symbols. The notion of "understanding," like the notion of "ethical choice," may well be an artifact of programming. Philosophers like Daniel Dennett argue that there's no good reason to assume that other, human "minds" that appear to be understanding are not simply "zombies," who act that way without true "understanding" as Searle conceives it. Scientists such as Marvin Minsky argue that the Chinese Box is simply another mind, a virtual one, which processes information just as other minds do. Other, similar criticisms point out the overall problem of philosophical criticisms of artificial intelligence, namely: there will always be an empirical gap, and it is the age-old philosophical problem of "other minds" which must always remain black boxes, of a sort, not accessible to our direct observation.

If we're concerned with the question of whether or to what degree robots might be truly "ethical" then we are stuck with the problem of the Chinese Box. Given we can never delve into the realm of intentions and beliefs held by other minds, whether human or robotic, we are left with only external behaviors, and pragmatic considerations. Does the system we are exploring *appear* to be acting autonomously? Does it believe it has a choice, and does it express this belief coherently? Can it engage in ethical argument, justify its positions, and even come to change its "mind" in the face of good, contrary arguments? These are the measures that we use when judging the moral capacities of other humans. Why will they not suffice when it comes to our robots or even alien robots from the planet Cybertron?

The Promise of Moral Machines

The Transformers act in ways that are clearly ethically measurable. The Autobots do good, the Decepticons do bad. Even while they entertain, they offered for kids of my generation, and now for an entirely new generation, models of virtue worthy of mimicry. Moral education is, after all, only undertaken with the notion that it is our external acts that serve as the measure of our characters, and even while we often try to infer intentions from those acts, the intentions of others will always be a mystery. But we can take comfort in the fact that this is a problem not just for robots, but for other minds generally. If you appear to be behaving morally to me, and I have no contradictory evidence about your internal mental states, then what other practical reason might I have to doubt your morality or ethics?

Our kitten-preserving washing machine and our safety gun that won't kill civilians are well-designed, and they help enable us to do good, or at least do better, so does it ultimately matter whether the good is truly *motivated* by the machines or by a wise designer? The kitten and the civilian don't care, as long as their lives are preserved. The tough part is still in devising the algorithms that will conduct our tasks in the real world with the care and precision of Transformers and with the appearances of virtue cast by the Autobots. In the end, whether we build our robots with more than the mere appearance of virtue is an interesting philosophical question, but no more puzzling than the question of whether other humans have the same virtues, rather than merely *seeming* to have them.

As long as our machines exhibit behaviors that work, that succeed in furthering our values, and doing so predictably, then the problem of the Chinese Box as applied to robot ethics will remain a question for philosophy students to ponder. It's worth noting, and the nature of the puzzle must be acknowledged to apply to other minds in general, but engineers continue to design more flexible machines, which will be more and more autonomous. We should take heed of the fictional examples ranging from *I, Robot* to *Transformers*, and ensure that even while we cannot guarantee that we engineer good into our machines, we engineer them as well as Optimus Prime and Bumblebee.

16

Freedom Is the Right of All Sentient Beings

GEOFFREY ALLAN PLAUCHÉ

The *Transformers* television series and toys were, as far as I can remember, my first encounter with science fiction. In *Transformers*, the human characters are confronted with the reality of an alien robotic civilization. The 1986 movie, which serves as a bridge between Seasons Two and Three of the series, was set in 2005 and the 2007 live-action movie was set in the present-day.

We viewers are ourselves confronted with the possibility of encountering an alien civilization based on artificial intelligences. Consider the vast interstellar distances that members of an alien civilization would have to travel to meet us. Consider also the relative slowness and the rigors of space travel. Any alien civilization we meet is likely to be very advanced scientifically and technologically. Unless they find a way to bend, break, or circumvent the limit that the speed of light places on space travel, we might be more likely to encounter artificial intelligences created by another biological species or beings who have traded biological life for artificial life.

What might such beings be like? We take it for granted that human beings are capable of being moral and that they should be. But will an alien robotic civilization develop or have any need for morality? If so, what kind of moral code might they have? Is it possible for our two or more species to live beside one another in peace, to co-operate and trade with one another rather than to make war and subjugate or destroy one another? If such alien artificial intelligences were superior to us in every way, what benefit could they possibly derive from associating with us? Why not ignore us, or enslave us, or destroy us instead?

Provided the alien artificial intelligences in question are sufficiently intelligent and possess volition, that is, a relatively human degree of free will not bound by rigid programming as non-human animals are by their instincts, then they will possess a moral code or codes. For all we know, they may even be more consistent in sticking to them than we humans tend to be. I am even hopeful that they *can*, though not necessarily will, have a moral code that is compatible with living in peaceful and mutually beneficial co-existence with us. Crucial to such an interspecies relationship is the mutual recognition that we each possess equal and absolute individual rights to life, liberty, and property. In the 2007 live-action *Transformers* film, Optimus Prime, leader of the Autobots, says, "Freedom is the right of all sentient beings." What reason could he have for believing this?

I think that the political philosophy of Aristotelian liberalism is best able to answer this and the other questions I have posed. Aristotelian liberalism synthesizes what are arguably the best aspects of Aristotle's philosophy with what are arguably the best aspects of the political philosophy of liberalism, particularly of its classical liberal roots and its modern libertarian incarnations. From Aristotle we draw on an ethical theory focused on the natural end that all rational beings pursue: a life of well-being or flourishing. Integral to a flourishing life are certain goods and virtues that we must pursue and possess which are determined by the particular kind of being we are. From liberalism we draw on an understanding of natural rights, including their importance both to our own individual flourishing and to bringing about and maintaining a free and flourishing society.

But, even if these ideas are true for human beings, what would make us think that they are true of all rational beings as well? Even of intelligent alien robots like the Transformers?

Flourishing, Virtue, and Artificial Life

Aristotle began his great treatise on ethics by observing that the good is "that at which all things aim."[1] This is an irrefutable conceptual truth. Anyone who attempts to deny it necessarily accepts its truth in so doing, for he who seeks to deny the claim that 'the

---

[1] *Nicomachean Ethics*, Book I, Section 1, line 1094a3.

good is that at which all things aim' is himself aiming at an end he necessarily perceives as worth attaining (an apparent good)—proving the claim to be wrong.

The important question is, what is the good? Or rather, which things are good and which are bad? When we ask whether something is good or bad, we are compelled to ask also: good (bad) for whom? and for what? When we say that food is good, what do we mean? Do we mean that food is good, period? No. What we mean is that food is good *for us*. And it is good for us for the reason that we need it in order to survive and because, if it is tasty, we usually enjoy eating it. Not all food is equally good for us, however. In fact, what counts as food for us depends on the kind of beings we are. Some animals can digest things that we cannot. What suffices as adequate nutrition for a plant will not suffice for human beings. We require particular amounts of certain kinds of nutrients and minerals not only in order to survive but, more importantly, to flourish. Moreover, while a certain amount of something, such as carbohydrates or certain fats, may be good for us, too much can be unhealthy. What's more, just as there are differences in food requirements between species, so too are there differences within species between males and females, different body types, different lifestyles, and so forth. Thus, goodness or badness is something that depends both on the thing in question and on universal and particular aspects of individual moral agents, it is not something that just exists independently.

Transformers also need some source of energy to fuel their bodies. The source of energy they depend upon is called Energon, in its raw form a type of crystal ore. In order to use it for fuel or other purposes the Transformers need to process it. This requires creativity and labor. Like our food, the "food" of the Transformers is scarce and requires effort to obtain and use. We need ethical principles and legal rules to guide and regulate our actions toward each other with respect to food, and all other scarce things we need or want, and so do the Transformers. And so will any rational artificial life-forms.

Morality is a code of values and principles that serves to guide our choices and actions both when we're alone and with respect to other people. Morality pertains only to matters of choice, for we can only rightly be praised or blamed for that which is in our power to control. All of our choices and actions are taken to pursue some end or other. The very fact of life necessitates the employment of scarce means, such as time and resources, to achieve certain ends. All life is conditional, even artificial life. We must act, and act wisely, in order to maintain and further our lives. So life both makes possible the existence of values and makes it necessary that we pursue them. It is our ultimate and natural end, that for the sake of which everything else is done.

Any code of morality needs a standard for judging what actually counts as a value (or a good) and what the proper means are for pursuing it. There is no better standard of value than that for the sake of which we make every one of our choices and actions. Our natural end, life, is our standard of value. This will be as true for artificial life-forms as it is for biological life. But while there are universal characteristics of life shared by all forms of life, there are also important particular differences between biological species, between biological and artificial life, and between different types of artificial life.

I have suggested that what I mean by life as one's natural end and ultimate standard of value is not mere survival but a life of flourishing. It's not enough, surely, merely to survive. On the face of it mere survival seems an awfully thin reed on which to hang the whole of morality. Everything and everyone would be reduced to being a mere means toward the end of survival. Even if there were a set of rules based on this standard, which one could follow, that would be both conducive toward long-term survival and correlate well with a fulfilling, moral life, the explanation still seems a shallow and unconvincing one. Do we love our friends and family merely because doing so is conducive toward our long-term survival? Moreover, what robust reason, or what reason at all really, could a mere survival standard offer for giving one's own life to save the life of a loved one, for instance? Even those who do choose death, such as a hero or a suicide, must necessarily see a life ending in the time and manner of their choosing as being preferable to a life ending in a different time and manner. In other words, a mere survival standard is inadequate for explaining the choice to die and even those who choose death must necessarily hold a flourishing life as their standard of value.

What is meant by a life of flourishing or well-being is health and development to maturity. As Philippa Foot points out, we determine what counts as flourishing the same way for humans as we do for plants and other animals. "The structure of the derivation is the same whether we derive an evaluation of the roots of a particular tree or the action of a particular human being. The meaning of the words 'good' and 'bad' is not different when used for features of plants on the one hand and humans, on the other, but is rather the same applied, in judgments of natural goodness and defect, in the case of all living things."[2]

When it comes to more complex life, particularly rational life, determining what is good and bad becomes more complicated and fraught with controversy, but it is nevertheless the same procedure in essence. The same can also be said for intelligent artificial life. To clarify further what is meant by a life of flourishing, some shallow goods and virtues can serve as mere means to the end of survival but with the flourishing standard, the various goods and virtues are conceived as being *parts of* a life of flourishing rather than something external to it. An example of this notion may be how buying a guitar is external to playing Stan Bush's "The Touch" while playing particular chords in a specific arrangement is part of what it means to play the song.

Bearing all of the foregoing in mind, let us turn to exploring some of the goods and virtues of which human flourishing consists, and to speculating about the nature of flourishing for artificial life-forms. We can start with the easier stuff first and revisit the point that life is conditional. Physical health is one good, necessary not just to make continued survival more likely but also for well-being—health is a natural state, and we derive enjoyment from it as well as from the things it enables us to do. We've discussed the fact that just as humans need fuel for their bodies so too will artificial life-forms. If organic life-forms do not eat enough food their functioning will become impaired and eventually they will die. The same will probably be true of artificial life. However, most if not all organic matter decays quickly; the same will probably not be true of whatever comprises an artificial life-form's body. Thus it may be possible to revive an artificial life-form after years, decades, or even longer, of its being without power; but even non-organic parts decay over time and so death by starvation still seems possible for artificial life. The ability to produce or acquire energy, as well as the tools useful for this purpose, will therefore be highly valued not only for this aspect of good health but for all the other things for which energy can be used.

[2] Foot, *Natural Goodness* (2001), p. 47.

Organic life is generally very fragile, highly vulnerable to injury and disease. While artificial life is likely to be far more durable, it will not be immune to such threats and may possess some weaknesses that organic life does not. Consider one such vulnerability somewhat amusingly dramatized in the *Transformers* cartoon:

> **STARSCREAM:** It looks like some kind of . . . rust!
>
> **MEGATRON:** Impossible! We are rust-proof!
>
> **STARSCREAM:** Perhaps you're made of shoddy materials, Megatron!
>
> **MEGATRON:** That's ABSURD!

Even artificial life can suffer from the equivalent of ill-health. Even artificial life can be damaged, sometimes beyond repair, or even destroyed. For these reasons weapons, armor, and shields of some kind as well as tools for the diagnosis and repair of damage, and the skills necessary for employing these things, will be of value.

As rational beings we observe things in the world and develop abstract ideas, or concepts, that refer to them. These concepts and their interrelations form the basis of our knowledge about the world. Knowledge does not come automatically to us. We must actively seek it out by observing the facts of reality, abstracting from them and integrating them into concepts, theories and stories about the world. We are neither infallible nor omniscient, and so we can make mistakes or even willfully evade the truth.

Accurate knowledge and good judgment are vital to improving the chances of our continued survival but more importantly also to improving our quality of life. It's the continual accumulation of knowledge that has enabled our species to develop from a primitive rock-and-spear-wielding, cave-dwelling existence to one that is today marked by an abundance of food, advanced medical care, plentiful clothing and comfortable shelter, instantaneous communication and swift transportation around the globe, and explorations into outer space. In light of this, intellectual ability and intellectual pursuits are valuable, although not everyone need specialize in scientific or other academic disciplines. Any alien artificial life-forms we happen to encounter in the near future will share these limitations and needs even though they will likely be more advanced scientifically and technologically than we are, and so they will probably value these things highly as well.

We have so far discussed a number of final goods or ends that comprise a life of flourishing—health, wealth, reason, intellectual ability and pursuits—as well as some of the intermediate goods that contribute to them. We can now identify some of the virtues that tend to produce these goods and that, being valuable in themselves, are also a part of flourishing. We can follow Aristotle in distinguishing between intellectual virtues on the one hand and moral virtues (traits of character) on the other. One reason to do so is that it helps to avoid intolerant moralizing about intellectual error. It's not necessarily a moral failing to make a mistake, hold incorrect ideas, or have poor math skills, for example. Among the intellectual virtues, and here I am not sticking precisely to Aristotle's list, are technical knowledge and skill, scientific knowledge, philosophical wisdom and knowledge, and practical wisdom (or prudence). Practical wisdom might be considered the master virtue, for it is the integrator of all the goods and virtues into a complete life and it guides the proper application of the other virtues. Aristotelian prudence is not pure, calculating prudence, however; while the moral virtues without practical wisdom are blind, practical wisdom without the moral virtues is empty.

And what moral virtues are central to a flourishing life? Well, assuming that our alien visitors are individual, autonomous beings like us, then the virtue of independence is one they might and should cherish. While many critics of liberalism fear the development of an excessive individualism and of a "me! me! me!" attitude that will lead to the breakdown of social cohesion and cultural norms, the human propensity to fall in with the herd is much more worrisome and prevalent. The virtue of independence recognizes that we are separate persons with our own minds that we must use to make decisions. It means that if we are to live a flourishing life that is our own, we must take the responsibility to think and work for ourselves rather than abdicate this responsibility to others. The virtue of integrity touches on this responsibility too. It means endeavoring to have a consistent set of principles and holding to them whatever temptations one might face, be they other people, unfortunate situations or one's baser inclinations. In a social context, it also means keeping one's promises; other people make plans in the expectation that you will do so.

Another important virtue is honesty. While honesty does in part mean that it is generally right to tell the truth and wrong to lie, it has a more fundamental meaning that is relevant here. Philosopher-novelist Ayn Rand argues that, given the way we as rational beings acquire knowledge, and given our fallibility and facility for engaging in willful evasion, honesty means "one must never attempt to fake reality in any manner" (to himself or to others).[3] And this involves not attempting to acquire values via fraud and not shying away from the facts, including one's proper hierarchy of values. If our alien artificial beings are capable of some analog to human emotion, or if they have an equivalent to a relatively opaque subconscious as do we, where automatic mental processes take place, then they too may be capable of evasion and self-deception. Even if they are not, they may still be capable of acting without principles and of deceiving others. So we have reason to expect that the virtue of honesty can and should be part of their flourishing as well.

And then there is the virtue of courage. Courage is the proper response to fear and potential harm. Fear is a very useful survival mechanism but even if our artificial visitors lack an analog to human emotion, the part about potential harm will still be relevant to them. They will still have to make risk assessments balanced against the value of the ends they aim to achieve and the requirements of the other virtues. Being too risk averse—being cowardly—can lead to frequent failure to achieve their ends as well as to fully exhibit and properly apply the other virtues. Being too insensitive to risk—being rash—can lead to the same problems in different ways.

We have also seen that productive work is necessary both for survival and flourishing. Our previous focus had been on the role of productive work in producing and acquiring fuel for our bodies, weapons, defenses, clothing, shelter, and other useful tools that better our chances of survival and improve our quality of life. As valuable as productive work is for creating these things, it serves another useful function as well. It also, chosen wisely, provides us with a sense of purpose, a core personal identity with which to integrate and determine the hierarchy of all our other values. Hence, productiveness too is a virtue, and an important one at that.

Rational beings are also capable of communication and conscious, purposeful cooperation. For human beings, at least, being social and political beings is also part of what it means to be a ratio-

---

[2] Rand, "The Objectivist Ethics," in *The Virtue of Selfishness* (1964), p. 28.

nal being. We are born in a social environment. We derive enjoyment from being in the company of other human beings who share our ideas and interests. We acquire much of our knowledge from other human beings. We depend on exchanging the values we produce for the values others produce in order to survive and flourish. Social existence enables the division and specialization of labor responsible for the continual expansion of knowledge and economic progress that we benefit from today. We naturally form into groups to co-operate in the pursuit of shared ends. A solitary existence is dangerous and impoverished in comparison to a social existence; imagine having to live off of what you alone could produce without modern tools, having to protect yourself from predators and natural disasters without any help and with only what weapons you can make yourself, having to treat your own injuries and illnesses, and what will happen as a result of your being less able or unable to defend yourself and provide for yourself when injured or sick. Together we accomplish much more, and live much better lives, spiritually and materially, than we would alone. Most or all of these things will probably be true of alien artificial intelligences as well. With the Transformers, we see all of these aspects of a social and political nature; the Autobots and Decepticons are opposing political organizations with a leader and other members who each possess specialized knowledge and abilities that suit their role within their respective group.

There are a number of virtues made possible and required by human social existence to which an artificial intelligence civilization could well have analogs. Some of the virtues we have already discussed have readily recognizable social dimensions. Other important social virtues include benevolence and several more that can be subsumed under it: sensitivity, generosity, civility and tolerance. Benevolence means having a habitual disposition of goodwill towards others. Sensitivity involves being alert to the interests, feelings, concerns, needs and so forth of others, particularly our friends and family. Generosity is that virtue in which we give of ourselves to others out of a sense of fullness or overflowing, without any expectation of receiving anything definite in return. Civility involves being polite and courteous in myriad ways and the virtue of tolerance involves enduring ideas or practices with which we disagree. It's easy to see how these virtues serve to grease the wheels of social relationships, so to speak, while their lack can cause friction and even grind cooperation to a halt. Civility and tolerance, in particular, are also necessary for the joint pursuit of truth because they facilitate open discussion and debate.

The Law of Association

At this point you may be thinking, "All right. I buy that there are good reasons for thinking that an alien race of artificial intelligences will probably have some sort of moral code that enables peaceful co-existence and mutually beneficial cooperation among themselves. But what reason do we have to think that they will have a moral code that will allow such a relationship between them and us?" Well, for one thing, given the understanding that the basis for morality lies in a being's capacity for rationality, I can think of no coherent reason to treat only one's own species, rather than all rational beings whatever their species, as moral agents worthy of respect as persons. More can be said about this but perhaps you will find an appeal to material self-interest to be more reassuring. Economic theory tells us that even an individual or group that is more efficient in every way than another individual or group can benefit economically from co-operation. The English economist David Ricardo originally expounded this law in 1817 in his theory of comparative advantage (or comparative cost). The great economist of the Austrian School, Ludwig von Mises, however, has argued that Ricardo's law of comparative advantage is but a particular instance of a more general law as it is applied to the problem of international trade; Mises dubbed this the law of association.[3]

The Law of Association might not hold if the aliens in question were so superior to us in every way that we were no more significant to them than ants, but barring this they could derive some material advantage from trade with us. To illustrate the law, let's use as an example the Autobot medic-mechanic Ratchet and a human I've just made up named John Smith. Both Ratchet and John are capable mechanics and also capable of building their own tools and parts. Suppose that Ratchet is a much better mechanic than John, however, and can earn $10,000 per hour as a mechanic but only $1,000 per hour making and selling the tools and parts a mechanic needs for his craft. Suppose also that John could earn

[3] See Mises, *Human Action: A Treatise on Economics* (1949; Scholar's Edition 1998), pp. 158–163; http://mises.org/resources/3250.

$100 per hour as a mechanic or $500 per hour making and selling the tools and parts a mechanic needs for his craft. Ratchet is a hundred times more efficient than John as a mechanic and twice as efficient than he is as a maker of tools and parts. Perhaps they both plan to work twenty hours per week and divide their time equally between doing mechanic work and making tools and parts. Their total output would look like this:

RATCHET: 10 hours mechanic work X $10,000 per hour = $100,000
10 hours making tools and parts X $1,000 per hour = $10,000
Total output: $110, 000.

JOHN: 10 hours mechanic work X $100 per hour = $1,000
10 hours making tools and parts X $500 per hour = $5,000
Total output: $6,000

Between them Ratchet and John have produced $116,000 worth of output. Now let us examine what the situation would be if Ratchet focused exclusively on working as a mechanic while John focused exclusively on making tools and parts.

RATCHET: 20 hours mechanic work X $10,000 per hour = $200,000
Total output: $200, 000.

JOHN: 20 hours making tools and parts X $500 per hour = $10,000
Total output: $10,000

The total output that Ratchet and John can produce has risen to $210,000. Even more importantly, both Ratchet and John are individually better off. John, who was worse at both jobs, was able to nearly double his output; likewise Ratchet, who was better at both jobs. This analysis we have applied at the individual level involving only two actors can be applied by straightforward extension to groups, to international trade, and even to interstellar trade. This means that it's possible, even likely, that humans and artificial lifeforms can live in peace with one another and benefit from co-operation, competition, and trade.

All right, so trade is more beneficial than doing everything yourself. But what about war? Why not just invade us, enslave or destroy us, and plunder our resources? To continue the appeal to material self-interest: war is an incredibly costly undertaking. A war is bound to result in massive loss of life, quite possibly on both sides even if they are more advanced than we are. While we are physically weaker than the Transformers, for example, we can and do make up for it, at least to a degree, with technology. Remember the exo-skeleton Daniel uses in the animated movie? And the sabot rounds used to good effect against Scorponok in the live-action movie? Even if we don't stand a chance, military expenditure is costly. It diverts creativity, labor, capital, energy and other resources away from productive uses into dead-end assets. A war would result in destruction of human lives and capital and, to the extent that it does, our attackers will lose the benefits they otherwise would have gained through trade. If they commit xenocide, purposefully causing the extinction of our species, all they will have gained will be the resources of our planet and whatever remains of our creations to be salvaged. If they enslave us, then they take on the burden of clothing, feeding, sheltering and training us, of directing our labor, and of suppressing the inevitable rebellions. When you think seriously about it, and presumably advanced artificial intelligences will be able to think very well, is war really worth it? On the other hand, ignorance of economic principles is not the only reason people might choose violence and war over peace and trade, so let us now turn to a discussion of liberty and justice.

Liberty, Justice, and the Autobot Way

Justice (which is both a good and a virtue) and liberty are of central importance to political philosophy. To the extent that they are absent, a life of flourishing and a free and flourishing society are made impossible. As it is conceived in the classical liberal tradition, liberty is freedom from aggression; more precisely, liberty is freedom from the threat or use of initiatory physical force. The act of coercing someone with the threat or use of physical force—such as by violence, murder, fraud and naked theft—imposes the aggressor's desires, interests, preferences, choices, actions, on the victim without his consent. To the extent that this occurs, the victim exists not for his own sake but for another's: his desires, interests, preferences, choices, actions, are no longer truly his but are alien to him. More to the point, to the extent that this occurs his actions are not self-directed. A person being physically coerced by another is not able to make the choices and take the actions he judges necessary for the maintenance and furtherance of his life. And he is not being respected as a person.

In the Aristotelian tradition, remember, morality is a matter of choice. For an action to count as virtuous it must be done freely, by choice, both for the right reasons and because it is desired. Thus, it is not enough simply to possess the goods, and it is impossible to possess the virtues, one needs in life without self-directed action. In other words, an act of mine does not count as virtuous and therefore contributory toward my flourishing if you force it upon me, even if it otherwise would have contributed to my flourishing had I desired and freely chosen it for the right reasons. To the extent that one's liberty is infringed upon, one is unable to flourish.

The importance of free choice is recognized several times in the 2007 live-action *Transformers* film. Consider this exchange involving Bumblebee, who during most of the movie had been unable to speak because of some damage inflicted by Megatron in the back story:

Bumblebee: [*fully repaired*] Permission to speak, sir?

Optimus Prime: Permission granted, old friend.

Sam Witwicky: You speak now?

Bumblebee: I wish to stay with the boy.

Optimus Prime: If that is his choice.

Sam Witwicky: Yes.

And here's another, from an exchange between Optimus Prime and Megatron while they fought:

Megatron: Humans don't deserve to live!

Optimus Prime: They deserve to choose for themselves!

Megatron: Then you will die with them! [*throws Prime away and primes his cannon*]

Megatron: JOIN THEM IN EXTINCTION!

What the liberals bring to the table, as a matter of political justice, is a greater recognition of this central importance of liberty and a more consistent protection of liberty in the form of an ethical, political, and legal principle: the right to liberty (and all of its corollaries and consequences). A right is a legitimately enforceable moral claim against the prior obligation of others not to threaten or use initiatory physical force against you. Not all the moral claims we have on the obligations of others are legitimately enforceable via the law or vigilantism. In the liberal tradition, only the moral claim to freedom from aggression can be consistently upheld as legitimately enforceable. The rights to life and property are two of its corollaries. A right to liberty is a right to a life of our own. And our right to liberty cannot be exercised if we are not allowed to keep and use the fruits of our labor as we see fit, provided we do not use our property to violate the equal rights of others to their own life, liberty, and property.

But so far we have not gotten deeply enough into the reasons, at the level of personal ethics, for why rational beings have rights and why we must respect them. I have said that our rights derive from a prior obligation of others. What gives us this obligation? Ultimately, what gives us this obligation not to aggress against others is our obligation to pursue a life of flourishing. To put it in a nutshell, since we are rational, political, and social beings, we ought to deal with other such beings through reason, discourse, persuasion, and co-operation (except when necessary to protect our own right to liberty, or the rights of others), rather than through violence and force. To do so is a matter of justice.

Consider the virtue of justice; it means accepting and granting the earned and deserved, and never seeking or granting the unearned and undeserved.[5] What do other rational beings deserve from us? Again we can look to Aristotle for some illumination. Aristotle argues that justice is complete virtue practiced in relation to others and because of this it is the greatest of the virtues. In other words, what other rational beings deserve from us is for us

---

[4] David Schmidtz argues that desert is not merely backwards-looking, given only as a compensatory reward; it can also be forward-looking, promissory: we can come to deserve something on the basis of what we do after receiving it. Deserving and earning are not interchangeable, however. Something can only be earned after the work is done. Nevertheless, it is possible to do justice to unearned opportunities. See Schmidtz, *Elements of Justice* (2006), pp. 31–70.

to possess integrity, to be prudent, independent, honest, productive, brave, benevolent, sensitive, generous, civil, tolerant, and so forth. We owe virtue first and foremost to ourselves, and because we are political and social beings we owe virtue to others as well. Virtues are not rigid rules, however; they are abstract principles and traits of character whose proper application is highly dependent upon context. While the virtues are, in the abstract, universal principles, Aristotle reminds us that what virtue demands of us will depend on our talents and abilities, the cultural traditions we accept (so long as they do not contradict what our nature as a human being (or artificial intelligence) demands of us), our particular circumstances and the particular conditions at the time of action.

Finally, we may follow Aristotle in his wisdom in another way. He makes a useful distinction between what he calls general justice and particular (or special) justice. General justice is, for Aristotle, the complete virtue we have just been discussing. Particular justice pertains more to political matters, such as violence, theft, fraud, and the like. With some tweaking, this distinction can be adapted to the liberal conception of justice and rights. An Aristotelian liberal must disagree with Aristotle that it is just that the law be used to require all virtue and prohibit all vice. The only vices that we recognize as crimes are those that involve aggression—those that involve the violation of rights. We also recognize that even particular justice is informed by all of the other virtues as general justice is. So an Aristotelian liberal sees particular justice as pertaining to what I earlier called political justice, which involves protecting the right to liberty and rectifying violations of it. Aristotelian liberals see general justice as pertaining to obligations we have to others that are not legitimately enforceable. To keep the difference between the two types of justice clear, it will help to rename them: 1) We have political justice which pertains to rights and is legitimately enforceable. 2) And we have social justice which pertains to our other moral obligations to others and is not legitimately enforceable.

Will alien artificial intelligences possess such a moral code as I have described and recognize us as persons, granting us the promissory respect we deserve in the name of political and social justice? Will we do likewise for them? There are no guarantees, but there is reason to hope that they will display the wisdom and goodness of Optimus Prime, rather than the imprudence and evil of Megatron, displayed in the recent live-action film:

IRONHIDE: Why are we fighting to save the humans? They're a primitive and violent race.

OPTIMUS PRIME: Were we so different? They're a young species. They have much to learn. But I've seen goodness in them. Freedom is the right of all sentient beings. You all know there's only one way to end this war: we must destroy the Cube. If all else fails, I will unite it with the spark in my chest.

RATCHET: That's suicide! The Cube is raw power, it could destroy you both!

OPTIMUS PRIME: A necessary sacrifice to bring peace to this planet. We cannot let the humans pay for our mistakes. It's been an honor serving with you all. Autobots, ROLL OUT!

What better way to end this chapter than with more words of wisdom from Optimus Prime?

> With the All Spark gone, we cannot return life to our planet. And fate has yielded its reward: a new world to call home. We live among its people now, hiding in plain sight, but watching over them in secret, waiting, protecting. I have witnessed their capacity for courage, and though we are worlds apart, like us, there's more to them than meets the eye. I am Optimus Prime, and I send this message to any surviving Autobots taking refuge among the stars. We are here. We are waiting.

About the Authors

Robert Arp earned his PhD in philosophy from St. Louis University, and has many interests including ontology, philosophy of mind, and philosophy of biology. He now works as an analyst for The Analysis Group LLC with the US Air Force on their information sharing system. He may have met a transformer, in the guise of a fighter jet, but he never would have known!

Adam Barkman is an assistant professor of philosophy at Yonsei University. Like his first *Transformer*, Bluestreak, Adam doesn't stay idle long: he has published over twenty essays on popular culture and philosophy in various books and journals and has traveled to some forty countries. He's the author of *C.S. Lewis and Philosophy as a Way of Life: A Comprehensive Historical Examination of His Philosophical Thoughts* and the co-editor (with Josef Steiff) of *Manga and Philosophy*. Adam lives with his wife and children in South Korea and is happy that despite being in their late twenties to early thirties, he and his bros, Jon and Joe, still have all their old *Transformers*.

Kevin S. Decker is an Assistant Professor of Philosophy at Eastern Washington University. He's the co-editor (with Jason Eberl) of *Star Wars and Philosophy*, *Star Trek and Philosophy*, and (with Richard Brown) *Terminator and Philosophy*. He has written on philosophical topics in popular culture such as James Bond, the films of Stanley Kubrick, *Star Trek: The Next Generation*, and *The Colbert Report*. When the clock strikes twelve midnight, he turns into a giant gun; now he's just waiting for someone to pick him up off the ground.

Karl Erbacher spent some of his youth in Okinawa, Japan, where the appearance of giant robot cartoons and toys were everyday expectations. Having seen many of the early cartoons in their 'original' Japanese (or so he thought), he was eager to participate in this book project. Karl is currently an undergraduate student at Eastern Washington University, and has aspirations to one day be a Professor of Philosophy. He's hoping that his chapter in this book will help his writing career 'transform and roll out'.

M.R. Eyestone has been a fan of Transformers cartoons, toys, and comics since the 1980s. Perhaps as part of a general refusal to grow up, he still passes a fair amount of time watching cartoons, collecting toys, and reading comics. He's currently at the University of Colorado at Boulder, working towards a PhD in philosophy, teaching, and doing a lot of thinking. He keeps a figure of Optimus Prime next to the statue of Socrates above his desk.

J. Storrs Hall is president of the Foresight Institute. He is the author of *Beyond AI: Creating the Conscience of the Machine*, the first full-length non-fiction treatment of machine ethics, and *Nanofuture: What's Next for Nanotechnology*. Josh was the founding Chief Scientist of Nanorex Inc, is a Research Fellow of the Institute for Molecular Manufacturing, and is an associate editor of the International Journal of Nanotechnology and Molecular Computation. He builds shape-changing robots in his copious spare time.

David R. Koepsell is an author, philosopher, and attorney-bot whose recent research focuses on the nexus of science, technology, ethics, and public policy. He's Assistant Professor, Philosophy Section, Faculty of Technology, Policy, and Management at the Technology University of Delft, in The Netherlands, and Senior Fellow, 3TU Centre for Ethics and Technology, The Netherlands. He is also the author of *Who Owns You? The Corporate Gold-Rush to Patent Your Genes* (2009) and *The Ontology of Cyberspace: Philosophy, Law, and the Future of Intellectual Property* (2000), as well as numerous scholarly articles on law, philosophy, science, and ethics.

Nicolas Michaud lives his life under the impression that he is, in actuality, Optimus Prime. Despite the obvious problem that he is far to short to be a giant robot, he spends his time at the University of North Florida, Jacksonville University, and the Art Institute of Jacksonville try to convince his philosophy students of this truth. They do not believe him, yet. . . .

Corey Neil has an M.A. in Mental Health Counseling, a B.A. in Psychology, and has extensive experience working in the mental health field. Corey is an athletic coach and is president of the Western New York Outdoor Adventure Club. He currently works at the Center for Inquiry Research Park in Amherst, New York.

Matthew Pike is currently a Ph.D. student in Philosophy at the University of Colorado, Boulder. His childhood obsession with Transformers probably helps to explain the years he spent working as a computer programmer, secretly (or not so secretly) hoping to accidentally create artificial intelligence. In addition to his (perhaps unhealthy) interest in sci-fi and fantasy, he enjoys music composition and performance, martial arts, hiking, and arguing with friends and colleagues about a wide range of philosophical topics, including epistemology, metaphysics, science, and the philosophy of mind.

Geoffrey Allan Plauché grew up with the Transformers cartoons, animated movie, and toys. He watched the movie on VHS so many times that he literally wore out the tape. Geoffrey recently received his Ph.D. in political science with a concentration in political philosophy from Louisiana State University. His dissertation is titled "Aristotelian Liberalism: An Inquiry into the Foundations of a Free and Flourishing Society". He has published in the *Journal of Value Inquiry* and *Journal of Libertarian Studies.*

Gabriel Rye is an independent scholar who studied philosophy at Eastern Washington University. This is his first (of many) philosophical endeavors, as his abilities are more than meets the eye.

John Shook recalls watching many of the original cartoons when he should have been studying in college. Despite his best efforts, he managed to tear himself away enough to graduate, and he is now a professional philosopher working at the Center for Inquiry in Amherst, New York, as Vice President for Education and Research. He contributed to *Bruce Springsteen and Philosophy* and writes books about pragmatism, naturalism, and humanism.

Michael Spicher wishes he had taken better care of his Transformers action figures because they would be quite valuable now. He's currently a Ph.D. student in philosophy at the University of South Carolina in Columbia. Michael is convinced that the location of the All Spark is a metaphysical problem and that 'the light will save us all'. He transforms into a harmonica and bass wielding blues musician to defend his spark against the pressures of graduate school.

Josef Steiff is probably not a robot in disguise, but he obviously has hopes for the car sitting in his driveway. Currently the Associate Chair of Film and Video at Columbia College, Joe is the author of *The Complete Idiot's Guide to Independent Filmmaking* and co-editor of *Battlestar Galactica and Philosophy: Mission Accomplished or Mission Frakked Up?* Joe somehow managed to miss the whole Transformers craze when growing up, but that's what midlife crises are for—he sure loves getting to have a second childhood so he doesn't have to put away his toys.

ERIC SWAN has an M.Ed. in Guidance and Counseling from Loyola University in Maryland and is committed to helping unruly teenagers transform into respectable adults with promising futures. Eric's personal All Spark is the beauty and poetry of life, which he expresses in his photography, poetry, drawings, love of nature, and his Seventies-plus songs. His favorite writers are Hunter S. Thompson and Jack Kerouac who he wishes were still around to critique his Transformers essay. Eric lives in the Rocky Mountains with his lovely wife (and co-author) Liz Stillwaggon Swan. He does a perfect headstand.

LIZ STILLWAGGON SWAN has been enchanted with artificial life since age four, when Santa left a little robot in her Christmas stocking. In graduate school, Liz wrote an essay tracing the contemporary fascination with robots back to the medieval obsession with automata and the alchemical recipes for creating homunculi. She has a recent article in *Biology and Philosophy* that she hopes will incite some philosophical interest in what artificial life can teach us about organic life. Liz lives in Colorado with her wonderful carbon-based husband, Eric Swan. She has a pretty good sticker collection.

JAMIE WATSON loved Transformers toys when he was younger, but was never very good at transforming them. Recognizing that prospects for a career in engineering were grim, he opted for philosophy. He is currently ABD at Florida State University. In addition to his dissertation in epistemology, he's co-authoring textbooks on ethics and critical thinking. Jamie also wrote "The Beast in Me: Evil in Cash's Christian Worldview" for *Johnny Cash and Philosophy*.

Index